Schizophrenia

To our patients and their families

Schizophrenia
Symptoms, Causes, Treatments

Kayla F. Bernheim
Livingston County Counseling Services, New York

Richard R. J. Lewine
University of Chicago, Pritzker School of Medicine and *Illinois State Psychiatric Institute*

W · W · NORTON & COMPANY

New York · London

We gratefully acknowledge Tavistock Publishers Ltd. and Pantheon Books, a division of Random House, Inc., for their permission to reprint selected excerpts from *The Divided Self,* by R. D. Laing.

W. W. Norton & Company, Inc., 500 Fifth Avenue, New York, N.Y. 10110
W. W. Norton & Company Ltd., Castle House, 75/76 Wells Street, London W1T 3QT

Printed in the United States of America.

Library of Congress Cataloging in Publication Data
Bernheim, Kayla F
    Schizophrenia.

    Includes index.
    1. Schizophrenia   I. Lewine, Richard R. J., joint author.   II. Title.
RC514.B47   616.8'982   78–13040
ISBN 0-393-01174-7
ISBN 0-393-09017-5 pbk.

4 5 6 7 8 9 0

Contents

Preface

Schizophrenia. The word itself conjures up disquieting images—images as varied as the people who experience them. Dr. Jekyll and Mr. Hyde; violence; stupor; walking nude in the streets; staring at walls behind bars in a hospital. The term, shrouded in mystery though used in everyday language, has come to carry such frightening connotations that the burdens of secrecy and isolation are frequently preferable to the social repercussions of admitting to being schizophrenic. Indeed, the social stigma accompanying schizophrenia, the widespread lack of understanding, and the misuse of the word compound the problems faced by the schizophrenic. Further, the effects of schizophrenia, like the effects of other disorders, are not limited to the individual. Social, vocational, and emotional relationships are all altered, often in inexplicable ways. The behavioral changes that occur are diverse, often seem illogical, and do not appear to be attached to any observable cause. That these changes may occur many months or even years before the disorder is labeled, and before any semblance of an explanation is given, adds further to the problems of coping with schizophrenia. This, of course, has widespread ramifications for family members, friends, and even associates.

The purpose of this book is to provide a basic understanding of schizophrenia—its symptoms, its course, its treatment, and its prognosis. We wish to answer as simply, yet as fully, as possible those questions repeatedly asked by schizophrenics, their families, and the concerned general public.

We begin by addressing the myths and mystique surrounding this complex illness and by providing a general model for understanding why and how schizophrenia develops. There follows a description of schizophrenic signs and symptoms from the perspective of the observer and also from the perspective of the schizophrenic individual. Included is a comparison of schizophrenia with other disorders with which it may be confused.

We move then to an exploration of the causes of schizophrenia. This section includes a description of research strategies and findings as well as a discussion of the roles of heredity, biochemistry, and environment in producing schizophrenia.

The treatment of schizophrenia is covered next. Following a review of the medical and psychological treatments available to the schizophrenic person, the role played by the family and by social institutions in an individual's recovery from schizophrenia is addressed. A major focus here is on the problems faced by families with a schizophrenic member. These problems are treated in detail, and suggestions are offered whenever possible. The section ends with the presentation of a general treatment strategy in which all of the therapeutic interventions previously discussed are combined.

Recovery is then examined as a process with highly variable outcome. Factors that influence this outcome with respect to the individual case are explained.

We conclude with a look to the future, summarizing advances that have already been made in our understanding of schizophrenia and speculating about directions for future research and treatment.

This book is written for three audiences. The first includes those people for whom schizophrenia is of personal interest. Schizophrenia is diagnosed in approximately 1 percent of the general population. This means that one out of every hundred persons will, at some time, be diagnosed as schizophrenic. It is estimated that many times that number go undiagnosed. When this figure is multiplied by the number of people who come into significant contact with each schizophrenic, it becomes clear that extensive social networks are affected. It is our belief that information and advice can help patients as well as families and acquaintances of schizophrenics to make well-informed decisions about their own lives and to behave in ways that will advance rather than impede the patient's recovery.

The second audience includes professionals and students who plan to work with schizophrenic individuals and their families. It is our hope that this book will sensitize these helpers to the complexity of the issues involved in our understanding and management of schizophrenia.

Finally, what follows will also be of value to students of psychology and human behavior. Our study of schizophrenia evokes issues of widespread significance. Is behavior governed by genes or environment? What is the nature of mental disturbance? What is the relationship between thinking and feeling? What are the sociological and cultural aspects of an individual's behavior? These questions and others are addressed and refined in schizophrenia research but are applicable, as well, to a much larger subject matter. Thus, people who are acquainted with the framework within which we study schizophrenia will find that their conceptualizations about other aspects of human behavior are enhanced.

A popular story circulated around the state psychiatric hospital where we both worked several years ago. One day, a schizophrenic patient challenged one of the professional staff members to a game of chess. After the patient won the first game the staff member concentrated harder, attributing the outcome to sloppy playing. After the patient won the second game, the professional was visibly surprised. After the patient won the fourth game in a row, the staff member walked away in frustration. The patient told the professional's receding back, "I may be crazy, but I'm not stupid."

We would like to thank those people who have taught us what it means and, just as important, what it does *not* mean to be schizophrenic. A number of bright, articulate patients and their families have been especially cooperative and helpful in sharing their experiences with us. We must acknowledge their contribution anonymously due to the still considerable stigma associated with schizophrenia. We are also indebted to our past academic and clinical supervisors for providing models for studying and understanding schizophrenia. We hope that they will recognize their influence throughout the book.

The actual preparation of the manuscript has involved the able help of several people. Irving Gottesman, Leonard Horowitz, Paul Rozin, Norman Watt, Robert Liberman, and Caroline Beale have read the manuscript at various stages and have provided very useful and thought-provoking comments. Rhea Cabin, Marilyn Fischer, Laurie Teraspulsky, and Judy Hansen have contributed invaluable help in typing and tracking down references. Some of the work required for writing this book would not have been possible without the National Institute of Mental Health Training Grant #MH00042, by which the second author was supported. We especially appreciate the way in which Norton editor, Don Fusting, carried out the difficult task of editing and coordinating our efforts. We wish also to thank our spouses, Joseph W. Bernheim and Janice F. Lewine, not only for their helpful suggestions, but also for their unflagging support throughout this project.

Finally we must assume the ultimate responsibility for the choice and presentation of material, any errors that remain, and the view of schizophrenia that we present.

March 1, 1978   Kayla F. Bernheim
                                                        Richard R. J. Lewine

Schizophrenia

1

FACTS AND FICTIONS
An Overview

At a cocktail party two strangers are introduced. They shake hands and say they are pleased to meet each other. Quickly they search for and find an area of common interest they can discuss. During their brief conversation, they look at each other frequently, smile, and nod. Within a short time, one of them sees a friend, ends the conversation politely, and moves away. The other turns and joins a nearby discussion.

Human behavior is, in general, quite predictable. We know a great deal about how strangers will behave—at a party, at a movie, in a classroom, on the street. As we get to know somebody well, we are able to predict how he or she will behave in many more situations. The extent to which we are comfortable with other people depends, in part on how predictable we perceive them to be.

Even when people behave in unexpected ways, we are comfortable if we can create a scenario in which their behavior makes sense. Gregarious John is quiet tonight because he's tired. Mary is wearing a dress today instead of jeans because she wants to impress her companion. Jerry is shouting because he feels unfairly treated by Bob.

Occasionally, however, we come across people whose behavior in neither predictable nor comprehensible. Acting as if they live in a radically different world, they make us feel uncomfortable and even frightened. A man stops in the middle of the street to yell at unseen oppressors; a woman smiles vacuously and begins to hum when asked for her ticket in a train. We, as observers, search for an explanation for these behaviors, and, finding none, we say these people are "crazy" or "mentally ill."

As far as we know, there have been people in all cultures at all times who behaved in bizarre, unpredictable, inexplicable ways.[1] Today, such behaviors are seen as evidence of schizophrenia, a disorder in which mental and emotional processes are seriously disturbed. However, even now understanding schizophrenia is no easy matter. Public misconceptions abound, and even professionals are not yet in complete agreement about what schizophrenia looks like let alone what causes it. Still, we now understand much about schizophrenia. We have a general idea about how and why the disordered behaviors develop, and we know something about how to change them. In the future we will know how to prevent them from occurring.

Let us begin our discussion with a brief description of schizophrenia, one which will be expanded later in this chapter. *Schizophrenia refers to disturbances in thinking, feeling, and relating.*

THOUGHT DISORDER

Each of us has had periods in which we were unable to "think straight." Fatigue, overwork, and emotional stress can impair concentration and cause thoughts to race. The schizophrenic individual appears more susceptible to this problem than other people. Thinking may be confused and disjointed a great deal of the time, and for no apparent reason. In addition, most of us engage in fantasizing some of the time. Both enjoyable and frightening fantasies occur to us from time to time, but we are able to separate fantasy from reality fairly easily. The schizophrenic may be overwhelmed by fantasy, unable to distinguish

---

1. Brown and Menninger, 1940; Deutsch, 1937; Gerard, 1964; Salzinger, 1973; Zilboorg, 1941.

between what is real and what is not. The thinking disturbance in schizophrenia can range from mild confusion with fleeting, unrealistic ideas to an almost complete inability to understand and respond appropriately to events in the environment.

EMOTIONAL DISORDER

The ability to feel normal emotions is disturbed in schizophrenic people. Emotions may be *dulled,* resulting in an apparent indifference to situations and events to which most of us would react strongly. Life frequently seems boring and empty to the schizophrenic. Sometimes, however, schizophrenics react intensely, but in an *inappropriate* way. They may laugh, cry, or become enraged for no apparent reason. Not only do these feelings appear unrelated to the situations in which they occur, they may be unrelated to the thoughts the person is having as well. So a schizophrenic person is likely to think about events in an abnormal way and to respond emotionally to situations in an abnormal way.

DIFFICULTY IN RELATING TO OTHERS

The ability to engage in social relationships is also impaired. Again, many of the experiences of the schizophrenic are ones all of us have had at some time or another: a desire to be alone, a need for social withdrawal, ambivalence regarding intimat relationships, difficulty in making life decisions, existential bo dom, and feelings of passivity and of living lives beyond own control. The schizophrenic differs, however, both pervasiveness and intensity of these feelings. Whereas us continue to love, play, and work in the face of the the schizophrenic frequently withdraws from many

At his core, the schizophrenic is socially isolated. We do not mean this in a physical sense. Rather a schizophrenic may be surrounded by people yet feel lonely, misunderstood, and all alone in the world; there are no "intimates," no shared secrets or joys.

Perhaps as a result of these difficulties in thinking, feeling, and relating, self-esteem is very low. The schizophrenic's self-perception may include feelings of disgust and failure. Turned primarily inward to a world of fantasies and dreams, the schizophrenic will often withdraw from others and from reality.

VARIABILITY: THE PROBLEM OF DIAGNOSIS

Describing the common symptoms of schizophrenia in general terms does not adequately answer the question: What is schizophrenia? Specific symptoms may vary from person to person and within one person over time. Some people develop symptoms gradually over many months while others, seemingly well adjusted, become severely disorganized over a few days time. Some people experience symptoms for a limited period of time and appear to recover spontaneously without treatment. For others, schizophrenic symptoms recede gradually with treatment, often leaving behind a residue of problems in living. Are all of these people schizophrenic? If not, who are and who are

The question is important because if we study several
~rders while believing that we are studying only
little about the causes and cures of any of

the beginning of the twen-
,856–1926), a German
he "father of psychiatry,"
of what he called *dementia*
oration.[2] In distinguishing

this disorder from others, he pointed out that dementia praecox was a single disease, which occurred predominantly in the young, was marked by a progressive deterioration, and resulted in a very poor outcome in most cases. The clinical picture painted by Kraepelin emphasized a chronic (long-term) illness with increasing mental disorganization, hallucinations, delusions, and inability to care for oneself. According to this view, a schizophrenic who spontaneously recovers has been misdiagnosed in the first place.

In contrast to this dismal outlook, Eugen Bleuler, a Swiss psychiatrist (1857–1939), suggested three major revisions in the concept of dementia praecox.[3] First, he changed the name to schizophrenia, a term derived from the Greek words *schizein* ("to split") and *phren* ("mind"). Thus, literally translated, *schizophrenia* means "split mind," a phrase that Bleuler felt captured the breaking up of normal thought proc sses that occurs in schizophrenia. Second, Bleuler proposed t'.at schizophrenia was really a group of related disorders rather than a single disease. The common features of all schizophrenias were disorganization in the way thoughts were related to one another, emotions that were either dulled or inappropriate to the schizophrenic's verbal statements, a preoccupation with fantasy life, and the simultaneous existence of opposite thoughts or feelings. Finally, Bleuler emphasized that schizophrenia did not necessarily result in a progressively deteriorating course. From this point of view, a person with the symptoms described above suffers from one of the schizophrenias regardless of the prognosis for recovery.

Continuing Diagnostic Differences

Current differences in diagnostic systems reflect historical differences in the concept of schizophrenia. At one extreme are the heirs of Kraepelin who restrict their use of the diagnosis to those who exhibit well-defined symptoms and generally place emphasis on the biological etiology of the disorder. At the other

3. Bleuler, 1950.

extreme are those who, like Bleuler, acknowledge several types of schizophrenia with varying outcomes, consider one's developmental adjustment in making a diagnosis, and place emphasis on social and psychological forces in the development of schizophrenia.[4] Not surprisingly, those holding the narrower view of schizophrenia diagnose it less frequently than those who take the broader developmental view.

The more restricted systems for diagnosing schizophrenia emphasize the presence of thought disorder.[5] There are various symptoms of disordered thinking, the presence of any one of which is sufficient for diagnosing schizophrenia. These thinking disturbances include hearing one's thoughts spoken aloud, hearing others' voices talking or commenting about one, believing that another's thoughts have been put into one's head, having one's thoughts taken away, having one's thoughts broadcast, and believing that one's feelings, thoughts, and actions are not one's own, but rather dictated by outside forces.

A broader, more flexible diagnostic system is represented in the *Diagnostic and Statistical Manual II* (DSMII),[6] the official source of diagnoses in most mental-health facilities in the United States. According to DSMII, schizophrenia represents a group of disorders marked by "misinterpretation of reality," "delusions and hallucinations," "inappropriate emotional responsiveness and loss of empathy with others," and behavior that "may be withdrawn, regressive and bizarre."[7] On the one hand, the manual provides for narrowly defined categories of schizophrenia— for example, catatonic schizophrenia, characterized either by "violent motor activity and excitement" or "stupor, mutism, negativism or waxy flexibility." [8] On the other hand, the categories "chronic undifferentiated" and "other" are designed for those patients judged to be schizophrenic, but not fitting the more narrowly defined groups. Thus, the clinician has much leeway in assigning the diagnosis of schizophrenia.

4. Carpenter, Strauss, and Bartko, 1974.
5. Schneider, 1959.
6. *Diagnostic and Statistical Manual II,* 1968.
7. *Ibid.,* p. 33.
8. *Ibid.,* pp. 33–34.

Debate over diagnosis continues because compelling evidence that would allow us to decide the question does not exist. There is, at present, no known medical or psychological test which can confirm the diagnosis of schizophrenia, although certain procedures may suggest its presence. The disorder is *inferred* from behavior, which is subject to multiple influences, and from responses to treatment. Thus multiple diagnoses and misdiagnoses still occur with frustrating frequency. Readers may well have had the experience of having had family members diagnosed and treated as schizophrenic by one practitioner, but not by another. This is frequently due to differences in the criteria used to diagnose schizophrenia.

Some professionals have pointed to the unreliability of the schizophrenic diagnosis—that is the inability of clinicians and researchers to agree among themselves on a definition of schizophrenia. These professionals suggest that we drop the label altogether.[9] However, a recent international study, including nine countries of diverse cultural, social, economic, and political backgrounds, has provided convincing evidence to dispel the notion that schizophrenia cannot be reliably diagnosed.[10]

Sponsored by the World Health Organization, the objective of the study was to determine if schizophrenics from different countries are alike when diagnosed by a group of clinicians using the same interviewing techniques and trained to use the same decision rules. Although there was disagreement about schizophrenic subtypes, the diagnosis of schizophrenia was very similar among all participating centers. A schizophrenic, whether living in China, Colombia, Czechoslovakia, Denmark, India, Nigeria, the United Kingdom, the USA, or the USSR, exhibited lack of insight, inadequate description of problems, suspiciousness, unwillingness to cooperate, false ideas, emotional dullness, poor rapport, and auditory hallucinations. Given common training, clinicians can indeed reliably diagnose schizophrenia. This does not necessarily prove that the concept of schizophrenia is useful, only that we can be consistent in its

9. Sarbin, 1972; Szasz, 1961.
10. World Health Organization, 1973.

application. We cannot proceed in our understanding of schizophrenia, unless we agree on its definition.

Our use of the term *schizophrenia* is closer to Kraepelin's than to Bleuler's. There are certainly people who, having been apparently well adjusted, lose touch with reality during a highly stressful situation and who recover completely. However, we are unconvinced that such episodes indicate the presence of schizophrenia unless other evidence exists to corroborate this view. Such evidence might take the form of a family history of schizophrenia, a long-standing history of social withdrawal or maladjustment, or a history of similar psychotic episodes. Most (but not all) of the data we will cite and the conclusions we will draw concern patients whose social, psychological, and familial history are consistent with the presenting symptoms, and whose prognosis generally includes some residual impairments. The extent to which these discussions are applicable to those well-adjusted persons who experience an "acute psychotic episode" remains a topic for research.

We are now in a position to expand our original definition: *schizophrenia refers to a chronic disorder in which thinking, feeling, and relating tend to be disturbed in characteristic ways.* Before going on to discuss the causes of schizophrenia, let's be clear about what schizophrenia does not mean.

SCHIZOPHRENIA DOES NOT MEAN SPLIT PERSONALITY

Perhaps the most widespread misconception is that schizophrenia means a split personality: Dr. Jekyll and Mr. Hyde, "the three faces of Eve," the mild-mannered man who suddenly murders his wife. While such behavior does occur (and is called a "dissociative reaction") it is *not* what is meant by schizophrenia. While the root of the term *schizophrenia* does mean "split mind," the split refers to a breakup of the personality components (thinking, feeling, and relating) rather than a split into two or more separate, coherent personalities.

In particular, the "split" refers to two phenomena. First of all, the schizophrenic is "split from reality." While the professional term for this condition is "psychotic," such lay terms as "crazy," "out of one's mind," or "out of touch" describe the same state. When psychotic, a person's perceptions of and feelings about his world are at marked variance with those of other people. He may hear voices when no one is speaking; he may think he is a famous scientist; he may feel that the radio is sending him special messages; he may perceive that parts of his body do not belong to him. Our world, the world we all agree on, has changed for him in mysterious, often frightening and occasionally beautiful ways. However, schizophrenics are not constantly psychotic, nor do they perceive everything about them in a psychotic way. The word *psychotic* refers to a temporary state in which various aspects of the environment are falsely perceived or interpreted. It does *not* refer to a stable personality trait, like the word *shy*. Thus, schizophrenics may be psychotic at times and "sane" (in proper touch with the environment) at others. Nonetheless, it is the behavior resulting from their psychotic perceptions that is usually most upsetting to those around them.

The second "split" experienced by the schizophrenic is between the thinking processes and the emotional processes. For most of us, thinking and feeling are consistent with each other most of the time. When sad, we usually wear a sad expression, have sad thoughts, tend to move slowly and with effort, and cry. People tend to think, feel, and act "all of a piece." In schizophrenia, thinking, feeling, and acting become fragmented in relation to each other and in relation to the events of the world. The schizophrenic individual may feel sad when thinking happy thoughts. Or he may feel nothing at all.

Hence, the "split" in schizophrenia refers not to a transformation into separate people, but rather to the dissolution of the functions of a single person. "Split personality" is, therefore, a misnomer and really refers to a separate disorder.

SCHIZOPHRENICS ARE NOT DANGEROUS

A second, widely held misconception is that schizophrenics are invariably unpredictable, aggressive, and dangerous. This is not so. While schizophrenics are sometimes dangerous, due to the psychotic ways in which they misperceive their environment, they are much more often withdrawn, apathetic, and frightened. Indeed, the public is in less danger from mental patients, as a group, than from the "normal" people in our environment.[11]

As with normal people, the best predictor of future behavior is past behavior (other things being equal). One would have good reason to be wary of a nonschizophrenic person who has been aggressive in the past. Likewise, if a schizophrenic has been aggressive at times when he was particularly disturbed, there is a reasonable probability that he could become so again if his illness worsened. However, schizophrenics who are not aggressive (the large majority) are not likely to become so unpredictably.

Part of the confusion about this point probably stems from the interchangeable use of the words *psychotic* and *psychopathic* in the mass media. A "psychopathic killer" is a killer who has no conscience. He is not irrational, not disorganized as the psychotic is. Rather, he does not feel that killing is wrong. While it is possible to be schizophrenic *and* psychopathic, the great majority of schizophrenics have learned to make normal moral judgments. If they hurt someone, it is usually because of their misperception of environmental events or the meaning of those events. Schizophrenic aggressiveness tends to be motivated by fear that one is being threatened in some way, rather than by a desire to hurt another person. Indeed, they are most often horrified by such acts when they regain normal perceptions. In summary, while schizophrenics may, at times, behave aggressively, they are, as a group, *less* aggressive than the general population.

11. Wahl, 1977.

SCHIZOPHRENIA IS NOT CONTAGIOUS

A misconception rarely stated but often acted upon is that schizophrenia is contagious. People are frightened of contact with schizophrenics, not only because the person's behavior is sometimes bizarre and unpredictable, but because they feel it might somehow "rub off." This is understandable in light of how precarious our own hold on reality sometimes seems to us to be at moments of stress. But, the fear is groundless. One *cannot* become schizophrenic simply through contact, however extensive, with someone who is disturbed. Families and friends need not be wary that contact with the patient will, of itself, make them ill.

SCHIZOPHRENICS ARE NEITHER HELPLESS NOR HOPELESS

One other misconception ought to be laid to rest—the notion that schizophrenics are totally unable to function and must be consigned to an institution for. life. While this conception had some validity in the past, when untreated schizophrenia often resulted in progressive mental deterioration and institutional care was commonly a necessity for those seriously afflicted, it has little validity now. Recent advances in treatment procedures have made life-long incarceration a rarity. While not presently a *curable* condition, schizophrenia is a highly *treatable* one. Patients who become ill at this time can expect, by and large, to lead their lives outside of institutions. Indeed, many schizophrenics have made, and maintained, a high level of adjustment to their own and their community's expectations. While the level of maximal adjustment varies from individual to individual, total disability is the exception rather than the rule.

These myths and misconceptions interfere with the ability to provide an environment that is conducive to recovery. To the extent that one holds these false beliefs, one will be frightened and suspicious of schizophrenic people. One would be unwilling to offer a schizophrenic person a job, to live next door to him, to interact with him socially. The effect of this social ostracism is to make return to the community a difficult and fearful prospect.

MODELS OF MADNESS

What causes schizophrenia? It is common to discuss the various descriptions and explanations of schizophrenia in terms of models—that is the system of beliefs within which one ascribes causation. In the Middle Ages, for example, the religious model was used to account for mental illness. All mental illness was explained by the presence of demons. The sufferer was said to be "possessed," and the goal of treatment was to drive out, or exorcise, the evil spirit. The physically less distressing treatments involved insulting the devil. This might be done in the following way: "Thou lustful and stupid one, . . . thou lean sow, famine-stricken and most impure, . . . thou wrinkled beast, thou mangy beast, thou beast of all beasts the most beastly."[12] This went on until either the demon or the patient gave up.

It was not until the early 1800s, when people began to look at the brain rather than at the soul as the site of disturbance, that the concept of disease replaced the concept of possession as the presumed cause of behavioral and emotional disorders. Though the medical treatments of the 1800s and early 1900s might appear inhumane by current standards, this was a critical turning point in the history of psychiatric disorders. Since a physical disorder was thought to underlie mental illness, abnormal behavior was subject to careful observation and clinical investigation. The science of psychiatry and our understanding of psychiatric disorders is, therefore, less than two hundred years old. Schizophrenia itself has been studied for fewer than

12. White cited in Brown and Menninger, 1940, pp. 29–30.

one hundred years. Today, there are many models from which to choose.

The Medical Model

At one extreme is the medical model, by which schizophrenia is labeled as a disease caused by an, as yet, unknown physical process. The schizophrenic individual is seen as sick. Behaviors occurring as a function of his illness are presumed to be out of his control. He is not held responsible for them. He is, however, held responsible for accepting the appropriate social role—that of patient. He is expected to seek medical help and to cooperate with the physician's attempts to cure or control the illness. Researchers working within this model search for biological causes of schizophrenia while clinicians prescribe biological treatments.

This view has led to important advances in our understanding and treatment of schizophrenia. But, in its pure form, it neglects the ways in which psychological, social, and cultural factors interact with physiology to produce behavior. Its unmodified application often produces helpless, dependent, passive behavior which may be antithetical to recovery.

The Moral Model

At another extreme are those who maintain that schizophrenia is merely a myth created by the labeling of patients. It has been argued that mental illness—and schizophrenia in particular—reflects a misapplication of the medical model to social and interpersonal problems.[13] It is said that different human beings, because of different values, ideologies, needs, and styles, will necessarily come into conflict with each other. Some people handle these conflicts well: others do poorly. Within this model "mental illness" is an inappropriate label for incompetent handling of problems in living. It describes people with faulty judg-

13. Szasz, 1961.

ment who make mistakes with reference to how they should behave and who are responsible for those mistakes. The label, then, essentially refers to a moral failing, and schizophrenics are simply behaving irresponsibly. Society reinforces their irresponsibility by imputing their behavior to an "illness" that is outside of their control. Indeed, it has been argued that the "cure" for such difficulties involves admission of guilt and repayment of damages.[14] The schizophrenic ought to take responsibility for his misbehavior, admit that it is wrong, change it, and attempt to make amends for whatever suffering he has caused others.

There is little doubt that schizophrenic behavior proves burdensome for those with whom the disturbed person interacts. Families may be embarrassed, frightened, and upset by such behavior. They typically accept financial responsiblity for the support and treatment of the schizophrenic person who may not hold a job or develop a secure peer group or live independently. However, the difficulties inherent in the moral model are analogous to the difficulties involved in blaming a blind man for bumping into someone. That is, physical impairments do exist. Further, they often affect behavior. The inability to demonstrate a specific physical basis for a given behavior doesn't mean that one doesn't exist. In fact, research in the area of schizophrenia yields strong evidence that a physiological basis for at least some schizophrenic symptoms is highly probable.

The Sociological Model

Why should a society label someone as ill, if indeed, he is not ill? According to one view, the label is used to shut out and lock up people whose behavior society finds offensive. The label thus serves the same political purpose as the label "witch" did during the Inquisition.[15] This argument is part of a wider view according to which the fabric of society is held together by laws and by social mores, including manners and customs. People who

14. Mowrer, 1960.
15. Szasz, 1961.

break laws are called criminals, and people who violate mores are called mentally ill. Both groups are treated in much the same way: society attempts to "rehabilitate" them through coercive control. Indeed, the distinction between "criminal" and "mentally ill" becomes more and more blurred as criminal behavior is accounted for in terms of childhood rearing, responses to poverty, and even to genetic predispositions.

One cannot deny the plausibility of this argument, nor is it possible to deny the fact that the label "schizophrenia" has been used for political purposes in some instances and has been inaccurate in others. However, it is illogical to argue that because a label can be misapplied it has no value. Racial and religious labels are analogous. The label "Jewish," for example, refers to a person with a certain set of religious beliefs and cultural values and traditions or whose parents are Jewish. However, some people think that Jews are sneaky and greedy, just as some people think that schizophrenics are invariably dangerous. In Hitler's Germany, the label "Jewish" was used to scapegoat people. Some people were made to bear the label inappropriately, for political purposes, in much the same way that some people have borne the label "schizophrenic" for the family's or society's purposes.

If the label "schizophrenia" has some important implications for the person to whom it applies, the fact that the community responds to these individuals in one way or another is a separate issue and should not be confused with what is going on within the individual.

The Antipsychiatry Model

According to another extreme view, sometimes called "antipsychiatry," schizophrenic behavior is seen as an island of sanity in a society that sets "crazy" standards of behavior:

> The condition of alienation, of being asleep, of being unconscious, of being out of one's mind, is the condition of normal man.[16]

16. Laing, 1967, p. 28.

And

> social adaptation to a dysfunctional society may be very
> dangerous. The perfectly adjusted bomber pilot may
> be a greater threat to species survival than the hospi-
> talized schizophrenic deluded that the Bomb is inside
> him. Our society may itself have become biologically
> dysfunctional, and some forms of schizophrenic alien-
> ation from the alienation of society may have a socio-
> biological function that we have not recognized.[17]

The schizophrenic is thus seen as a prophet, whose heightened state of awareness represents "true" sanity.

The behavioral symptoms of schizophrenia have remained
remarkably constant across time and across cultures. If schizophrenia is, indeed, a "sane response to an insane world," different cultures ought to produce varying amounts and kinds of
responses. This has not been the case.

However, since this argument is essentially a definitional one,
it can't be refuted on grounds of logic or evidence. If a person
uses the word *table* to mean "a container for holding liquids,"
we can only insist that, for us, the word has a different meaning.
The same is true of the words *sane* and *insane*. They are used
here in the way they are commonly used, but we cannot prevent
someone from using them in a different way.

Most professionals would agree that an adequate explanation
of the complex phenomenon called schizophrenia involves aspects of many models. The role of heredity, constitution, learning, motivation, social conditions, and societal expectations in
determining one's mental health are all acknowledged. Schizophrenia results from the interaction between factors inside the
individual (his biochemistry and his personality traits) and factors outside (environmental stress).

17. *Ibid.,* p. 120.

THE ROLE OF BIOCHEMISTRY

Schizophrenia probably has its roots in a biochemical abnormality within the body. While there are those who dispute this view,[18] the evidence at this point appears highly persuasive and comes primarily from two sources. First, a large body of research data indicates that schizophrenia has a genetic component.[19] That is to say, the tendency to manifest schizophrenic symptoms under stress is, in large part, genetically based. While it has been known for many years that schizophrenia tends to run in families (and, indeed, this knowledge has been causal in the suspicion that faulty family rearing practices cause schizophrenia), it is only recently that adoption studies and twin studies have helped to tease apart the genetic and environmental contributions to the illness. While the genetic contribution is clear, nongenetic factors have also been implicated by these same studies. Nonetheless, insofar as genes provide us with our basic physical equipment, a genetic predisposition toward schizophrenia means that some part of the body is malfunctioning or likely to malfunction under a certain set of circumstances. Analogies with other medical diseases are common. Both diabetes and hypertension run in families. They are not *solely* genetically determined. Rather, what is inherited is a *predisposition* to become ill in this way, given the right set of factors.

The other major source of evidence for a biological predisposition to schizophrenia comes from a recent treatment innovation. In 1955, clinicians in the United States began using chlorpromazine (Thorazine®) to treat schizophrenia. The results were overwhelmingly positive. Many patients who had been withdrawn became communicative; many patients who had been assaultive became calm; many patients who had lost touch with reality regained it. Both recent clinical experience and controlled scientific studies have confirmed the initial impression that the symptoms of schizophrenia are markedly and

18. Laing and Esterson, 1964; Szasz, 1961.
19. Rosenthal, 1968; Rosenthal, 1971; Gottesman and Shields, 1972.

lastingly reduced in many patients through the use of chlorpromazine and other related drugs. We need only compare Census figures of mental hospitals over the last two decades to become convinced of the importance of medication in the treatment of schizophrenia. The number of inpatients in state and county mental hospitals (the majority of whom were diagnosed schizophrenics) in the U.S.A. climbed steadily for several decades to a peak of 559,000 in 1955. Then, for nineteen consecutive years the number fell until, in 1974, fewer than 216,000 people inhabited these institutions.[20] While the mechanism of the drugs' effect is still unclear and while many problems with their use remain, the way has been paved toward a biochemical explanation for at least some of the phenomena we call schizophrenia.

Thus, while much research remains to be done, it is reasonable to expect that schizophrenia has, as one of its components, a biochemical abnormality. We can also be sure that this approach will not yield the *whole* answer.

THE ROLE OF PERSONALITY TRAITS

Each individual is different—in intelligence, in upbringing, in values, in adaptability. Thus, each individual responds to and copes with illness in a different way. This may well account for the wide variety of ways in which schizophrenia is manifested and is certainly related to the relative success each individual has in overcoming the effects of the illness.

By way of example, consider Sam and John, both middle-aged men who have recently had a heart attack. Sam's life has been single-minded. His career has been his only interest. While he has a wife and two children, he has related to them only superficially for many years. He is proud that he has been able to provide them with a comfortable, even luxurious, life style, but he has never taken much interest in giving, or receiving,

20. Becker and Schulberg, 1976.

emotional support. Rather, he has always seen himself as "strong" and has tried to raise his children to be strong as well. He hasn't cried since he was an adolescent, and he has always minimized or ignored pain or physical impairment in himself and in his family. Sam has many business acquaintances with whom he is on excellent terms. They see him as an extremely capable businessman.

Sam's heart attack comes as a massive shock to his self-image. Unable to communicate his very real fears to anyone or to accept them himself, he works hard to convince himself that they do not exist. As usual, he is successful. He is so successful that he cannot take his physician's advice seriously. His values, attitudes, and coping style all dictate that he go back to work quickly and that he work at least as hard as he did before.

John has also worked very hard and has been financially successful, and he is also proud of himself. But he has always been more invested in relationships with people than with his career. He sees himself as a fallible, and at times a weak, person who depends on his wife and other family members for help when he is in emotional or physical pain. He has accepted his weaknesses as well as his strengths and has attempted to teach his children that they need not be perfect. John does not have a large number of acquaintances. He spends much of his time with a small group of friends whom he has known many years. Together they make music (John plays the violin), play cards, or discuss their feelings about personal or community issues. John's friends see him as a warm, affectionate person.

John's heart attack also comes as quite a shock. He becomes quite depressed and discusses his fear of dying with his wife and with one of his close friends. When the doctor tells him that he can expect to live a long and comfortable life if he will slow down a bit at work and take certain other precautions, he agrees readily, even though the reduced family income will mean no more summer trips. His wife doesn't seem to mind about that, and John begins to think, with pleasure, of the additional time he will be able to spend with family and friends.

Sam and John are very different people. They respond to the same event quite differently. The outcomes of that event will be predictably different, and will depend as much on *how* they respond as on *what* they are responding to.

THE STRESS FACTOR

Both clinical experience and research have indicated that environmental events may be quite important with respect to the timing and frequency of schizophrenic "episodes." Stress can take many forms. For most of us, a death in the family is perceived as stressful. But the birth of a child or promotion to a better job, like other happy events, can produce stress too. In fact, any change in life circumstances requires some adjustment in the individual, and people vary in their capacity to adjust.

The role of stress in the development of schizophrenic symptoms is particularly hard to study since what is stressful for one person may not be stressful for another. Nonetheless, two conclusions can be drawn. First, the biological predisposition to become mentally disorganized lowers a schizophrenic's resistance to stress in general, although some people who are so predisposed can tolerate more stress than others. Second, the issue of becoming independent from one's family of origin appears to pose special difficulties for individuals predisposed to schizophrenia. This is not surprising in view of the fact that mental, emotional, and social competence are requirements of successful completion of this task. The predisposed individual may be impaired in each of these areas.

THE DIATHESIS-STRESS MODEL

Schizophrenia occurs as a result of three factors: internal physiological and psychological predispositions, and environmental stress. Whether or not a person who has no genetic predisposition for schizophrenia can become schizophrenic (versus experiencing an acute psychotic episode) due to stress alone is still a disputable point. In such cases where no genetic evidence is apparent, it is more likely that familial schizophrenia went undiagnosed for a variety of reasons or that family members carried a predisposition without showing symptoms themselves. The latter situation is analogous to the one in which two short parents have a tall offspring. These arguments form the basis of the "diathesis-stress" model. The "diathesis" refers to the biochemical predisposition toward the illness (schizophrenia) which *must* be present in order for the illness to manifest itself. However, the diathesis alone is not enough. It must be activated by a stressor. Thus, while a person with no diathesis for schizophrenia can become disturbed under severe stress—with anxiety, with ulcers, with neurotic manifestations—he will not become schizophrenic. Further, while a person *with* a schizophrenic diathesis (which may or may not include overtly schizophrenic family members) may enjoy good health, he carries a *tendency* to become schizophrenic under the right set of circumstances. At present, we have no way to measure the strength of this tendency to become ill.

At the same time, having a schizophrenic relative *does not* mean that one is necessarily carrying the predisposition for the illness. The family inheritance patterns indicate that schizophrenia may well be a multigenic phenomenon, with many family members carrying no "schizophrenic genes," some family members carrying a small number, and a few unlucky family members carrying a significant number.

Schizophrenia refers to characteristically disturbed ways of thinking, feeling, and relating that develop in biologically predisposed individuals under certain personal and environmental circumstances. Schizophrenia is a complex phenomenon that has existed in all cultures at all times. It is not a purely medical disorder, nor is it a purely social, or political phenomenon. Rather, it evolves through an interaction between genetic, personal, environmental and cultural factors. In Chapter Two, we begin to describe the symptoms of schizophrenia.

2

SYMPTOMS OF SCHIZOPHRENIA

Kate sits at her typewriter, unable to concentrate. The ticking of the clock and the whispering of her co-workers are too loud. She senses, with some anxiety, that they are talking about her—again. Finding their behavior interesting, she starts to make some notes for "The Book," which will, once and for all, explain human behavior. She is flooded, suddenly, with an intense feeling of power and well-being. A co-worker approaches to see if she is all right, worried because Kate has been staring into space for twenty minutes. At the sound of her name, Kate looks up but finds herself unable to understand what is being said to her. She hears each of the words, but cannot figure out which of a hundred meanings to attach to them. Frightened and mute, she continues to stare as the face of her co-worker begins to dissolve into unrelated features.

There are two perspectives from which to view this episode. From Kate's, the world is changing in confusing and terrifying ways. From ours, Kate is experiencing symptoms of schizophrenia. In this chapter, we describe schizophrenic symptoms from the point of view of the observer.

Schizophrenia can affect virtually all areas of personal and social functioning. It has multiple symptoms, many of which are also seen in other disorders. Further, schizophrenia tends to have a fluctuating course, with symptoms waxing and waning over time. Thus, it is rare that a person will exhibit *all* of the symptoms of the illness at any one time. More typically each patient shows a cluster of some of the symptoms while other symptoms may be absent entirely. In addition, symptoms may vary in content and intensity from the grossly abnormal to the tolerably deviant. Nevertheless, there are commonalities running throughout which identify schizophrenia. This chapter will both describe the symptoms of schizophrenia upon which a clinical diagnosis is made and show how other disorders that may resemble schizophrenia are sometimes erroneously labeled as schizophrenia. While there are a number of clinical systems for diagnosing schizophrenia, we will consider disturbances of thinking, feeling, and interpersonal relationships.

SCHIZOPHRENIC THOUGHT

One of the defining characteristics of schizophrenia is disordered thinking. This is present, in one form or another, at one time or another, in all schizophrenics and is typically what makes schizophrenia often seem so bizarre. In our example, Kate experienced a number of symptoms of thinking disturbance. She believed, falsely, that she was writing a great book. She had difficulty concentrating and was unable to understand what a co-worker was saying to her. Her perceptions of the co-worker's appearance changed.

A major difficulty in studying thinking problems is that they are not directly observable and must be *inferred* from speech and behavior. There are some theorists who feel that the odd ways in which many schizophrenics attempt to communicate represent a purposely garbled message. Their view is that schizophrenic thinking is not disordered, but rather that the schizophrenic is motivated to disguise the meaning of his communications.[1] However, this is not the commonly held view. Others hold that schizophrenia can be characterized by the presence of certain beliefs.[2] Specifically, these beliefs are that thoughts are

1. Haley, 1959; Sullivan, 1953.
2. Schneider, 1959.

heard "aloud"; voices exist in the absence of people arguing or discussing; thoughts are "inserted" as if by some external force; thoughts are withdrawn as if by some external force; thoughts are being "broadcast"; and believing that personal feelings, behavior, and "will" are controlled from outside the person. A more general view is that while the *content* of schizophrenic thought may be environmentally or personally relevant, it is the *process* of disordered thinking that is central to schizophrenia.

For example, Kate believed herself to be writing an important book. Further, she believed that her co-workers disliked her and were saying disparaging things about her. Clearly, the content of these beliefs has personal relevance. We can surmise that Kate feels unimportant and unliked and has a need to see herself as especially intelligent, insightful, and worthwhile. We can guess that her thoughts about "The Book" are attempts at compensating for her lack of self-confidence. However, many people have these sorts of conflicts but they do not develop such deviant ideas. It is this uncontrollable tendency to develop bizarre, unrealistic ideas, not the underlying conflicts they may represent, that is characteristic of schizophrenia. Thus, in our example, while feeling worthless in the face of a strong need to achieve is not unusual, to believe that one is writing a book that will change the world is quite deviant.

To date, it has not been demonstrated that the schizophrenic can be taught or coerced or convinced not to have these thoughts. Clinically, we have had some success in teaching the schizophrenic not to talk about bizarre ideas and helping him to see that they do not represent reality and, therefore, should not be acted upon.

Patients' descriptions of their thinking processes support the view that thinking is disturbed. They complain, for instance, of disturbances in their ability to concentrate and to organize their thoughts. In its mild form this tends to appear as distractibility. A schizophrenic may have more difficulty than other people concentrating on a telephone conversation when people are conversing in the background. He may have trouble reading because the activity prompts thoughts that seem to go off in their own direction. He may become confused if asked to follow a series of instructions.

These interruptions in thinking are part of our own experience, too. We become distracted in just these sorts of ways when we are overtired or emotionally upset. We can begin to understand, then, how distressing it must be to find one's mind wandering, out of control, much of the time. We can also appreciate how tiring is the effort to sustain concentration under these circumstances.

More fundamentally, the schizophrenic finds it difficult to organize thoughts and direct them toward a goal. It appears as if associations lose their logical continuity. Where most of us would simply give our age in response to the question "How old are you?" a particularly disturbed schizophrenic might answer "Twenty-four, which is one less than twenty-five, which if multiplied by four equals one hundred . . . ." Thinking, which is normally goal-directed, becomes fragmented. This sort of disturbed thinking is called "loose associations."

Normal thinking follows certain logical rules, and, until recently, it had been thought that schizophrenic thinking was guided by a different set of rules rather than by no rules at all. It was thought that, if only these rules could be discovered, schizophrenic thinking would become comprehensible. For example, what can we conclude from the premises "all basketball players are tall" and "John is tall?" While these statements tell us nothing about a relationship between John and basketball, if schizophrenics typically conclude "John is a basketball player," then they would be illustrating the use of a different sort of logical rule called "predicate logic." However, when schizophrenics were compared with nonschizophrenics of similar intelligence, no consistent differences in logic were found.[3]

During the last few years, there has been growing evidence that schizophrenics' thinking may represent an "accentuation of normal response biases."[4] In other words, the tendency of nor-

3. Broen, 1968; McGhie, 1969.
4. Chapman and Chapman, 1973.

mal people toward certain types of errors is exaggerated in schizophrenia.

One example of a normal response bias is the "halo" effect. If, for instance, there is one thing we don't like about a neighbor (perhaps the statues in the front yard), it will usually carry over, against reason, to judgment about other things (a dislike for the neighbor's style of humor). This is a "negative" halo effect. This can also occur in a positive way, as represented in the saying "love is blind." These are both normal biases operating against objective information. In the schizophrenic, however, the process is extreme. Where most people can learn to overcome the pull of a halo effect, the schizophrenic sometimes appears swept away by it, unmindful of appropriate reaction. Thus, the neighbor with the statues on the front lawn may be perceived as haughty, aloof, showing off, really trying to ridicule the schizophrenic, and perhaps being part of a systematic attempt to bring about the schizophrenic's downfall. From this view, schizophrenic thought is not guided by a different set of rules, but is rather an extreme form of normal thinking. In either case, lack of goal direction or "accentuation of normal response biases," the thought of the schizophrenic is sometimes difficult to follow because of its disjointedness.

Bleuler, whose turn-of-the-century characterization of schizophrenic symptoms remains unsurpassed, describes the disorder this way:

> In the normal thinking process, the numerous actual and latent images combine to determine each association. In schizophrenia, however, single images or whole combinations may be rendered ineffective, in an apparently haphazard fashion. Instead, thinking operates with ideas and concepts which have no, or a completely insufficient, connection with the main idea and should therefore be excluded from the thought-process. The result is that thinking becomes confused, bizarre, incorrect, abrupt.[5]

5. Bleuler, 1950, p. 22.

Thus, thoughts may be connected simply because they occur together in time. For instance, if one asks a patient a question, he may respond with an idea he happened to have at the time, with little reference to the meaning of the question. Words may come together in sentences because they have similar sounds, rather than appropriately related meaning. Fragments of thoughts may lead to other fragments of thoughts so that, before long the original intent of the communication is lost. Our example of the schizophrenic's response to the question of how old he was is bizarre, not because the associations are bizarre but because the original goal is lost while one thought leads to another. It is as if thinking gets waylaid, leading forever down divergent paths and either failing to get to the point quickly or going beyond it. A schizophrenic patient describes the state this way:

> My thoughts get all jumbled up. I start thinking or talking about something but I never get there. Instead, I wander off in the wrong direction and get caught up with all sorts of different things that may be connected with the thing I want to say but in a way I can't explain. . . .
>
> My trouble is that I've got too many thoughts. You might think about something, let's say that ashtray and just think, oh! yes, that's for putting my cigarette in, but I would think of it and then I would think of a dozen different things connected with it at the same time.[6]

Two Models of Disordered Thinking

There are two primary ways of describing disordered thinking. One is that the normal brain has a filter mechanism which prevents the intrusion of unwanted or irrelevant thoughts. As you read this book, for example, you are relatively unaware of

6. McGhie and Chapman, 1961, p. 108.

the noises of the outside world. You might not have noticed the grumblings of your stomach (if it is near mealtime). You have probably put out of mind a difficult decision you have to make in the near future or a disturbing interaction with a friend that occurred recently. You are able to focus your attention on this page, more or less at will, and you can direct your mind to shut off extraneous thoughts and feelings.

The schizophrenic person appears to have a faulty "shut -off" mechanism, a faulty filter. He tends to be flooded by information, by thoughts and feelings from within and by stimulation from without. Patients' descriptions, like the following from a recovered schizophrenic, lend credence to such a view:

> Each of us is capable of coping with a large number of stimuli, invading our being through any of the senses. It's obvious that we would be incapable of carrying on any of our daily activities if even one hundredth of all these available stimuli invaded us at once. So the mind must have a filter, which functions without our conscious thought, sorting stimuli and allowing only those which are relevant to the situation in hand to disturb consciousness. What happened to me in Toronto was a breakdown of the filter, a hodgepodge of unrelated stimuli were distracting me from things that should have held my undivided attention—irrelevant, completely unrelated events became intricately connected in my mind.[7]

Researchers have come up with a view that encompasses what has been expressed by patients themselves. They suggest that there is a disruption in the ability to attend selectively. When schizophrenics must choose to attend to certain stimuli and ignore others, they become confused and their performance is impaired. For instance, in one study, schizophrenics were compared with normal people with respect to their ability to repeat a message they had heard. When the target message was presented alone, patients had no difficulty but when the target

7. MacDonald, 1960.

messages occurred simultaneously with one or more distractor messages (presented through earphones, one or more messages to each ear), schizophrenics performed poorly compared to the normal subjects.[8] Should this descriptive model eventually prove to be accurate, we still have a long way to go before understanding exactly how and why such a filter system works.

The second, more recent, interpretation of schizophrenics' thinking is that they either lack or fail to use optimal strategies in their thinking.[9] Each of us organizes incoming material in some way so that we can remember it more easily, while the schizophrenic person may not have useful organizational principles available. For example, you are given the task of memorizing the following words: *cat, chair, fish, linen, sunny, desk, cotton,* and *cloudy.* The way to optimize your performance would be to recall the words by categories, like weather conditions, types of cloth, animals, and furniture. The schizophrenic is not as likely either to perceive these organizing relationships or to use them consistently. Regardless of the ultimate outcome of these two views—filtering and thinking strategies—in explaining schizophrenic thought, it is agreed that schizophrenics during their ill periods have poorly organized thoughts.

Thought Blocking and Repetition

Another common symptom is thought blocking. Schizophrenics complain at times of being totally without thoughts. They may "go blank" in the middle of a sentence, often starting up again on a totally new theme. There appears to be a poverty of ideas, with the common result that the same theme may be repeated over and over again with little, if any variation. Consider the following in which a patient attempts unsuccessfully to communicate a thought.

> Certain objects have to be tested to get their answers whether they are bad or good to increase. After certain

8. Rappaport, 1967.
9. Koh and Kayton, 1974; Russell, Bannatyne, and Smith, 1975.

objects have been examined their answers say they are
bad to increase. Objects with solitude names of their
own kinds are bad for pluses. When it's 9:40 the small
hand is between the 9 and 10 or it's 20 of 10.

. . . Two hands on 7 is just 6:35 and it will never
have any more figures. This form of increasing is not
plain. Most increasing is plain. Even small hand on 9,
large hand on 8 is only called 8:40 and it won't have
any more names. 8:40 is 20 of 9. This name will always
be odd. 4:35 is always small hand on 5, large hand on
7 because:

     a. in ordinary counting there's something between
1 and 12.

     b. 5 follows 4, so when it's 4:35 it's 25 of 5 so the
small hand is between 4 and 5.

This line of thought goes on for many pages.

Sometimes, patients are so disturbed that they are unable to
answer simple questions. Instead, they repeat the question in
parrotlike fashion. It is almost as if the overworked filter mechanism had shut down the system entirely for a time. However
we describe it, there is no doubt that many schizophrenics are
aware of thought blocking and find it highly distressing.

Hallucinations

Both loose associations and thought blocking tend to be characteristic of most, if not all, patients' experience. There are a
number of additional ways in which thought disorder may be
manifested. By far the most common is hallucinations. Hallucinations are sensory experiences in the absence of the appropriate external stimuli. The schizophrenic may hear voices talking to or about him when no one is speaking. He may see a
vision of a dead relative. He may feel insects crawling over his
body or an electric current running up and down his spine.

Patients may or may not be aware that their experiences do

not match reality. When they are aware of this fact, they are often able to "ignore" the disruptive voices or sensations more or less successfully. Indeed, a number of recovered schizophrenics are able to carry on with their personal and vocational activities while still hearing voices occasionally. They remind themselves that the voices are not real and are able to reorient themselves to the job at hand. Clearly, such a strategy, while possible, is difficult to carry out and requires strong motivation. Many schizophrenics, on the other hand, are unable to distinguish their faulty sensations from reality so that their behavior is seriously disrupted. Some will carry out voices' commands to hurt themselves, to refuse to speak, or to engage in other inappropriate behaviors.

Delusions

A similar symptom is the tendency of some schizophrenics to misunderstand the *meaning* of real stimuli. They personalize events that are not really related to them. A patient like Kate may think that people are talking about her when their conversation is about an entirely unrelated matter. She may believe that a song on the radio is being sung specifically to her for some reason. She may feel that policemen who drive by her door think she is a criminal and are plotting to trap her. These sorts of false ideas are called *paranoid* or delusional ideas. They differ from the occasionally paranoid thoughts that we all get insofar as they are not correctable by reasoning or by proof. The schizophrenic tends to be unshakable in his faulty beliefs while we will generally change ours when new information comes our way.

Finally, the schizophrenic may be unable to differentiate between thinking about an action and actually doing it. He may be unsure about whether he has actually called somebody a name or simply thought about doing so. Fantasy and reality can become hopelessly intertwined.

Coping with Thought Disorder

The thinking disorders described earlier vary widely from person to person and from time to time with respect to severity. In seriously disturbed people, communications can be so disordered that strings of seemingly unrelated words result and comprehensible conversation is impossible. On the other hand, recovered schizophrenics may show little, if any disturbance in concentration and thinking. Typically, these activities continue to require more than normal effort and are more easily disrupted than in persons without the illness. Therefore, it is important for patients and their families to be aware of the problem and to develop appropriate strategies for reducing external distraction.

In order to read or study, for example, a schizophrenic usually has greater need for a quiet, nondistracting setting than his normal peers. He may well take instruction more easily in a one-on-one setting than in a group where other activities may be going on. He will probably be more competent and at ease among a small group of people than at a large, bustling party. He is likely to perform better in a job where he is not asked to do a number of different things simultaneously.

Family members and friends are often most dismayed by the paranoid aspect of the schizophrenic's disorder. And well they might be, since false ideas about family and close friends are quite often prominent. How should we behave in the face of false accusations or with respect to other false representations of reality? This is a difficult question since the answer is dependent on the patient's condition. If the person is highly disturbed and appears to rigidly adhere to his false beliefs and perceptions, denials of accusations and statements about reality will probably do no good and may even serve to further alienate the patient. In this circumstance, prompt professional attention will serve the patient better than the family can serve him by reasoning with him.

In many instances a schizophrenic may be unsure of his perceptions and actively seek reassurance about what is true and what is false. This is particularly true of partially recovered patients who may continue to experience hallucinations and misperceptions of reality even after appropriate treatment. For such patients, careful and nonemotional statements about reality can be of help. It is important, however, to present reality as it is. It should not be distorted to protect the patient.

Let's suppose for a moment that a schizophrenic acquaintance complains that he is uncomfortable riding buses because he feels that everybody is staring at him. He further feels that they all know he has been hospitalized for mental illness and are thinking that he is stupid or sick. What can you say? First, you have to decide if it is likely that people stare at him. If, for instance, he dresses quite strangely (or is very unkempt and sloppy), or tends to behave oddly in public situations, or has a noticeable physical defect of some kind, people on buses may indeed stare at him. In such a case you help by saying:

> People probably do notice you because you wear cut-off jeans and no shirt and need a shave. But they *don't* know about your illness unless you *tell* them. People can't read minds. They might think you look sloppy, but they aren't thinking all those other things.

If there is nothing conspicuous about the person and you are sure that people don't stare at him you could say:

> Your illness doesn't show. If people glanced at you on a bus they would only see a normal, everyday guy. There is nothing about you that would make people stare at you and think bad thoughts about you. They can only see what you let them see.

It is important to keep in mind that the person is genuinely uncomfortable. He is not making it all up nor trying to exasperate you. In fact, it is a credit to him and to your relationship with him that he will share these feelings with you at all. Thus, your statement about reality is best offered in a sympathetic, helpful way rather than in a way which would convey that he was stupid for misperceiving things like he does.

Let's consider a situation that may be harder to deal with. Suppose a schizophrenic person walks into a room and asks accusingly: "Were you talking about me?" If you were, it is best to say so and to tell him what you were saying. If you were not, it's appropriate to tell him you were talking about something different and to give him a general idea of the topic if you can. If you try to respond honestly to the request for information rather than to the accusation, you will find yourself less upset over the interaction and more able to be understanding. Remember that disordered thinking is involuntary, and that the patient may be disturbed, confused, and frightened. These and other coping strategies can be developed as the need arises once the impairment in thinking is recognized and understood.

EMOTIONS IN SCHIZOPHRENIA

It is not known at this time whether disturbances in feeling come from disturbances in thinking, whether disturbances in feeling cause thinking disruptions, or whether they are separate disturbances. Regardless of the eventual solution to this puzzle, it is clear that the schizophrenic has emotional experiences that parallel the thought disturbances.

Just as the train of thoughts is often fragmented and disconnected from reality, so is the emotional stream disrupted and unrelated to real-life events. This emotional disruption can be most upsetting to both the patient and his family and friends. For the patient, it is exhausting and confusing. For those who know him it is frightening in that they are no longer able to predict how he will respond. They find themselves unable to calm him, to influence him in expected directions. They are deprived of the ability to make the patient feel better.

The Acute Phase

The emotional disorder tends to take one of two forms depending, apparently, on the phase of the illness. During periods of acute upset, emotions tend to shift rapidly and are often inappropriate to the circumstances. These are also the periods when thought seems most impaired.

Typical of this phase are the responses of a young woman who was asked to describe the happiest time of her life. She described a family picnic during which she felt safe and protected. Yet, she cried piteously as she described the day's events and her happy feelings on that occasion. When asked a few minutes later to describe the most unhappy event in her life she laughed almost uncontrollably while describing an incident in which her father, drunk, beat up her mother as she watched. She was totally unable to explain the inconsistency between her thought and feelings, and was quite disturbed by the mixed message she was giving.

Patients will often smile or giggle inappropriately, become incensed for no apparent reason, or appear depressed and tearful during happy circumstances. They appear unable to sustain a mood as they are unable to sustain a directed thought sequence. In many cases, the entire personality seems to change as the emotions change, and this may happen frequently over a brief period of time.

While these intense, alternating feelings have their negative aspects, they can also be extremely exciting. Euphorias and mystical experiences occur which can hardly be matched by what the sane world has to offer. The disparity between Kate's real and fantasied situations is an example of this problem. She experiences being able to read minds, to understand and predict fully the behavior of other people. At such times she feels powerful, omnipotent, even godlike. These feelings provide such a striking contrast to her nonpsychotic judgments of herself as, at best, no better than millions of other young women and, at worst, less worthwhile and less in control of her life than most people, that she has been unable to tolerate the loss of her psychotic ideas for more than a few months at a time. As a result she characteristically stops taking her medication immediately after each discharge from the hospital. Many patients, like Kate, report missing these episodes intensely when the illness abates.

The Chronic Phase

Emptiness and lack of feelings are manifestations of the chronic phase. Outside of occasional episodes of excitement, schizophrenia tends to produce a flattening of the entire emotional system. The patient appears not to experience the highs and lows of normal feelings. Indeed, he may act as if nothing matters at all. He is unable to experience pleasure and, therefore, loses his motivation to achieve positive goals. He is somewhat insensitive to pain, and may not be motivated to avoid it. During the chronic phase of the illness the schizophrenic often stops taking care of his physical appearance, ceases to work, and avoids social and recreational activities. He becomes lethargic, withdrawn, and unmotivated.

This severe constriction of the emotional range is far more common overall than are the episodes of active disturbances. For many patients the illness first manifests itself in this way and they may never again experience the highs and lows of normal emotion, nor the superhighs and superlows of the acutely disturbed schizophrenic. Further, even in patients who are prone to active periods, these periods tend to diminish in length, frequency, and intensity over the years, with a nonresponsive emotional system usually being the final outcome in untreated cases. It is as if the emotional system is destroyed by continuous overstimulation.

The crucial feature of the schizophrenic's emotional life is the apparent split between thought and feeling. It is as if the two had somehow become separated, where in most of us, how we feel and what we think are of a piece. If we think "sad" thoughts, we feel sad; if we think "happy" thoughts, we feel happy. Such is not the case for the schizophrenic, who, in his disordered world, exhibits behavior that suggests that thought and feeling are no longer related. Thus, the split in schizophrenia refers to the lack of connection among thoughts, feelings, and reality rather than to the formation of two distinct personalities.

Coping with Emotional Disturbance

During the acute phase of the illness, the schizophrenic may have little control over his rapidly changing expressions of feeling. This can be frightening and confusing for the individual and for the family as well. A general strategy of attempting to reduce emotional stress while securing professional help as quickly as possible is probably in order. Getting angry, questioning the person about his feelings, and attempting to reduce emotional distance (by hugging or talking it out) are usually counterproductive. In general, interactions that are emotionally stimulating should be avoided at this time.

During the chronic phase, when lethargy and unresponsiveness may predominate, families can offer and encourage activities which are designed to be rewarding. However, emotional dullness may be a feature of the illness and not a reflection on the worth of the people with whom the patient interacts.

INTERPERSONAL RELATIONS AND SCHIZOPHRENIA

Probably the most common schizophrenic behavior is social withdrawal. Perhaps in response to the onslaught of uncontrollable thoughts and feelings, schizophrenics tend to withdraw into a world of their own. Formerly gregarious and extroverted individuals may become seclusive and quiet; formerly shy individuals appear even less responsive to social stimuli. While it used to be thought that schizophrenia was most likely to develop in already "schizoid" (that is, shy and withdrawn) individuals, it is now clear that there is no special predisposing personality. It is an oversimplification turned to myth that a shy child has a greater chance of developing schizophrenia than a highly social child. Indeed, recent evidence suggests that children eventually treated for schizophrenia as adults may be abrasive and aggressive as well as withdrawn and quiet.[10]

As the illness develops, an inner world of fantasy comes to replace the outer world of reality. This process tends to be gradual and to precede the development of more obvious symp-

10. Watt, 1972.

toms, and so is often hard to detect. But it may occur abruptly and with little warning or reason. Often, but not always, social withdrawal is accompanied by loss of interest in personal hygiene and loss of motivation to work or study. The withdrawal can become extremely marked, such that the person may refuse to come out of his room or to communicate with anyone at all. More often, the person appears distracted and preoccupied. He may appear to become extremely interested in a solitary hobby (perhaps reading or stamp collecting) that had only occupied a moderate amount of his time previously. Families tend to search in vain for a reason for the change in behavior, often ending by labeling it a phase. This is certainly quite natural since each of us withdraws from time to time. Mental illness is, and probably should be, our explanation of last resort. It is only when this withdrawal becomes prolonged or extremely marked or when it is accompanied by disordered thinking or acute emotional episodes that families become concerned enough to get a professional opinion.

Though we have presented the signs and symptoms of schizophrenia within separate spheres of experience, an overall picture is important as well. In all areas, the schizophrenic is variable and disorganized. Thoughts seem to lose their goal of social communication. Thinking becomes disconnected, and confusing. Similarly, emotional responses begin to lose their connections with thoughts and environmental events. The schizophrenic, withdrawing from interpersonal contact, relies further and further on his internal processes; the distinction between fantasy and reality lessens. No longer responding to external, environmental stimuli, the schizophrenic often appears inappropriate in his thoughts, feelings, and interpersonal experiences.

At this point, readers are probably developing a severe case of "medical student's disease," in which many of the symptoms appear to apply to self or to friends. Since we all have had some of these experiences, are we all schizophrenic? The answer is emphatically *no*. The diagnosis of schizophrenia is made on the basis of *clusters* of these symptoms which are either *quite long-*

standing or *marked in severity*. Since many of the symptoms occur in other disorders as well as in normal people from time to time, the total picture must be considered by an experienced, mental-health professional in order for an accurate diagnosis to be made. Even then, the picture is not always clear so that a diagnosis may be used as a "working hypothesis." While this situation is certainly frustrating, it is by no means limited to the diagnosis of schizophrenia. It occurs with great frequency, for example, in many areas of medicine.

SCHIZOPHRENIA "SUBTYPES"

Schizophrenic symptoms tend to cluster, yielding subtypes of the disorder that are conceived of as "ideal types." It is rare that a person fits a particular subtype exactly. The fit is more often imperfect so that the subtype label carries less information, in general, than the label "schizophrenia."

Chronic Undifferentiated Schizophrenia

Mary is thirty-seven years old and has been hospitalized eight times since she was nineteen. She is unmarried, lives in a boarding home, and works in a factory. She has few friends and spends most of her free time watching television. Her hospitalizations have always resulted from the same set of symptoms. She becomes agitated, finds it difficult to organize her thoughts, fears that she may be turning into a man. She begins to talk out loud to herself, to rock back and forth in her seat at work, and to wander aimlessly through the streets in the evenings. She stops saying "good morning" to co-workers and appears confused if they address her. Usually, after a few weeks in the hospital, she feels and looks better and is discharged to resume her solitary life on the outside.

Mary's diagnosis is *chronic undifferentiated schizophrenia*. This is the most commonly diagnosed form of schizophrenia. The label carries a number of implications. The word *chronic* implies that the illness is of long-standing duration. Often, prolonged or multiple hospitalizations have been necessary. The illness is presumed to have existed months or even years before the diagnosis was made. An additional implication is that the illness will continue as a chronic condition, even though it might be brought under adequate control with treatment. The underlying assumption here is that schizophrenia is much like diabetes—it is controllable, but not curable. The word *undifferentiated* simply means that no one symptom dominates the picture—that is, that no finer distinction in symptom pattern can be made. Often, patients with other subtype diagnoses in the early years of their illness will show a less differentiated symptom picture over time. Thus, an older patient is more likely to be diagnosed as having chronic undifferentiated schizophrenia than a younger one.

Paranoid Schizophrenia

Jim is twenty-four years old. He is a third-year medical student. Over the last few weeks he has been noticing that older men appear to be frightened of him when he passes them on the street. Recently, he has become convinced that he is actually the director of the Central Intelligence Agency and that these men are secret agents of a hostile nation. Jim has found confirmatory evidence for this idea in the fact that a helicopter flies over his house every day at 8:00 A.M. and at 4:30 P.M. Surely, this surveillance is part of the plot to assassinate him. He neglects his studies and spends most of his time figuring out how to evade his enemies.

After engaging in many subtle tests of her loyalty, Jim finally confides in his girl friend. Dismayed and frightened, she telephones Jim's parents, who convince him, with great difficulty, to see a psychiatrist.

Paranoid schizophrenia is diagnosed in patients who exhibit a fairly well-formed, coherent delusional system. We have described delusions as false ideas that are not correctable by reasoning. When such ideas are prominent in the symptom picture, the patient is labeled paranoid. This group includes people who consistently believe that they have a different identity from their real one, who believe that they have a function that they do not have, or who believe that other people are plotting to harm them. Delusional systems tend to have two related aspects. They tend to be grandiose, in that the patient believes himself to be special, to be powerful, often to be magical. The other side of this coin is intense mistrust of others—since he is so important, his enemies are trying to harm him. It is possible for a patient to show only one or the other of these aspects, but more often they are both apparent.

We might ask at this point about the relationship between paranoid delusions and overt hallucinations. There are two ways to think of this. First, hallucinations may be overt, though camouflaged, expressions of an internal conflict. In our earlier example of the patient who felt grandiose and persecuted, we might find hallucinations like hearing special messages coming from the radio. In this case, the hallucinations would represent feelings of powerlessness. Second, this false perception might then be incorporated as another piece of environmental information, in typical paranoid style. Thus, "since I'm being controlled, I must be pretty powerful." While this formulation makes clinical sense, there is no research evidence either to support this view or to explain the mechanism of hallucinations and delusions.

Many schizophrenic patients show some paranoid-type symptoms like believing that people are talking about them or believing that the radio is sending them messages. However, it is only when these symptoms converge into a false *system* of beliefs that paranoid schizophrenia is properly diagnosed.

Simple Schizophrenia

Although Ted is thirty-four years old, he still lives with his parents. He has held a full-time job pumping gas since he graduated from high school. Ted has never created any serious difficulties at home. He insists on taking meals alone in his room and sometimes giggles for no apparent reason, but his parents have not been upset by these behaviors. Ted has no friends, except for a cousin with whom he goes bowling occasionally. However, he is unfailingly polite and well liked.

Due to financial difficulties, Ted's boss is forced to close down the station, and Ted is laid off. Despite prodding from his parents he refuses to look for another job. On the contrary, he takes less and less interest in his personal appearance and spends the greater part of each day in pajamas sitting around the house. His mother, who now spends more time with him than she ever has before, notices that when he thinks he is alone he often smiles, frowns, or gestures as if he were engaged in conversation. After six months, she is unable to tolerate the strain of having Ted around all the time, and takes him to the family physician.

In cases where the outstanding symptom is gradual but severe interpersonal withdrawal, *simple schizophrenia* is diagnosed. Usually, the most florid symptoms are absent, although thought disorder and an overabundant fantasy life may be apparent to the trained observer. It is likely that the majority of cases of simple schizophrenia go undiagnosed, since schizophrenia in this form appears not to significantly disrupt a person's ability to work at routine tasks, even though his social life may be severely limited. Thus, simple schizophrenics may come into treatment only when stressed by the loss of a person who has taken care of them or the loss of a job around which they have structured their lives, for example. Sometimes, a diagnosis of simple schizophrenia is made in persons who enter the mental-health system with other psychological or social problems like alcoholism or vagrancy. Because of the subtle ways in which schizophrenia manifests itself in this form, diagnosing simple schizophrenia may be quite difficult. In principle, thought disorder must be demonstrable before this diagnosis is accepted; interpersonal withdrawal alone is not enough.

Schizo-Affective Schizophrenia

June, age twenty, has come to see her doctor. She is extremely depressed, cries copiously, and says that she is afraid she will kill herself. The physician has difficulty following June's train of thought. At one moment she says that voices are instructing her to cut her wrists; at the next she says that she thinks she may have been raped when she was asleep so that she is dirty and deserves to die. She is quite pale and says she hasn't eaten anything at all for a few days. Her thoughts race and always come back to the same idea—she is not fit to live.

The label, *schizo-affective schizophrenia,* is applied when disorders of mood (elation or depression) appear to rival thought disorder for domination of the symptom picture. The difficulty here is in deciding whether the person has a schizophrenic illness with associated emotional features, or a mood disorder, known as affective psychosis, with associated disturbance in thinking. The most common alternate diagnoses for such a person are "manic-depressive psychosis" and "psychotic depressive reaction." In each of these mood disorders thinking may be impaired, although in principle thoughts should be consistent with the prevailing mood even if they are inconsistent with reality. This distinction is important in that the effective treatment procedures for schizophrenia and the affective psychoses are quite different, but it is often a difficult distinction to make in practice. It is sensible in these cases for the practitioner to take an "educated guess" and to try one set of treatments, falling back on the alternate diagnosis if necessary.

Catatonic and Hebephrenic Schizophrenia

Catatonic refers to a set of symptoms primarily concerning abnormalities of body movement. A patient who takes one pose and holds it for a long period of time without moving and for no obvious purpose is said to be catatonic. Such a person appears unable or unwilling to move about and is often mute as well. He may appear partially or totally unresponsive to external events, responding to neither questions nor commands. Occasionally, such a period may be interrupted by an excited phase in which the patient may behave assaultively, with neither insights into nor control over his behavior. However, these "frenzies" are quite infrequent.

The term *hebephrenic* is applied to extremely childish, silly, inappropriate behavior. Making faces in the mirror and giggling, peeking around corners to wave gaily at strangers, and acting out nursery rhymes are all examples of hebephrenic behavior as it is presently defined.

Diagnoses of *catatonic schizophrenia* and *hebephrenic schizophrenia* were quite common in the early 1900s but are quite rare today. While patients often show catatonic or hebephrenic symptoms, these symptoms rarely dominate the total picture. Thus, in modern practice, chronic undifferentiated schizophrenia is usually the diagnosis of choice for patients with these symptoms. Whether the symptom picture has actually changed over time or whether different diagnostic criteria are presently in vogue is a moot point.

SCHIZOPHRENIA AND MANIC-DEPRESSIVE PSYCHOSIS

At this point, it is probably clear that schizophrenia may affect all areas of functioning, including thinking, feeling, and acting. Further, it may affect them in a variety of ways depending on the person's genetic endowment, the environment, and one's individual personality and strategies for living. Thus, it is not surprising that schizophrenia may be confused with other disorders on the basis of certain similarities in the symptom pictures. For instance, the distinction between schizophrenia and the affective psychoses may be quite a difficult one.

What is manic-depressive illness, and why is it so hard to distinguish from schizophrenia? First, manic-depressive psychosis, one of the affective psychoses, is similar to schizophrenia in that the sufferer is "psychotic," that is, split from reality. He behaves on the basis of unrealistic perceptions about himself and his social environment. In the case of manic-depressive psychosis, unrealistic thoughts and actions stem from an abnormally euphoric or depressed mood. Thus, one important way in which to distinguish between the disorders is to see whether thoughts and mood are related (manic-depression) or are unrelated (schizophrenia).

In the "manic" phase of the illness, the patient may feel so good that he believes himself to be omnipotent—he can do anything at all without worrying about the consequences. He may feel that he no longer needs to eat or sleep to stay alive and may, indeed, stop doing one or both. He may believe that he has unbounded financial resources and may squander money, plunging him and his family into debt. He may believe that he has made a world-shattering discovery and call the president numerous times a day to share his find. Obviously, these behaviors may closely mirror the grandiosity often seen in the paranoid schizophrenic.

When depressed, the manic-depressive may believe that he is suffering the pains of hell. He may describe sensations of being burned or torn apart. He may confess to outrageous crimes he did not commit. He tends to become extremely withdrawn and slowed-down, or he may become agitated and suicidal. Again, many of these behaviors resemble schizophrenic symptoms.

How, then, can we tell the disorders apart? The answer, in general, is to look beyond the symptoms themselves and at the development and course of the illness. In manic-depressive psychosis, the psychotic episodes tend to be separated by periods of *normal functioning*. These periods may be quite short (a matter of days), they are often of several months or even years duration. Untreated schizophrenia, on the other hand, may wax and wane, but some symptoms are almost always apparent.

Another diagnostic tool for distinguishing between the psychoses may be to evaluate the response to drug treatment. Among patients identified as schizophrenic, some respond well to phenothiazine and others either do not respond or actually become worse. Those schizophrenics who seem to respond well are those who more closely approximate what we have called the "classical" schizophrenic. While using this type of approach to further our diagnostic understanding may eventually prove of value, there is no guarantee that classifications of "medication responders" and "medication nonresponders" will relate to our present clinical descriptions of schizophrenic features in a systematic fashion. That is, some people who show the clinical symptoms of schizophrenia may not respond to phenothiazines, while some people who are not presently diagnosed as schizophrenics may benefit from these medications.

SCHIZOPHRENIA AND DRUG-INDUCED PSYCHOSES

A substantial number of diagnosed schizophrenics enter the treatment network initially because of alcohol or drug abuse. There appear to be certain perceived benefits for the schizophrenic in both drug use and in the milieu of the drug subculture. These benefits may account for the large number of schizophrenic individuals who use or abuse various substances. Many schizophrenics report turning to drugs in an attempt to decrease their confusion and already disturbed thinking. They tend to rely on opiates, alcohol, or barbiturates to "stop the voices," calm their feelings, or in other ways reduce their symptoms. Since none of these substances is very effective at reducing thinking disorder, schizophrenics often use a variety of drugs in a continuing attempt to find relief. They are, in essence, attempting to medicate themselves, although generally unsuccessfully.

Further, the drug subculture tolerates deviant behavior and does not typically demand a high level of vocational or interpersonal functioning. The schizophrenic individual may thus feel less out of place and less pressured to perform within this milieu. For such patients, drug abuse is a *symptom* of underlying thought disorder.

However, nonschizophrenics who abuse certain substances may develop symptoms resembling those seen in acute schizophrenia. In particular, both hallucinogens and amphetamines can induce schizophreniclike symptoms. LSD, mescaline, and other such drugs often produce alteration in thoughts, feelings, and behavior that resemble acute schizophrenia. Drug users may hallucinate and misperceive themselves and their environment in dangerous ways. They may feel, for instance, that they can fly, and proceed to leap off a building. Typically, these symptoms follow ingestion of the drug and remit when the drug effect has worn off, thus making a differentiation from schizophrenia relatively easy. Occasionally, after multiple drug experiences, users may experience "flashbacks" or simply a continuation of the drug's effect during drug-free periods. Under these circumstances, it is difficult to decide whether the drug use has precipitated a true schizophrenic process or whether the drug has some long-term deteriorative effect of its own with multiple ingestions. At this point, a differential diagnosis becomes quite difficult to make with a high level of confidence.

Amphetamine abuse may produce an *amphetamine psychosis,* which closely mirrors symptoms of paranoid schizophrenia. The user becomes hostile, suspicious, and withdrawn, and may develop ideas of persecution. Again, these symptoms typically disappear following cessation of drug use and so are differentiable from schizophrenia.

SCHIZOPHRENIA AND ORGANIC BRAIN SYNDROMES

Finally, a number of organic conditions may resemble schizophrenia. Neurological dysfunctions of many kinds as well as metabolic disorders can produce psychological and behavioral symptoms of the kind we have been describing. Examples of this would include *senile dementia* in which confusion, disorientation, childish emotionality, and misperceptions of reality are common, and *Korsakoff's psychosis* (associated with long-standing alcohol use), with symptoms of memory impairment, disorientation, and, occasionally, delusions. Hence, a thorough physical examination is crucial in any diagnostic process. Even then, many of these organic conditions are difficult to detect and may be missed.

THE VALUE OF DIAGNOSIS

We may well ask, as others have done, what is the value of diagnosing schizophrenia? Doesn't it do more harm than good? The label "schizophrenia" can be misunderstood, misused, and abused by professional as well as lay persons. That this has happened, however, does not mean that schizophrenia is a "myth"[11] or a political tool.[12] Schizophrenia can be reliably diagnosed.[13] When used appropriately, it describes a disorder affecting thought, feeling, and behavior that may take a variety of surface forms, all of which have in common (a) disruption in thought process or content, (b) social withdrawal and isolation, (c) a splitting of thought from affect, as well as emotional experiences that parallel those in thinking. To turn our heads from the existence of schizophrenia is to deny the schizophrenic individual consensual validation of experiences, thoughts, and feelings that exist for that person. This can only serve to further isolate him.

11. Sarbin, 1972.
12. Szasz, 1961.
13. World Health Organization, 1973.

3

INSIDE SCHIZOPHRENIA

In Chapter Two, we described schizophrenia from the point of view of the observer. In this chapter, we try to describe the experience of schizophrenia as it is felt by patients.

> I am in no small degree, I find, a sham—a player to the gallery. Possibly this may be felt as you read these analyses.
>
> In my life, in my personality, there is an essence of falseness and insincerity. A thin, fine vapor of fraud hangs always over me and dampens and injures some things in me that I value.
>
> . . . It may be that the spirit of falseness is itself a false thing—yet true or false, it is with me always. . . . This element of falseness is absolutely the very thinnest, the very finest, the rarest of all the things in my many-sided character.
>
> It is not the most unimportant.
>
> I have seen visions of myself walking in various pathways. I have seen myself trying one pathway and another. And always it is the same: I see before me in the path, darkening the way and filling me with dread and discouragement, a great black shadow—the shadow of my own element of falseness.
>
> I cannot rid myself of it.
>
> I am an innate liar.[1]

1. MacLane, 1902.

This nagging, constant feeling of falseness is perhaps the most striking aspect of the inner life of the schizophrenic. It is a feeling we have each had on occasion, the sense of "playing games," of being "phony," hypocritical, or insincere. But for the schizophrenic this feeling is pervasive and insistent. While the normal person is generally able to "play a role" (for example, a dutiful wife or aggressive businessman) and to switch roles with relative ease, the schizophrenic is unable to make these adjustments without feeling a threatening assault on personal integrity. It is as if all that one does, thinks, or feels is in the service of role playing. The feeling of "self," which provides unity, consistency, and security, is painfully absent. Most of us, if asked "Who are you?" could come up with some reasonable answer. No doubt, we would include aspects of our love, work, and play relationships as well as describe some ongoing personal characteristics. We are in touch with ourselves. In sharp contrast, the intense, postadolescent struggle to find an answer to the question "Who am I?" represents the existential core of schizophrenia.

In this chapter we attempt to describe the set of self- and social perceptions that typically accompanies schizophrenia. These perceptions, and the feelings accompanying them, lead to some of the most significant problems in living that schizophrenics encounter. They are subjective, often subtle, and expressed in different ways by different patients.

Furthermore, they are not treatable by medication. In fact, they tend to emerge *after* drug therapy has controlled the acute symptoms of the disorder. It is clear, however, that medication does not *cause* these subjective symptoms to emerge because untreated schizophrenics in whom the disorder has spontaneously abated report similar feelings as do treated patients. Rather, the medication appears to *allow* these perceptions and feelings to surface by controlling the runaway thinking process. Thus, a successfully medicated patient stands at the beginning, rather than at the end, of the rehabilitation process.

That medication is the beginning rather than the end point of recovery is an important point to consider and should not be taken lightly. It is, by and large, unrealistic to expect that a properly medicated schizophrenic can immediately take a place in society and function at the level that would have been expected if he had never become ill. Much more often, self-esteem and social relationships continue to be impaired and continue to interfere with many aspects of functioning. It is with respect to these internal issues that psychotherapy and environmental manipulations can be of significant value.

THE FEELING OF BEING UNREAL

Schizophrenics often lack a *sense of self*. Typically, patients report that the feeling of being "unreal" has been with them for a long time. In exploring their childhood feelings they are often unable to recall any period of time in which they felt comfortable with their identity. It would seem that, in most cases, this basic insecurity about one's place in the world predates the onset of any florid psychotic symptoms by many years. What does it mean, to lack a sense of identity, a sense of "self"? Scottish psychiatrist R. D. Laing has probably offered the most comprehensive descriptions of the subjective aspects of schizophrenia in his book *The Divided Self:*

The individual, then, may experience his own being as real, alive, whole; as differentiated from the rest of the world in ordinary circumstances so clearly that his identity and autonomy are never in question; as a continuum in time; as having an inner consistency, substantiality, genuineness, and worth; as spatially coextensive with the body; and, usually as having begun in or around birth and liable to extinction with death. He thus has a firm core of ontological security.

This, however, may not be the case. The individual in the ordinary circumstances of living may feel more unreal than real; in a literal sense, more dead than alive; precariously differentiated from the rest of the world, so that his identity and autonomy are always in question. He may lack the experience of his own temporal continuity. He may not possess an overriding sense of personal consistency or cohesiveness. He may feel more insubstantial than substantial, and unable to assume that the stuff he is made of is genuine, good, valuable. And he may feel his self as partially divorced from his body.[2]

Many patients have referred to the same self-perceptions in various ways. Throughout this chapter, we will rely heavily on descriptions by three articulate young adults who are diagnosed schizophrenics. The first, Jim, age twenty-six, has been coping with schizophrenia for seven years and has had multiple hospitalizations. He describes himself as "plastic man." He is aware that his behavior in many social situations does not reflect his "real self." He despises "plastic man," wants, as the goal of psychotherapy, to learn to "be real," but is not at all sure what that means. He is generally unable to make a single statement about his feelings or values without qualifying it past meaning. He says, for example, "I handled it well . . . I think . . . maybe . . . sort of . . . well, okay." Occasionally, he is unsure whether his behavior is "plastic" or "real."

The second patient, Rita, became ill at age twenty and spent five years in a mental hospital before returning to the community. While in the hospital, Rita insists that she only exists in the presence of others. When she is alone she is "not alive." She is frightened of sleeping at night for fear of becoming nonexistent. Rather, she spends the nights watching television and conversing with hospital attendants. She sleeps much of the late afternoon and evening, when the activity of others around her reassures her that she is real.

Dorothy, a bright, charming twenty year old, has been in and out of the hospital since she was eighteen. She describes herself as "smoke," and perceives herself as light, insubstantial, intangible. She has neither substance nor merit. Each of these people describes the same feeling in slightly different terms.

2. Laing, 1965, pp. 41–42.

The following description was written by a twenty-two-year-old woman during the early period of her recovery.

> In order to explain the feeling of not being real, it is necessary to go into a long unreal definition of the feeling, for it is so far from reality that, in order to be made into a concrete real definition, it has to be described in an abstract, unreal way, if it is to be fully understood. Probably, it is not worth fully understanding, for the feeling itself is one of unworthiness, in the way that a counterfeit bill might feel when being examined by a banker, with a good understanding and appreciation of real currency . . . like watching a movie based on a play and, having once seen the play, realizing that the movie is just a description of it and one that brings back memories and yet isn't real and just different enough to make all the difference. . . . The important things have left and the unimportant stay behind, making the loss only more apparent by their presence.[3]

Note that it is not one's *products* that are judged unworthy, but one's *existence*. This theme comes up again and again.

CRISIS OF FAITH

Lack of self-definition may encroach upon a number of specific aspects of one's being. For instance, lacking a clear set of religious or idealistic values, the schizophrenic may experience an almost constant "crisis of faith." Such crises occur with some frequency among normal people, but for them, questioning usually leads to a reaffirmation of the old or to the embracing of a new set of principles which help to define one's "self" and yield standards with which to judge one's behavior.

3. Meyer and Covi, 1960, pp. 215–217.

For the schizophrenic, such a crisis of faith is much more difficult to resolve. Jim, begins to wear a cross. He finds himself obsessively concerned with being a hypocrite; he begins to perceive others as being highly attentive to the cross he wears and he believes them to be as critical of him as he is of himself. He believes that his inner lack of religious conviction shows, and he becomes more and more agitated.

Dorothy moves from creed to creed, searching for some external guide that can fill the emptiness within. She floats from Eastern mysticism to Catholicism to vegetarianism to Judaism. She finds herself unable to incorporate any of these into her "self"; each disappointment leads to another search. We can get a glimpse of how painful and disorienting such protracted crises of faith must be by recalling our own adolescent "crises" and search for self-identity.

SEXUAL IDENTITY

Lack of confidence with respect to sexual identity is another common aspect of the phenomenon. Schizophrenics may be unsure about what it means to be a man or woman. Having no clear conception of the ideal, they are constantly unsure of how well their behavior matches up with the expectations prescribed by their relatives, friends, and society.

Again, such feelings commonly occur in normal adolescence. But normal people are usually able to resolve the issue to their satisfaction with time. The schizophrenic, unable to see himself as clearly male or herself as female, may become overly concerned about occasional homosexual or affectional feelings. This person may withdraw from interaction with the opposite sex due to the confusion about gender role and the appropriate behavior that accompanies each role. Such withdrawal, of course, only robs the person of practice and experience, and this serves to further block the development of a clear sense of sexual identity.

LACK OF COMMITMENT

In all areas of identity development, including religious, sexual, vocational, and social identities, what is lacking is a sense of commitment. Each person has a set of roles that provides standards by which to judge behavior. For example, one such set might include the following roles: woman, psychologist, humanist, liberal, wife, friend, colleague, pianist, and so on. The person who accepts these roles gives them meaning and is commited to acting in ways consistent with each of them. She not only has a relatively clear sense of what they mean to her, but she also feels they *are* her. The schizophrenic lacks this clear sense of "self"; he "plays" roles but is unable to internalize them. He is relatively unable to commit himself to ideals, to standards, to goals. It must be understood that we are not here talking about laziness or voluntary nonparticipation. Rather, the schizophrenic's sense of self is fragile at best—he is caught in the vicious cycle of being unable to commit himself to behaving in ways consistent with his self-image and is unable to develop a self-image that would allow him to commit himself. Cutting through this cycle is one of the goals of the rehabilitation process.

DEPERSONALIZATION

In addition to having a deficient self-concept, these patients typically experience the phenomenon of watching themselves behave, for which the clinical term is *depersonalization*. Laing describes the process in this way:

> The schizoid individual exists under the black sun, the evil eye, of his own scrutiny. The glare of his awareness kills his spontaneity, his freshness; it destroys all joy. Everything withers under it . . . the schizoid individual depersonalizes his relationship with himself. That is to

say, he turns the living spontaneity of his being into
something dead and lifeless by inspecting it.[4]

The schizophrenic tends to be acutely aware of his own mental and bodily processes with the result that the emotions that
normally accompany activities appear to be separated and unreal as a patient describes below.

> It is as if everything that is done during the day is
> done automatically and, then, examined by the feeling
> that would have been put into the act, had it been
> committed in a reasonably normal way . . . the feeling
> that should dwell within a person is outside, longing
> to come back and yet having taken with it the power
> to return.[5]

Jim habitually falsifies his feelings. He describes behaving "as
if" he were happy. He then, immediately and involuntarily,
observes his behavior objectively, without feelings, and con-
cludes that his behavior was phony. In thus acting as an unin-
volved, unemotional observer of himself, he is robbed of the
spontaneity, of the "realness" of his actions. He is occasionally
trapped and paralyzed within this vicious cycle. He describes
this as "being blocked" or "blocking." At such times he is unable
to express himself at all.

Dorothy also describes watching herself behave. While engaging in conversation she experiences her "self" as standing aside
saying things like "Here is Dorothy, acting like an intellectual.
Look at her try to think of smart things to say. Isn't she absurd!"
She is not hallucinating. She knows that these are her "own"
thoughts but she is unsure whether to "own" the behaver or the
observer. In the end, she is split apart, unable to "own" either
self. She describes herself as "empty."

Again, the patient is caught in a vicious cycle. Since a schizophrenic's behavior is often inappropriate, a recovering patient
must, of necessity, watch himself behave in order to learn and
evaluate social skills. In order to improve, he must, as we all do,

4. Laing, 1965, p. 112.
5. Meyer and Covi, 1960, p. 217.

function as an observer of his own behavior. Yet, to the extent that he does so, he is unable to see himself as the originator of the behaviors which he observes. Normal people have little difficulty in seeing themselves as *both* the actor and the observer. The schizophrenic, however, apparently must *choose* between the actor and the observer.

EMPTINESS AND DEPRESSION

The feeling of emptiness that Dorothy describes is a classic feature of the subjective life of the schizophrenic and is invariably experienced by patients whose sense of self is deficient and who act as observers of their own behavior. Such patients are able to differentiate this feeling from normal depression quite easily. They describe being alienated from their feelings, rather than feeling sad. It is as if feeling empty leads to a kind of second-order depression. That is, while the patient does not like feeling empty and may be upset and unhappy about it, he does not *experience* the unhappiness; rather, he *thinks* it. Thus, when depression does exist, it comes from a *judgment* that emptiness is abnormal or unsatisfying.

Depression of this kind may well be a good prognostic sign insofar as it indicates a desire and ability to develop meaningful relationships and a capacity for future commitment to such relationships. For the schizophrenic who experiences himself as empty but does not judge the experience as a negative one, motivation to engage in the business of life may be minimal or nonexistent.

Many patients appear to be highly ambivalent about their lack of feelings. They may wish to be like others and, at the same time, feel that they cannot be.

> If the patient contrasts his own inner emptiness, worth-lessness, coldness, desolation, dryness, with the abundance, worth, warmth, companionship that he may yet

believe to be elsewhere (a belief which often grows to fantastically idealized proportions, uncorrected as it is by any direct experience), there is evoked a welter of conflicting emotions, from a desperate *longing* and yearning for what others have and he lacks, to frantic *envy* and hatred of all that is theirs and not his, or a desire to destroy all the goodness, freshness, richness in the world. These feelings may, in turn, be offset by counter-attitudes of disdain, contempt, disgust or indifference.[6]

FEELING DIFFERENT AND EVIL

If one is "blocked," empty of feelings, one is, in some important sense, nonhuman. Many schizophrenics perceive themselves as profoundly different from other people, as "nonhuman" in this sense. There is a deep and abiding sense of one's inability to meet the standards of being a person. There is constant comparison of oneself with others, accompanied by self-denigration and, often, the jealousy to which Laing refers above. Thus, "not real," "not full of life" translates, subjectively, as "not a person." At minimum, the schizophrenic feels impaired and alienated from the mainstream of living; at maximum, he may feel evil and capable of infecting others with evil.

In Hannah Green's novel, *I Never Promised You a Rose Garden* (1964), the patient, Deborah, puts it this way:

> "How did you destroy your sister?" Dr. Fried asked Deborah who was huddled on the couch, shivering in Yri's cold through the heat of Earth's August.
>
> "I didn't mean to—she was exposed to my essence. It's called by an Yri name—it is my selfness and it is poisonous. It is mind-poisonous."

6. Laing, 1965, p. 91.

"Something you say that destroys? Something you do, or wish?"

"No, it's a quality of myself, a secretion, like sweat. It is the emanation of my Deborahness and it is poisonous."

Suddenly Deborah felt an explosion of self-pity for the miasma-creature she was, and she began to elucidate, drawing larger and larger the shape of herself and the evidence of her substance.[7]

While Deborah is a character in a novel, she voices a sentiment that one hears over and over again from patients. Jim, whose mother had committed suicide when he was four years old, recounted the scene as he recalled it to his therapist. After some moments of silence, he was asked, "Did you kill her?"

"Yes," he replied.

"How?"

He answered, "I don't know . . . just by being." It must be understood that he was not giving voice to a psychotic delusion. Rather, he was expressing a deep sense of guilt and shame about his very essence.

Dorothy, during a psychotic episode, attached a meaning to each letter of the alphabet. The first letter of her therapist's name meant "safe from harm." Through this device she was able to maintain contact without fear of contaminating someone about whom she cared. Many months later, when her condition had improved significantly, she joked, "It's lucky you're safe."

"Do you still see yourself as contagious?" she was asked.

She replied in the affirmative. She was no longer joking.

A patient, in describing the process of psychotherapy, makes the following observation:

The patient is terribly afraid of his own problems, since they have destroyed him, so he feels terribly guilty for allowing the doctor to get mixed up in the problems. The patient is convinced that the doctor will be smashed too. It's not fair for the doctor to ask

7. Green, 1964, p. 82.

permission to come in. The doctor must fight his way in; then the patient doesn't have to feel guilty. The patient can feel that he has done his best to protect the doctor. The doctor must say by his manner, "I'm coming in no matter what you feel."[8]

Each of these patients expresses the same sentiment, that one's essence can be dangerous. As much as the schizophrenic individual may wish to fill the emptiness within, his guilt and need to protect others from harm fosters the isolation that he finds so painful. This guilt is rarely related to specific thoughts or acts but is related, instead, to an all-inclusive sense of worthlessness. The person may feel as if he has no right to exist at all.[9]

To summarize, inside schizophrenia we find a core of frightening, depressing, and alienating self-perceptions. These include feeling separated from one's body and behavior (watching oneself behave), feeling separated from one's feelings (being nonhuman), feeling alienated from others, and feeling evil, worthless, and contagious. This is qualitatively different from the "poor self-image" encountered in many neurotic and normal individuals. Rather, it constitutes a lack of a coherent self-image. It is one thing to think of oneself as a bad, incompetent, or worthless person; it is quite another to think of oneself as not a person at all.

A PAINFUL CHOICE

What would life be like if we saw ourselves in this way? First, given the choice between the emptiness of a schizophrenic's sanity and the rich variety of his madness, we would experience great difficulty in committing ourselves to sanity. Kate (Chapter

8. Hayward and Taylor, 1956, p. 211.
9. Laing, 1965.

Two) once remarked: "You give me the choice of being functional and feeling empty or being dysfunctional and feeling
wonderful." Her perceptions were painfully accurate. Although
psychotic episodes can have terrifying aspects, they almost invariably provoke feelings of grandiosity, acute sensitivity, and
euphoria as well. Conversely, while treatment restores some
control over the thought processes, it can allow the experience
of lifelessness to emerge. In the face of this conflict, it is a rare
person indeed who opts, once and for all, in the direction of
sanity. Much more often, patients will periodically stop taking
their medication and will voluntarily provoke a psychotic episode. They simply cannot bear the emptiness and the loneliness
for an extended period of time. Typically, this behavior is ra-
tionalized in any number of ways: "I'm well now and I don't
need the medication anymore"; "I'll just take a little less 'cause
it slows me down too much"; "I forgot." But, in truth, the
struggle is to find a level of medication at which just enough
fantasy is allowed to slip through to relieve the suffering, while
at the same time maintaining enough control over thinking to
function effectively.

Unfortunately, therapists sometimes have a different definition of "optimum medication effect" from that of most patients.
While the therapist, with the support of the family, often aims
at getting rid of the thought disorder entirely, this goal is often
not consistent with the patient's felt needs. Thus, with no one
to understand the need for emotional experience, the patient
typically accepts medication while under the control of another,
and resists it when left alone.

In sum, while the psychiatrist's and family's goal for the patient is that he should achieve a maximal level of functioning at
job, school, and elsewhere, the patient's goal is often to find
some marginal level of adjustment wherein active fantasies, and
the feelings associated with them, can be preserved. A number
of different compromises is possible. Dorothy is content to work
sporadically as a waitress or typist, living on social security disability income in between times. While she still voices goals like
going to college or becoming a nurse, she takes them less and
less seriously as times goes on. She has tried, off and on, to

achieve maximal functioning, but has found the emptiness and loneliness too much to bear. She has always, at such times, reduced her medication and given up her goals. Her family is understandably disappointed and dismayed. They are well aware that she could achieve more of what they want for her, but they are unaware of the pain that prevents her from doing so.

Jim has found a somewhat different solution. He has decided that happiness is not his most important goal. Instead, he has chosen to live like other people and, in order to do so, has learned to tolerate a good deal of boredom and loneliness. He functions competently at his job and, unlike past years, takes his medication regularly. He is not willing to risk another hospitalization and the loss of self-esteem that that will bring, even if he has to give up the emotional intensity he believes that other people have. His family is understandably delighted at his progress, but, of course, they are unaware of how he feels inside.

The resistance to treatment exhibited by many schizophrenics is not a result of stubborness, recalcitrance, or lack of good sense. It is the result of a struggle that most of us would be hard pressed to resolve. It is our own experience that an understanding of this issue and the conflict it evokes by someone close to the patient (typically, a therapist) goes a long ways toward helping many schizophrenics opt for sanity, as Jim has done. But the patient who voluntarily becomes psychotic is neither bad nor stupid. Rather he is opting for what appears at the moment to be the best of two conflict-laden choices. Later, he will often opt for the other.

THE THREAT OF RELATIONSHIPS

The emptiness of daily living is exacerbated by the schizophrenic's need to withdraw from relationships. This need is at least partly provoked by the insecurity about self as well as by the fear of harming others. Thus, a second problem in living encountered by the schizophrenic is ambivalence toward close interpersonal relationships. For the schizophrenic, loving and being loved can be seen as terribly threatening. While "losing oneself" in a love relationship presents little problem for someone whose identity is secure, it can be devastating for one whose identity is not.

> A firm sense of one's own autonomous identity is required in order that one may be related as one human being to another. Otherwise, any and every relationship threatens the individual with loss of identity.[10]

The schizophrenic individual tends to be frightened of emotional intimacy. Being loved either exacerbates feelings of emptiness, differentness, and isolation rather than soothing away these feelings or is threatening to the already tenuous sense of self and must be avoided. Since the schizophrenic cannot trust the validity of his own feelings, he is unable to be comforted by the expressed feelings of others. Because of emotional isolation, the schizophrenic's relationships lack mutuality. The patient fears his inability to "keep up his end of the bargain." Being unable to love, to engage himself spontaneously in a relationship, he distrusts others' ability to do so.

Sometimes, the schizophrenic may feel that he has, in fact, turned others to stone. Feeling unreal, he perceives others as being equally unsubstantial. A young woman was discussing her painting with her therapist. When asked why she did not paint any portraits she replied: "I've always had trouble painting corpses." She had, quite clearly, projected her own feelings of lifelessness onto others.

At the same time, like all of us, the schizophrenic longs for close, satisfying relationships.

> The abundance *there* is longed for, in contrast to the emptiness *here;* yet participation without loss of being is felt to be impossible, and also is not enough, and so the individual must cling to his isolation—his separateness without spontaneous, direct relatedness—because

10. *Ibid.,* p. 45.

in doing so he is clinging to his identity. His longing
is for complete union. But of this very longing he is
terrified, because it will be the end of his self. He does
not wish for a relationship of mutual enrichment and
exchange of give-and-take between two beings "con-
genial" to each other.[11]

The fear of being swallowed up and the fear of hurting
others combined with the wish to relate in a genuine way leads
to a tremendously conflicted attitude toward relationships. The
following poem stanza, which Rita wrote to her therapist, illustrates the need for distance, for protection from and for the
loved one:

> You are a fortress of my heart
> And without you I would be lost and alone,
> Inside you is a wall,
> That kept a shell around you,
> So that I will not penetrate your love.

Here, the patient is not voicing a complaint. She is not bemoan-
ing the limits of the relationship. Rather, she expresses her
comfort that neither she nor her therapist will lose their "selves"
in the relationship; both are protected by the therapist's impen-
etrable inner shell. The therapist's strong sense of identity allows
the patient to relate without risking getting lost.

The conflict surrounding relationships typically precludes the
development of intimacy with others. As the schizophrenic fears
and avoids relationships, he avoids going through the trial-and-
error process by which we learn how to relate to others in a
satisfying way. The schizophrenic has typically avoided practicing social skills. This lack of experience and the lack of self-
confidence which accompanies it further complicate the problem. Thus, the lack of social skills that results from internal
conflicts feeds the feeling of incompetence and makes resolution
of the problem even more difficult. As can be seen, the vicious
cycle that is created leads to increasing withdrawal and isolation

11. *Ibid.*, pp. 91–92.

unless it is successfully interrupted. This is an issue to which psychotherapy can be addressed.

Relating at Work

Vocational difficulties are also, to some extent, a result of negative self-perceptions. The schizophrenic is acutely sensitive to the expectations of others, and tends to feel unable to meet these expectations successfully. When working at a job, he is likely to obsessively compare himself to other workers. He spends much energy worrying about what others may be thinking about him, and tends to believe that they see him as incompetent and as worthless as he sees himself. His concentration may be impaired, not only by the disturbances in thinking, which were described in Chapter Two, but by his own overconcern with the perceptions of his superiors and peers.

Since recovering schizophrenics are counseled (correctly) to begin work in a relatively nonstressful job, the individual may well feel that the work he is doing is beneath him. He may become jealous, angry, and frustrated. When these feelings are combined with the jealousy the schizophrenic may feel concerning others' ability to form relationships, to "be alive," his behavior at work may become self-defeating. He may withdraw from interaction with other workers, thereby provoking discomfort in those around him. He may, on the other hand, concentrate all his energy on building relationships at work such that he doesn't attend properly to the job. He may quit, or work in such a way that he is fired, due to feelings of loneliness and alienation or due to feelings of anger and jealousy. Coming to work with an already precarious ability to concentrate, the schizophrenic may be defeated by his own sense of separateness.

In summary, the recovering schizophrenic faces the world with a set of self-perceptions that significantly interfere with his ability to feel and act like other people. Feeling empty, isolated, different, he finds it difficult to love, to be loved, to work, and to accept reality without withdrawing into fantasy. Medication does not cure these "symptoms" of schizophrenia. The success that an individual may have in overcoming and changing these self-perceptions depends, in large part, on his ability to behave as others do while feeling different and alone. To the extent that he has the courage and motivation to tolerate these feelings while participating in living, the increasingly positive responses from others may slowly ease the pain and allow the patient to begin to feel worthwhile. To the extent that the individual is unable to tolerate the feelings and, as a result, withdraws from the business of living, he will validate such feelings of emptiness.

SOME THOUGHTS ABOUT CAUSE

Where do these perceptions come from? While their etiology is presently unknown, a number of speculations have been offered. Theorists who presume that certain family interaction patterns cause schizophrenia would argue that a young child comes to see himself as a person only insofar as his family treats him as a person. If the family is unable to allow the child a separate identity, if they are insensitive to his individual qualities and needs, if they force him into a mold of their own making, the child will be unable to develop a secure sense of self.[12] However, as we will see, there is little reason to believe that any of these parenting styles can, by themselves, cause schizophrenia:

Some speculate that the process whereby a person comes to be labeled as schizophrenic is responsible for negative self-perceptions.[13] The child is progressively labeled as "bad" and then "mad" as his behavior becomes less and less consistent with parental and societal expectations. He, therefore, comes to see himself as bad (mean, selfish, unfeeling) and finally as mad (different, isolated, alone). Such an explanation is likely to be

12. See, for example, Bateson *et al.*, 1968; Bowen, 1960; Haley, 1959.
13. Szasz, 1961.

only part of the story. Schizophrenics typically relate having perceived themselves as different and strange long before their behavior deteriorated. They labeled themselves as "mad" well before others did. While these recollections may, of course, be inaccurate, they occur often enough to be taken seriously. However, there can be no doubt that the labeling process serves to validate the person's worst fears, thus strengthening the pre-existing negative self-perceptions.

Since schizophrenia often tends to surface in late adolescence and early adulthood, many patients are deprived of normal adolescent experiences. It is likely that this deprivation may be involved in the poorly developed sense of self. Often, by the mid-teen years, the first inner signs of schizophrenia are beginning to be felt. Concentration may be slowly deteriorating and the expected decrease in fantasizing at this time may not happen. Beginning to withdraw out of fear, the incipient schizophrenic is unable to engage in the turmoil, growing, and self-defining processes of adolescence. At a time when independence and self-worth are issues to be resolved, the schizophrenic is unable to fight the battle successfully.

Perhaps, the subjective symptoms are, in some mysterious way, a function of an underlying biochemical disorder. We don't know. All we can say at present is that they are commonly described by schizophrenic patients, that they interfere significantly with the person's health 'and happiness, and that they are chronic, although treatable problems.

4

CAUSES OF SCHIZOPHRENIA
An Overview

Whenever we seek to understand the causes of some phenomenon, especially when that phenomenon is as complex as schizophrenia, we must deal with many different areas of explanation. We may choose to explain the causes of schizophrenia in terms of biochemistry, physiology, precipitating events, family patterns, or societal factors. Which set of variables one chooses to study depends largely on one's own preconceptions about human behavior. By far the most common question asked about behavior in general, and about schizophrenia in particular, is whether it is "caused" by genes or by the environment. This is known as the *nature-nurture question*. How do researchers go about the business of answering this question?

THE GENAIN QUADRUPLETS

The case of the Genains is one of the classic examples of a family study of schizophrenia.[1] It provides a dramatic view of the impact of schizophrenia on a family, as well as of the great difficulty in separating heredity from environment in determining the causes of schizophrenia. The Genains are a set of iden-

1. Rosenthal, 1963.

tical quadruplets, all four of whom survived and became schizophrenic. The chance of being both a surviving quadruplet and schizophrenic is about one in one-and-a-half-billion births.

The Genains, a fictitious name derived from the Greek words meaning "dire birth" or "dreadful gene,"[2] first came to the attention of researchers at the National Institute of Mental Health when the quadruplets were about twenty-four years old. The four sisters are known by aliases chosen to represent the initials of the National Institute of Mental Health, NIMH. The girls, born within seventeen minutes of each other, are in order of their birth, Nora, Iris, Myra, and Hester. Three of the four (Nora, Iris, and Hester) were hospitalized at least once.

At the time of the first contact with NIMH researchers, the Genain household was in a turmoil. Mr. Genain, unemployed for some time, was a suspicious, irritable, withdrawn, and guarded person. He avoided social contact when possible and generally was uncommunicative when forced to interact with others. Mrs. Genain, while much more stable than her husband, nevertheless was overprotective with her children and was prone to distorted ideas about her daughters. Hester, the youngest and always the oddest of the four sisters, was totally disoriented. Clothes disheveled and torn, she often seemed oblivious to other people and generally disoriented in public. Iris was equally confused, had a glazed, faraway look in her eyes, and was clearly not capable of caring for herself. Somewhat less disoriented, but hesitant and anxious, Nora was shunned by her father during the family meeting. It was as if Nora did not exist. Finally, there was Myra, always the best liked and the least disturbed of the quadruplets. Though currently unable to care for herself, she had been the last Genain to lose her job.

Not surprisingly, the Genains could no longer manage to survive at even the marginal level of functioning that they had attained before Myra's unemployment. The offer of the NIMH to take the quadruplets into their clinic was, therefore, accep, ᵈ. During the three years that Nora, Iris, Myra, and Hester were at the NIMH, volumes of interview, test, and school and hospital

2. Rosenthal, 1971.

record material were collected. The story that emerges has enough characters and subplots to fit anyone's theory of schizophrenia, illustrating just how complex the nature-nurture question can be.

Though Mrs. Genain's side of the family was healthy, Mr. Genain's relatives were known to suffer frequent physical and mental disorders. His mother had had what was reported as a nervous breakdown during her teens, lasting three years. She also became extremely angry and depressed after her later pregnancies, frequently threatening to kill herself and her husband. She and her husband, a meek, hard-working man, had nine children, few of whom could fit anyone's definition of well adjusted. The oldest brother was not very bright, a slow learner, and never succeeded in learning a trade. He is reported to once have been found in bed with his thirteen-year-old daughter. The next brother, who remained single, was a very heavy drinker who became wild and irrational when angry. The next to youngest son had a history of mental illness including thinking people were talking to him, wandering about, and crying. He was described by the family as being "strange." Finally, there was Mr. Genain, the youngest of nine children.

The Genain household was characterized by an excessive degree of control over the quadruplets' lives. Both as children and as adults, Nora, Iris, Myra, and Hester were guarded, spied upon, and ruled by Mr. Genain's iron fist. Mr. Genain would insist, for example, on having lunch with and picking up Nora and Myra every day at work, even when the girls were in their twenties. He would become hostile, angry, and threaten them if they tried to establish independent social lives. Their entire childhood was constricted. They were not allowed to have friends visit or to visit other children's homes. The few times the girls managed to get away to a social event, Mr. Genain would barge in and take the girls home. Throughout school, they were considered as one unit, always together but isolated from other children.

By the time the girls had started school, they had been paired off into two sets of twins by their mother. Myra and Nora were considered to be more developed, bright, and pleasant than

Hester and Iris. Mrs. Genain generally perceived Myra and Nora as good, and Hester and Iris as bad. Hester and Iris became the targets for constant supervision, reprimand, and punishment. Much of Mrs. Genain's concern centered on the two girls' masturbation. After various attempts to stop them from masturbating, both Hester and Iris were circumcised at eleven years upon medical advice. This operation involved removing a flap of skin from each girl's clitorus. To prevent them from tearing their stitches out after the operation, the girls' hands were tied to the bed for thirty days. Despite the extreme measures, they did not stop masturbating.

There are many descriptions, events, and family interactions that one might hold up as abnormal in describing the development of Nora, Iris, Myra, and Hester Genain. Nevertheless, it is clear even from this brief description of the Genains, that family history, rearing practices, and physical trauma all play a role in the development of schizophrenia in the Genain quadruplets. At the time of the major publication about the Genains in 1963, Myra was living with her husband, and Nora, living with her mother, and had taken on a part-time job as a dance instructor although her social life remained limited. Both Iris and Hester were hospitalized.

SEARCHING FOR PATTERNS

What the case of the Genains so vividly illustrates is the fact that mental illness runs in families. This idea is certainly not new. It dates back to the sixteenth-century physician Paracelsus, who suggested classifying diseases on the basis of how they grouped in families. "Hereditary taint," defective human material thought to cause a great many unwanted attributes including insanity, had its greatest popularity in nineteenth-century Germany. Ever since the development of the concepts of disease and abnormal behavior, we have looked for other characteristics associated with a given disorder that might suggest a reason for its occurrence.[3] Such observations were not limited, however, to family patterns of mental illness.

During the middle of the nineteenth century, it was reported "that the 'pauper class' in Massachusetts furnished proportionately 64 times as many cases of [1]'insanity' as the 'independent class.' "[4] About the same time, it was observed "that women sooner yield (to insanity), but being more elastic recover again, while men being more firm, resist longer and then break without power to rise again as readily as females do, when they are cast down."[5] For some time it was thought that excessive masturbation could cause insanity, a belief presumably arising from an observation of frequent masturbation by psychotics.[6]

While some of these ideas may seem outdated, they represent two views very much alive today concerning the causes of schizophrenia—namely, the genetic and the environmental. Although in most current theories of schizophrenia the interaction between hereditary and environmental influences is recognized, the distinction is still made between geneticists and environmentalists. It has been stated that "the relative weight one places on the two classes of events leads to one being clustered in the genetic camp or the environmental camp; we seem to agree that there is no valid dichotomy but that these labels serve to identify preferred research strategies and data interpretations."[7] Thus geneticists would be concerned with the Genains' genetic background while environmentalists would emphasize family rearing practices as both sought to explain why and how the girls became ill.

ATTRIBUTING CAUSES

The research strategies of both geneticists and environmentalists require observing the rate of schizophrenia in different

3. *Ibid.*; Zilboorg, 1941.
4. Dohrenwend and Dohrenwend, 1969, p. 1.
5. Jarvis, 1850, pp. 150–151.
6. Ellard, 1977.
7. Gottesman, 1976, p. 3.

groups of people—families in the case of geneticists, and different segments of the general population in the case of environmentalists. The rate of schizophrenia in variously defined groups of people is then compared to that of approximately 1 percent over the general population.[8] If a group of people has a much greater rate of schizophrenia than one out of every one hundred, we may then conclude that some characteristics of that group are making it more susceptible to schizophrenia. Our concern in the remainder of this chapter will be to describe the characteristics of those groups having especially high rates of schizophrenia. As a caution against jumping to any conclusions about the cause of schizophrenia, we note that even if two events consistently are observed to occur together, it does not necessarily imply that one causes the other. In other words, if events A and B occur together it is possible that A causes B, that B causes A, that both A and B are caused by a third event, C, or that their joint occurrence is coincidental.

Consider, as an example of two phenomena that occur together but are not causally related, gout and high intelligence. Gout is a hereditary metabolic disorder that results in an excess of uric acid in the body, the swelling of joints, and often excruciating pain. Much of the swelling and pain (due to the accumulation of uric acid crystals) produced during an attack of gout is concentrated in the toes of the foot, especially the left big toe. It has also been noted that gout has struck people of intellectual achievement. Among them are such figures as Sir Isaac Newton and Charles Darwin.[9] There arose, not surprisingly, a theory suggesting that gout caused genius and creativity. However, as pointed out by an early investigator in the field, it is known that uric acid is not used by the brain and "we have no evidence at all that a pain in the toe stimulates the mind."[10] Similarly, while we have a great deal of information about how those people having high rates of schizophrenia differ from those having low rates, we must be cautious in making causal statements. For example, some people who have schizophrenia

8. *Ibid.*; Maher, 1966; Rosenthal, 1963; White and Watt, 1973.
9. Boyd, 1971; Roueché, 1947.
10. Roueché, 1947, p. 31.

are also quite creative. Yet we really cannot say that schizophrenia causes creativity, nor that creativity causes schizophrenia.

SCHIZOPHRENIA IN THE FAMILY—THE GENETIC VIEW

The genetic camp generally concentrates on the study of family patterns of schizophrenia. The Genain quadruplets were investigated primarily by a behavior geneticist and largely interpreted within an hereditary context insofar as many of the Genains' relatives were severely disturbed. Even a cursory consideration of the Genains, however, reveals that hereditary and environmental influences are inextricably mixed. In addition to a family history of psychiatric disorder, there were physical traumas and deviant rearing practices. One could quite literally cite the Genains as evidence for any theory of schizophrenia.

Aware of this difficulty, behavior geneticists over the last three decades have turned their attention to developing research strategies for separating genetic and environmental influences on schizophrenia. Underlying behavioral genetic research is the fact that different family members share varying amounts of genes. Each individual receives an equal amount of genetic information (in the form of chromosomes) from his father and his mother. Chromosomes, containing many genes, transmit a biochemical code responsible for determining the structure and activity of the body's proteins. At the biochemical level, differences in this genetic code lead to individual differences such as the composition of body fluids and tissues, requirements for nutrients, and response to specific drugs. Some traits, like color blindness, are determined by a single gene. One either has the trait or does not have the trait. Other traits, however, like height, are the product of a number of different genes and vary continuously over some range. Everyone, with the exception of identical (monozygotic, from the same cell) twins, represents a unique genetic—and, therefore, biochemical—make-up. As a very rough generalization, however, the greater the genetic overlap between two people, the stronger the similarity between them. However, there is a distinction between the genotype, the genetic make-up, and the phenotype, the observed behavior of a person. In the case of schizophrenia, we are limited to theories about the schizophrenic genotype since currently there are no genetic tests for schizophrenia. We are, in other words, restricted to observations of and experiments on behavior.

A good example of the relationship between genotype and phenotype is that of favism, a severe physical disorder characterized by anemia, fever, abdominal pain, and transmitted as a genetic trait.[11] Whether or not a person shows the clinical signs of favism depends on the presence or absence of the fava bean in the person's diet. Favism shows up in those persons who are both genetically predisposed to favism and who eat the fava bean. This "gene-bean" interaction varies in such a way that some susceptible groups exhibit favism because of a high genetic frequency and others because of a heavy diet of fava beans. However, susceptible individuals never suffer from favism if they avoid eating fava beans. In this case, the phenotype, favism, only results when the genotype, predisposition to favism, is exposed to an adverse environment, the eating of fava beans. Conversely, if one does not have a genetic predisposition for favism, then one will not develop favism no matter how many fava beans are eaten.

Ideally, we would like to have a similar understanding of schizophrenia—that is, a demonstrable genotype, and the expression of a reliably diagnosed set of clinical symptoms in the presence of environmental conditions known to be adverse. Because we cannot test for schizophrenia in the same way that we test for syphilis, for example, the accurate clinical diagnosis of schizophrenia is very important. Indeed, how one defines and diagnoses schizophrenia is essential to know in any study, genetic or environmental. Therefore, we shall indicate when appropriate the way in which differences in diagnosis affect the findings.

11. Gottesman, 1976; Rosenthal, 1971.

Overall, behavioral geneticists have used three basic strategies in studying schizophrenia: pedigree or family studies, twin studies, and adoption studies. Pedigree studies, the tracing of familial patterns of schizophrenia through several generations, could be important in identifying specific genetic locations involved in schizophrenia. However, because genetic and environmental factors are confounded in pedigree studies, they are of little value in distinguishing between genetic and environmental effects. Nevertheless, family studies have pointed to striking relationships which have been followed up by twin and adoption studies.

Twin studies are based on the comparison of identical or monozygotic, and fraternal or dyzygotic twins. Finally, in adoption studies the rates of schizophrenia among the biological and adoptive relatives of schizophrenics adopted at an early age are compared. Because genes and environment are not confounded as when biological parents rear their own children, the adoption strategy offers the best possibility of separating hereditary and environmental factors.

Family Studies

In family studies, one first identifies a group of schizophrenics, also called the probands or index cases.[12] The rates of schizophrenia among relatives of varying genetic similarity to the probands are then compared. From the genetic viewpoint, we would predict a higher rate of schizophrenia the closer in genetic composition the relative is to the schizophrenic. Shared genetic composition among different family members is as follows.

First-degree relatives, parents, siblings, and children, have 50

12. The family study figures, including proband, twin, and adoption studies, are based on the reports of Slater and Cowie, 1971; Gottesman and Shields, 1972; Gottesman, 1976; Keith *et al.*, 1976; Rosenthal and Kety, 1968; Rosenthal, 1971; Wender *et al.*, 1974.

percent of their genes in common. Half siblings, uncles and aunts, nieces and nephews, and grandchildren are second-degree relatives. They have 25 percent of their genes in common. Cousins, or third-degree relatives, have a 12.5-percent genetic overlap with one another.

If we now examine the average rates of schizophrenia among first-, second-, and third-degree relatives of schizophrenics, we find that the rates increase with increasing genetic similarity between the schizophrenic and the relatives. There is about a 3-percent rate of definite schizophrenia among second- and third-degree relatives of schizophrenics. The rate rises to about 9 percent for first-degree relatives. In some cases the diagnosis of schizophrenia is not definite. But if we include probable as well as definite cases of schizophrenia, these rates are about 4 percent, 3 percent, and 11 percent for the third-degree, second-degree, and first-degree relatives, respectively. The rate for the special case of children of two schizophrenic parents is approximately 36 percent for definite cases of schizophrenia and about 46 percent when including probable cases. Regardless of whether we choose to be stringent or somewhat flexible in our diagnosis, genetic similarity to a schizophrenic increases the risk of being schizophrenic oneself.

However, it is appropriately argued that first-degree relatives share more of their environment as well as genes than do distant relatives. In other words, parents and children will have spent much more time living together than grandparents and grandchildren. Similarly, having two schizophrenic parents not only increases the amount of common genetic material passed on to the children, but also increases the potential deviancy of the home environment. Thus, the different rates of schizophrenia among the various relatives of schizophrenics could well reflect environmental as well as genetic differences. One way to investigate this problem is to examine the rate of schizophrenia in identical and fraternal twins. As twins live in the same family environment, any difference in the rate of schizophrenia between the two types of same-sex twins may be attributed to genetic factors.

Twin Studies

There are two types of twins. Monozygotic, commonly known as identical twins, are produced from the same egg. Identical twins, therefore, are unique in being exactly alike genetically. Dyzygotic, or fraternal twins, are produced from two separate eggs. Fraternal twins share 50 percent of their genes, on average, just like any siblings. If genetic transmission is important in schizophrenia, we would expect both members of a set of identical twins to be schizophrenic more frequently than both members of a set of fraternal twins.

In order to test this, we first locate two groups of schizophrenics: those having identical twins and those having fraternal twins. Next, we compare the rate at which the identical twins of schizophrenics are also schizophrenic versus the rate at which the same-sexed fraternal twins of schizophrenics are also schizophrenic. About 22 percent of the identical twins of schizophrenics are also schizophrenic, including only definite cases of schizophrenia. In contrast, only about 7 percent of schizophrenics' fraternal twins are schizophrenic. Broadening the definition of schizophrenia to include those who are psychotic but fail to show the classical signs and symptoms of schizophrenia increases the rates to 41 percent for identical twins and 12 percent for fraternal twins. Twin studies over the last fifty years have been consistent in reporting a rate of schizophrenia two to five times higher for the identical than for the fraternal co-twins of schizophrenics. Once again, the greater the genetic similarity one has to an identified schizophrenic, the greater one's chances of also being diagnosed schizophrenic.

There is an objection to this genetic interpretation. We could argue that identical twins are both schizophrenic more frequently than fraternal twins because identical twins are reared more nearly alike than same-sexed fraternal twins. Identical twins often are dressed and treated alike. They frequently are mistaken for one another and have difficulties in establishing individual identities. Thus, if family environment were causing schizophrenia, then identical twins should both be schizophrenic more frequently than fraternal twins to the extent that they are treated similarly.

To answer this objection, schizophrenics who were adopted into one home at a very early age and whose identical twins were adopted into a different home were located. The identical twins, in other words, had only their genes in common. Of the twenty-seven pairs located to date, fourteen pairs, or 52 percent, are both schizophrenic. If we include "schizophrenialike" disorders among the co-twins, then seventeen pairs, or 63 percent, are both schizophrenic.[13]

Identical twins reared apart were more frequently both schizophrenic than identical twins reared in the same home. This is somewhat surprising, since we might expect that sharing both genes and environment would dispose both twins to be schizophrenic more often than if they shared only their genetic make-up. This discrepancy results from having only a small number of identical twins reared apart who are available for study. With larger numbers this discrepancy may disappear.

Finally, the risk for schizophrenia among the children of identical twins concordant for schizophrenia is about 6 percent. The risk among children of identical twins discordant for schizophrenia is about 13 percent.[14] Thus, even if a parent is not schizophrenic, being the identical twin of a schizophrenic (identical twins discordant for schizophrenia) raises the risk of schizophrenia in his or her children. This is interpreted as demonstrating that the nonaffected twin shares with the affected twin the genes responsible for the transmission of schizophrenia.

Adoption Studies

As in the case of the Genains, results from the family study of schizophrenia could be interpreted from either a genetic or an environmental viewpoint. While it has been demonstrated

13. Gottesman and Shields, 1972.
14. Cited in Gottesman and Shields, 1976, p. 374.

that schizophrenia runs in families, it is also true that an adverse home environment or deviant rearing practices might account for the occurrence of schizophrenia in more than one family member. Adoption studies deal with this problem by examining the rate of schizophrenia among the biological and adoptive relatives of schizophrenics who had been adopted at an early age by nonfamilial foster parents. This strategy allows us to investigate environmental influences in the form of the adopting family and genetic influences in the form of biological relatives. From the genetic viewpoint, we would predict a higher rate of schizophrenia in the biological relatives than in the adoptive relatives. From the environmental viewpoint, we would predict the opposite. The findings to date conform to the genetic predictions.

The rate of definite and probable schizophrenia among parents who gave up for adoption children who later became schizophrenic is approximately 12 percent. In contrast, the rate of schizophrenia among the adoptive parents of children who were schizophrenic as adults is about 2 percent.

One might argue that schizophrenics are more likely to give up their children for adoption than nonschizophrenics. This would result in a higher rate of schizophrenia among the biological than adoptive relatives of schizophrenic adoptees. Therefore, it is critical to also examine the rate of schizophrenia among the biological and adoptive relatives of people adopted as infants, but who do not become schizophrenic as adults. The rate of schizophrenia among both biological and adoptive parents of nonschizophrenic adoptees is about 5 percent. Biological parents of schizophrenics have a higher rate of schizophrenia than adoptive parents of schizophrenics, and both biological and adoptive parents of nonschizophrenic adoptees.

Another way of comparing the rates of schizophrenia among the biological and adoptive relatives of schizophrenics is to identify adoptees who have a biological parent diagnosed schizophrenic and to compare their rate of schizophrenia to that of adoptees whose biological parents have no history of psychiatric disturbance. There is approximately a 19-percent rate of schizophrenia (including both definite and probable diagnoses) among children adopted from a schizophrenic parent. The rate of schizophrenia among children adopted from parents with no psychiatric history is about 10 percent. Restricting the definition of schizophrenia to include only those having severe, long-term symptoms, little emotional responsiveness, and extreme social isolation reduces the rates to 8 percent for the schizophrenics' adoptees and 0 percent for the nonschizophrenics' adoptees. Once again, biological background is a stronger risk factor for schizophrenia than home environment.

Finally, can schizophrenic parents cause children who are not biologically related to them to become schizophrenic? In other words, can the behavioral, emotional, and interpersonal characteristics of a parenting schizophrenic cause schizophrenia in the children he or she raises? In response, we can point to a 5-percent rate of schizophrenialike behavior among twenty-one children of normal parents adopted into homes with one schizophrenic parent.[15] This is well within the range of a 10-percent schizophrenia rate among children put up for adoption by parents without a history of psychiatric disorder.

Thus, even using a less restrictive definition of schizophrenia, the rate of schizophrenia among the adopted children of schizophrenic foster parents is far below the 19 percent rate of schizophrenia among schizophrenics' biological offspring reared in foster homes. The presence of an identified schizophrenic in the rearing family does not increase the rate of schizophrenia in adopted offspring if there is no blood relationship to a schizophrenic.

The Case for Genetic Transmission

It is clear that genetic transmission plays an important role in schizophrenia (see Table 4:1). In terms of risk for schizophrenia, the identical twins of already identified schizophrenics and the children of two schizophrenics are the most vulnerable. Then, first-degree relatives of schizophrenics are at a substantially

15. Keith *et al.*, 1976; Wender *et al.*, 1974.

TABLE 4:1

Strategies and Findings of Genetic Research

METHOD	START WITH	LOOK AT	FINDINGS	INTERPRETATION
Pedigree studies	Schizophrenic individuals	All biological relatives	Schizophrenia runs in families; increasing genetic similarity increases the risk for schizophrenia.	Both genetic and environmental factors may be implicated.
Twin studies	Schizophrenics who have twins	Identical and same-sex fraternal twins	Forty-one percent of identical twins have definite or probable schizophrenia; 21-percent of fraternal twins have definite or probable schizophrenia.	Greater genetic similarity increases risk for schizophrenia, despite presumed similarity in rearing.
Adoption studies	(a) Adult schizophrenics who had been adopted as children	(a) Biological and adoptive parents	(a) Twelve percent of biological parents are schizophrenic; 2-percent of adoptive parents are schizophrenic.	(a) Genetic factors increase the risk more than rearing factors.

(b) Adults who have given up children for adoption	(b) Schizophrenic and nonschizophrenic children	(b) When a parent is schizophrenic, 19 percent of children are definite or probable schizophrenics; when a parent is not schizophrenic, 10 percent of children have probable schizophrenia.	(b) When rearing is presumed normal, having a schizophrenic biological parent increases the risk for schizophrenia in the offspring.
(c) Adult schizophrenics who have adopted children	(c) The adopted children	(c) Five percent of children have definite or probable schizophrenia.	(c) An adoptive schizophrenic parent does not increase the risk for the adopted child.
Adopted Twin studies — Adopted schizophrenics with identical twins adopted by different family	Twins	Sixty-three percent of twins have definite or probable schizophrenia.	Having a schizophrenic identical twin predicts schizophrenia, despite differences in rearing.

This table summarizes the ways in which genetic researchers have approached the study of schizophrenia and what they have found. Regardless of the approach, the risk for schizophrenia for someone increases as his or her genetic similarity increases. In addition, the evidence shows that environmental factors play a part since even genetic identity does not predict schizophrenia with 100-percent certainty.

higher risk for schizophrenia than the general population. Increasing genetic dissimilarity reduces the chances of schizophrenia drastically, so that most estimates of rates of schizophrenia among second- and third-degree relatives of
schizophrenics are not much above that for the general population. In our attempts to separate the environmental from the
hereditary influences, we generally have found biological relationships more predictive of schizophrenia than environmental
factors. This is, a close biological relationship to a schizophrenic
is much more frequently associated with schizophrenia than is
a close environmental relationship.

While the case for the genetic transmission of schizophrenia
is a solid one, it by no means accounts for all of schizophrenia.
"While the genetic risk strategy is obviously a heuristically valuable one, . . . roughly 90 percent of persons diagnosed schizophrenic do not have a parent (or parents) so labeled."[16] Likewise, there are many more relatives of schizophrenics who do
not show signs of schizophrenia than those who do.[17] It has
been pointed out in a recent clinical study that 73 percent of
143 children (over twenty years of age) of schizophrenic parents
were mentally sound.[18] Finally, as pointed out by behavioral
geneticists, "the fact that the concordance rate for schizophrenia
is very far from 100 percent in many studies is probably the
best single piece of evidence there is pointing to the general
importance of environmental factors—as yet unknown."[19] The
epidemiological study of schizophrenia primarily has been concerned with tracking down these "as yet unknown" environmental factors.

EPIDEMIOLOGY

Many contemporary ideas regarding the role of environment
in the development of schizophrenia have evolved from years

16. Keith *et al.*, 1976, p. 541.
17. Garmezy, 1974(a).
18. Bleuler, 1950.
19. Gottesman and Shields, 1972, p. 291.

of epidemiological research. Epidemiology is the study of the distribution of a given disorder, in this case, schizophrenia, over the population. Ideally, the goal of epidemiology is to uncover the causes of a disorder and, by doing so, to prevent its recurrence.

To illustrate the value of epidemiology in the search for causes, we can cite recent trends to identify groups of people at risk for work-related disorders. For example, the rate of lung cancer is significantly higher among asbestos workers than that in the general population. Based on the fact that persons regularly exposed to asbestos fibers have a higher rate of lung cancer than those not regularly exposed, we infer that asbestos fiber has a part in causing lung cancer. Yet many asbestos workers do not develop lung cancer. Further studies among asbestos workers reveal that people who both are exposed to the asbestos fibers and smoke have the highest rate of lung cancer. We may hypothesize that asbestos fibers are carcinogenic and especially potent in producing lung cancer in someone who is a cigarette smoker. Our knowledge of lung cancer epidemiology—that is, the pattern of lung cancer distribution among different groups of people—led us to reasonable hypotheses about one cause of lung cancer. It is the task of clinical researchers to follow up these leads.

As cancer is found more frequently among asbestos workers, a proportionately higher rate of schizophrenia is associated with the lowest social stratum is our society. Though socioeconomic status is defined in a number of ways, we generally use it in reference to employment status, degree of job prestige, education, and position in the social hierarchy. The actual rates of schizophrenia in the lowest social class have varied from as low as .45 percent to as high as 13 percent, depending on the definition of schizophrenia and the method for locating subjects.[20] The lower figure of .45 percent is substantially below the 1 percent frequently cited as the rate of schizophrenia over the general population. This discrepancy may be due to differences in the definition of schizophrenia or to different characteristics of the groups studied. The important point is that even with

20. Dohrenwend and Dohrenwend, 1969.

these lower figures, the lowest social class had the highest rates of all the classes studied. In contrast to these findings, most epidemiological studies investigating the distribution of manic-depressive disorders by social class have found the highest rates in socioeconomic groups *other* than the lowest. Thus, we can say that the lowest social class is associated not with more psychoses in general, but rather specifically with high rates of schizophrenia.

While this association between social class and schizophrenia has been known for some time, more recent work has suggested that the relationship primarily occurs in large, urban centers, not in rural areas or small towns. A review of the epidemiology of schizophrenia suggested the following:

> the relationship of socioeconomic status to schizophrenia has been demonstrated only for urban populations. Even for urban populations, a linear relationship of socioeconomic status to rates of schizophrenia[21] has been demonstrated only for the largest metropolises. The evidence, though, that there is an unusually high rate of schizophrenia in the lowest socioeconomic strata of urban communities seems to me to be nothing less than overwhelming. The proper interpretation of why this is so, however, is not so unequivocal.[22]

On this basis we would expect schizophrenics generally to be unemployed or have jobs with low prestige and poor salaries; to have less education than average; to live in lower-class neighborhoods; and to occupy the lowest positions in our society. This is not to say that schizophrenia is not also diagnosed and treated in the higher social classes. The situation is analogous to the high risk for lung cancer among asbestos workers. Though lung cancer occurs in the general population, it occurs at a higher rate in asbestos workers. Similarly, while schizophrenia

21. A linear relationship indicates that as one factor changes, the other does so in proportion to it. For example, with each increase in socioeconomic level, there is a decrease in the rate of schizophrenia.
22. Kohn, 1973, p. 62.

is diagnosed and treated at all social levels, the highest rate occurs in the lowest socioeconomic class in large, urban areas.

Social Class and Schizophrenia

Every large city has its "characters." The schizophrenic may be the woman wearing two overcoats in the middle of summer, stockings bunched around the knees, hat pulled down over her eyes to avoid direct eye contact, and gazing constantly to the ground in search of cigarette butts. Perhaps he is the man standing in the middle of traffic, oblivious to all about him except the message he preaches to an unhearing audience. The shuffling, unsure walk and the withdrawn, averted look seem to always mark this type of person. Even in the midst of big-city diversity where many styles of behavior are tolerated, this type of schizophrenic stands out.

Living on handouts and an occasional odd job, these people manage to survive. Home can be a tenement dwelling or a door step. Much of their time is spent wandering the streets, searching for others' discarded items. They frequently are hospitalized if their behavior is annoying to others or if it becomes too difficult for them to survive.

In contrast to this bleak picture, there are many lower-class schizophrenics who live in apartments of their own, in familial homes, or in halfway houses. Though not living on the street, they share the problems common to all persons of low social class: poor housing, erratic employment, fear of crime, and poor health care. They can make use of social services when necessary and often use the hospital as a refuge when stress becomes intolerable.

Regardless of the particular individual's degree of disorder, schizophrenia occurs far more frequently among those who live under conditions of social and economic instability and who must frequently scramble for the necessities of life rather than the luxuries.

Why are there more schizophrenics in the lowest social class than any of the other socioeconomic classes? There are three ways of answering this question. First, we may judge people to be more deviant on the basis of their social status. Second, because schizophrenics generally have trouble establishing social relationships and keeping jobs, they have few social and financial resources. As a consequence, they drift into the lowest social class. This is known as the *social-drift hypothesis.* Third, there is more stress and instability associated with lower-class life than life in the other classes, and, as a result, more people are likely to break down. This is called the *social-causation hypothesis.* [23]

Clinicians, researchers, and interviewers may expect more deviant behavior from a person of low social class than of high social class. We may be, in other words, ready to find behaviors conforming to our low socioeconomic stereotypes, such as lazy, unstable, and irresponsible.

Attribution theory, the position that our preconceived ideas and expectations influence our perceptions, has been shown relevant to sex differences in psychiatric research. For example, a written list of symptoms will be judged differently whether they are attributed to men or to women. [24] Anecdotally, we find this sort of behavior in parents, and others, when a child is expected to be telling a lie, and is treated as such, though the child is in fact telling the truth. When the child protests, the parents say, "See, you're lying again." The child's actual behavior in this case may only minimally bear upon the interaction between parents and child.

Likewise, it is possible that pre-established ideas about lower-social-class behavior puts us in a frame of mind to define more behaviors as abnormal. We might, for example, expect people in the lower social classes to have more superficial relationships, to be less inhibited, to think more loosely, and to be less conforming. If so, we could well focus on these sorts of behaviors, all of which are relevant in making a diagnosis, more in the lower social classes than in the upper ones. While stereotypes and expectancies are going to influence our perceptions, it is unlikely that attribution theory can account for such a large

23. Dohrenwend and Dohrenwend, 1969; Hare, Price, and Slater, 1972; Turner, 1968; Turner and Wagenfeld, 1967.
24. Broverman *et al.,* 1970.

difference as exists between social classes in the rate of schizophrenia.

The social-drift hypothesis states that schizophrenics, unable
to meet the social and work demands of the upper classes, drift
socially downward, thereby increasing the rate of schizophrenia
in the lowest social class. Support for this interpretation is found
in the relationship between geographical mobility and serious
mental disorder.[25] People with severe psychological disturbances
have been reported to move around a great deal, from residence
to residence, town to town, and state to state. The association
between geographic mobility and psychiatric disorder, however,
is not as well established as that between social class and schizophrenia. Additional evidence for the social-drift hypothesis is
provided by a study that found that schizophrenic males took
up occupations in a lower social class than their fathers more
frequently than was true in the general population.[26]

In contrast to the social-drift hypothesis, the social-causation
hypothesis maintains that low-social-class members face greater
stress and hardships than those in the higher social classes. The
disproportionate numbers of schizophrenics in the lowest socioeconomic status, therefore, are taken to reflect disproportionate stress. Recent work in this area has indicated that both social
drift and social causation may contribute to the high rate of
schizophrenia in the lowest social class.[27]

Other Risk Factors: Age and Sex

Up to now, we have concentrated on the relationship between
low social class and schizophrenia since it is the most consistent
finding to emerge from epidemiological studies. However, there
are two other characteristics of interest: age and sex.

It is generally agreed that the age of risk for schizophrenia
is roughly between the ages of fifteen and fifty-five. In other
words, if a person is going to experience a psychotic schizo-

25. Kohn, 1968; Ødegaard, 1936; Schwab and Schwab, 1973.
26. Turner and Wagenfeld, 1967.
27. Kohn, 1973.

phrenic episode, he is most likely to do so during this age period. Within this age range, the onset of schizophrenic psychosis and first hospitalization tend to predominate among adolescents and young adults.[28] In other words, of all persons diagnosed as schizophrenic at their first psychiatric hospital admission most tend to be below the age of thirty. We are not sure why this is so. It is possible that the symptoms of schizophrenia are genetically timed to appear at this point in development, much as secondary sexual characteristics are timed to appear in the early teens. It is more likely, however, that the developmental tasks of adolescence and young adulthood, separation from one's family of origin and the development of a new independent set of relationships, are particularly stressful for those people who are predisposed to schizophrenia. The risk for schizophrenia is then lower before these tasks arise and after they have been accomplished than it is during the transition.

Further, there is a reliable difference between male and female schizophrenics in the age at which they are first hospitalized. Although the overall rate of schizophrenia is about equal for the sexes, male schizophrenics are between five and ten years younger than female schizophrenics at first hospital admission.[29] This sex difference is especially marked when more stringent criteria for schizophrenia are adopted. The average age (across several studies) at first hospital admission is about twenty-five years for males and thirty-two years for females.

This suggests that in our ultimate interpretation of the development of schizophrenia, the onset of psychosis, and psychiatric hospitalization, we must take into account differences between the sexes. It is still too early to interpret this discrepancy between male and female schizophrenics in their age of psychosis onset. Perhaps the separation from family of origin is easier in general for women, who often leave home only when they marry, than for men, who are expected to be more inde-

28. Kramer, 1976; McCabe, 1975; Rosenthal, 1971.
29. Kramer, 1976; Lewine, Strauss, and Gift, 1978; McCabe, 1975; Pollack, Levenstein, and Klein, 1968; Rosenthal, 1971.

pendent. It is possible that more stress, for women, is produced, when their children begin school, and they are left alone a good part of the day, than when they physically leave their parents. If this hypothesis is true, the discrepancy in age of onset between men and women ought to change as societal sex-role expectations change. In any case, there is increasing evidence that sex-role expectations, sex-role stereotypes, and differences in developmental crises between men and women eventually will bear upon this issue.[30]

THE DIATHESIS-STRESS MODEL

We have approached the search for the causes of schizophrenia from two different viewpoints. In the study of biological and adoptive families of schizophrenics, we have emphasized the importance of genetic transmission in schizophrenia. Genetic similarity to a diagnosed schizophrenic substantially raises the chance of being schizophrenic oneself above that for the general population. The environment, whether defined in the narrow terms of the nuclear family or in the broader context of society, also is implicated in schizophrenia. Epidemiology has focused on the social conditions and individual characteristics associated with high rates of schizophrenia. The lowest social class has a rate of treated schizophrenia substantially above that of the other social classes. The onset of psychosis and first psychiatric hospitalization are concentrated among the young, with male schizophrenics breaking down in adolescence and female schizophrenics breaking down in young adulthood. While identifying these various groups of people at risk for schizophrenia is important for determining where to concentrate our mental-health resources. of greater long-term importance are the clues we now have about the causes of schizophrenia.

30. Broverman *et al.*, 1970; Chesler, 1972; Gove and Tudor, 1973; Linn, 1971; Raskin and Golob, 1966; Williams, 1977.

The diathesis-stress model of schizophrenia has evolved from a consideration of both genetic and epidemiological studies. It is hypothesized that schizophrenia results in those persons who have a genetic predisposition for schizophrenia, the diathesis, and who are exposed to an adverse environment, the stress. The model predicts that someone who has *both* the genetic susceptibility and a stressful environment will develop schizophrenia while someone who is subject to only one of the conditions will not.

THE PRACTICAL IMPLICATIONS

We have seen that the risk for schizophrenia is progressively increased as one shares more and more genes with a schizophrenic individual. Specifically, the data we have indicate that approximately 12 percent of children with one schizophrenic parent become schizophrenic, so that being schizophrenic oneself substantially increases the risk to one's children. However, a normal person who has a schizophrenic parent or sibling mated to a person with no schizophrenic family history will almost certainly produce a normal child. That is, the risk to a niece, nephew, or grandchild of a schizophrenic individual is not substantially above that of the general population.

Ought parents who have one schizophrenic offspring be concerned about the possibility of their other children becoming schizophrenic? The risk to siblings of a schizophrenic is about 8 percent. That is, a person with a schizophrenic sibling will become schizophrenic in approximately one out of every twelve instances. In general, the risk of becoming schizophrenic is increased only for first-degree relatives of a diagnosed schizophrenic—parents, siblings, children. The risk for more distant relatives is not substantially different from the risk for the population at large. In addition, schizophrenia is an illness of adolescence and young adulthood. Thus, the risk for schizophrenia decreases with time and is quite low by age forty, even for individuals with a schizophrenic family member.

We wish to caution against losing sight of the individual in our discussion of rates of schizophrenia and risk periods. In making statements about risk, we are doing so on an actuarial basis in the same way that insurance companies compile lists of features about people at risk for accidents or health problems. The individual may vary considerably from the statistical average of the group of which he is a member. In addition, there is at present no way of predicting which, if any, of the relatives of a schizophrenic person will develop schizophrenia. Thus, while the schizophrenic person ought to be aware that any children he or she may have will be statistically at increased risk for schizophrenia, we have no way of knowing whether any of those children will actually develop the illness.

Acknowledging this individual variability we turn now to the causes of schizophrenia.

5

CAUSES OF SCHIZOPHRENIA
Specific Factors

In Chapter Four, we found that schizophrenic symptoms occur as a result of the interaction between genetic and environmental factors. This general statement still fails to answer the question of what causes schizophrenia. Consider, for example, the case of a seriously disturbed paranoid schizophrenic who, when under stress and not on medication, believes he is God and is convinced that his parents are poisoning his food. When regularly taking medication, he does not hear voices and only mildly believes in his superhuman abilities.

What "causes" this person's beliefs? Do his parents, through their overconcern for his well-being, make him feel that they are out to get him? Has the failure to continue medication caused the paranoid's beliefs? Is there an underlying physiological or biochemical disturbance that renders the paranoid susceptible to fantastic beliefs when stressed? These questions, all of which could well be answered with a "yes," reflect different views and interpretations of the meaning of cause.

In this chapter, we adopt the view that genetic transmission is the *necessary*, but not *sufficient*, cause of schizophrenia which is then modified by environmental events (including learning, developmental crises, and stress) to result in clinical schizophrenia.[1] As a simple example of the differences between specific

1. Meehl, 1962.

94

and modifying causal factors, underlying predispositions and actual clinical picture, let us reconsider favism.

The necessary condition for favism is the presence of a single, sex-linked gene. Without this genetic transmission, one cannot develop favism. However, even if a person is genetically susceptible, the sufficient condition for producing the clinical signs of favism requires the eating of fava beans. The symptoms themselves are not genetically transmitted; it is the predisposition that is inherited. The distinction between underlying predisposition and clinical expression, as well as that between necessary but *not* sufficient and necessary *and* sufficient conditions for the manifestation of disorder must be kept in mind as we trace the hypothetical course of schizophrenia. The observable conflicts, feelings, thoughts, and actions exhibited by the schizophrenic are the end product of a very long and complicated series of interactions beginning in the genes and ending in society.

We examine, in the remainder of the chapter, some of the ways in which genetic transmission, biochemical processes, physiological systems, behavior, internal conflicts, and social stress may interact to lead to schizophrenia. Not all the pieces will fit together. Indeed, at times, one type of explanation will appear to have no obvious relationship to another type of explanation. We can be confident, however, that whatever the final picture is, it will have to include both genetic transmission and environment in explaining schizophrenia.

GENETIC AND ENVIRONMENTAL INTERACTION

Two general types of genetic theories exist to account for the underlying disorder in schizophrenia.[2] One is a "monogenic-biochemical" theory which posits that a genetic mutation causes a metabolic imbalance which, in turn, causes schizophrenia. To date, research data have not provided strong support for this

2. Rosenthal, 1963; Slater and Cowie, 1971.

theory. The second theory, the diathesis-stress model, hypothesizes an as yet unspecified genetic predisposition to schizophrenia (the necessary condition), which, in conjunction with an adverse environment (stress), eventually leads to schizophrenia.[3] This model is more consistent with the available evidence.

Stress, generally referring to reactions to changes in one's environment, such as a death in the family, marriage, birth of a child, or medical illness, that cause emotional tension, may come from many sources including family and social relationships, work demands, general developmental crises, and physical trauma.[4] A schizophrenic psychosis presumably occurs in those people who have a genetic susceptibility to schizophrenia and are exposed to a level of stress that exceeds some tolerable limit. Since the strength of the predisposition to schizophrenia can vary from very weak to very strong, schizophrenics will differ in the amount of stress they can tolerate. Those people with a very strong tendency toward schizophrenia may become psychotic under little or no stress, whereas those people with very weak schizophrenic predispositions might be able to tolerate a great deal of stress. According to the diathesis-stress view, no amount of external stress can cause genuine schizophrenia in a person who does not have the genetic predisposition.

Consider the hypothetical interaction between genetic predisposition and stress in Figure 5:1. The tendency toward schizophrenia is inherited and may vary in intensity. This genetic predisposition manifests itself as a biochemical imbalance, causing overresponsivity to the environment. That is, people prone to schizophrenia do not modulate or dampen their responses. This hyperresponsivity, in turn, results in extremely variable behavior, attentional difficulties, and highly fluctuating emotions. After some time, the schizophrenic begins to shut out the world to protect himself against his hypersensitivity. The biological limits set by the genetic predisposition restrict the schiz-

3. Erlenmeyer-Kimling, 1968; Gottesman and Shields, 1976; Kohn, 1972; Matthysse, 1976; Murphy, 1968; Rosenthal, 1963, 1968.
4. Mednick, 1970; Zahn, 1977.

FIGURE 5:1

A Diathesis-Stress Model for Schizophrenia

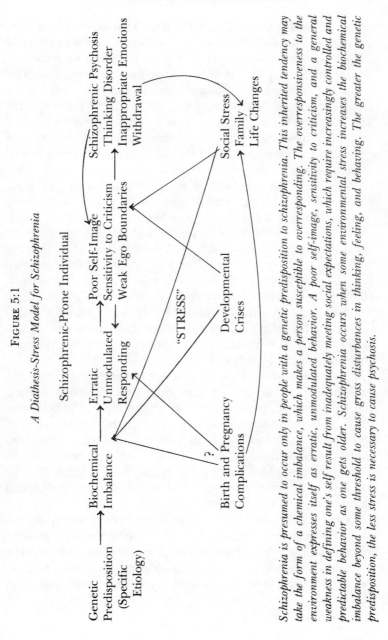

Schizophrenia is presumed to occur only in people with a genetic predisposition to schizophrenia. This inherited tendency may take the form of a chemical imbalance, which makes a person susceptible to overresponding. The overresponsiveness to the environment expresses itself as erratic, unmodulated behavior. A poor self-image, sensitivity to criticism, and a general weakness in defining one's self result from inadequately meeting social expectations, which require increasingly controlled and predictable behavior as one gets older. Schizophrenia occurs when some environmental stress increases the biochemical imbalance beyond some threshold to cause gross disturbances in thinking, feeling, and behaving. The greater the genetic predisposition, the less stress is necessary to cause psychosis.

ophrenic's ability to develop social and work skills. The schizophrenic's self-image suffers as he falls short of familial and social expectations. As demands from the environment increase, the schizophrenic may withdraw further to avoid more failure. The more the schizophrenic isolates himself, the lower his self-esteem. Other environmental stresses may take the form of birth and pregnancy complications, which further limit the child's physical development and the ability to meet developmental crises such as going to school for the first time, leaving home, or establishing independence from one's family.

Though we have explained schizophrenia serially, in other words starting with a genetic predisposition and moving in turn to a biochemical imbalance, erratic behavior, and, finally, withdrawal, interactions between the individual and the environment may occur at any point. We know, for example, that the effects of genes can be modified in response to the "environment," that external stress can cause radical biochemical changes. A family's tolerance of deviant behavior may increase the frequency of strange behavior by the schizophrenic. Reacting to a schizophrenic as a psychiatric label rather than as a person will lower his self-esteem and cause him to withdraw from people even further.

This interactionist view of schizophrenia should dispel the misconception that genes totally determine behavior. During the last century, "hereditary taint," or simply bad genetic material, commonly was thought to account for many types of socially deviant behavior. "Taint included most traits considered undesirable, such as left-handedness, stuttering, being hunchbacked, or using foul language to excess."[5] The effects of rearing, learning, life experiences, and unforeseen environmental circumstances generally were ignored.

Except for extreme and rare instances, genes simply do not *absolutely* determine behavior. In the case of favism, one who inherits a genetic predisposition for a serious disorder need not necessarily develop it. Indeed, the absence of the fava bean in the predisposed individual's diet ensures him protection from

5. Rosenthal, 1975, p. 1.

favism. Similarly, while genetic transmission may determine a schizophrenic predisposition, whether or not a person ultimately exhibits gross psychotic behavior depends on environmental circumstances.

Our ultimate task in understanding the causes of schizophrenia is to determine how individual characteristics affect and are affected by individual development, family, and society. For now, however, we are faced with the practical reality of pursuing this goal along many different, sometimes isolated paths.

BIOCHEMISTRY AND SCHIZOPHRENIA

A young person who has been taking large doses of amphetamines is brought into a hospital emergency room agitated, hallucinating, and shouting about a plot to kill him. Another person, after taking LSD, hallucinates, finds meaning in everything, and generally is very sensitive to the physical environment. A patient suffering from a neurological disorder known as Parkinsonism begins acting and speaking bizarrely after being treated with the medication, L-Dopa. All of these people have exhibited radical changes in thinking, feeling, and behaving after taking drugs that alter the chemical state of the brain. Such clinical observations have led to the belief that deviations from normal brain biochemistry underlie the symptoms of schizophrenia.

The nervous system, of which the brain forms a part, is composed of billions of neurons or nerve fibers. We perceive some environmental event, such as a noise or a light, because that event stimulates the appropriate nerves. The nerves carry this environmental information in the form of an electrical impulse, which travels along the length of the nerve fiber. Fibers are connected so that information is carried from the sensory organs, such as the eyes, ears, or nose, to the brain, where many as yet unknown processes occur that allow us to accurately perceive the environment. Although nerves transmit information electrically, the spaces (or synapses) where one neuron meets another transmit the environmental stimulation biochemically by changing the chemical make-up of the receiving nerve so that the electrical impulse can continue from one neuron to another. The amount of biochemicals, among which are norepinephrine, dopamine, and acetylcholine, present at the synapses influence the transmission of information. These biochemicals are called neurotransmitters. The same system mediates the transmission of information within the nervous system itself. We know, for example, that certain parts of the brain act to inhibit, as well as to excite, behavior and perception. Our interest in biochemistry is in assessing the effects on feeling, thinking, and behaving of varying the levels of neurotransmitters.

The Dopamine Hypothesis

Although there are several neurotransmitters of interest to those studying schizophrenia, dopamine recently has received the most attention.[6] Much of the research in biochemistry has had two goals: to systematically determine if increasing the amount of dopamine in the brain leads to feelings, thought, and behavior that mimic those of schizophrenia (as suggested by clinical observations), and to find out if schizophrenics do, indeed, have more brain dopamine than normal. These two objectives reflect the "dopamine hypothesis" of schizophrenia—namely, that an excess of dopamine in the brains of schizophrenics leads to their disturbances.

Excessive doses of amphetamines, which greatly increase the amount of dopamine in the brain, can result in a psychotic episode indistinguishable from paranoid schizophrenia in previously normal volunteers.[7] Moreover, when taken even in small doses, amphetamines can release a wide range of symptoms, like delusions of persecution and grandeur, or worsen already

6. Meltzer and Stahl, 1976.
7. Angrist *et al.*, 1974; Griffiths, Oates, and Cavanaugh, 1968.

existing symptoms in schizophrenics. This adverse effect of small doses of amphetamines on schizophrenics suggests that schizophrenics have a higher than normal amount of brain dopamine. Presumably, anyone with very large amounts of dopamine, whether as a result of excessive amphetamine use or by virtue of being schizophrenic, will experience the delusions, feelings of persecution, and anger of paranoid schizophrenia.

Animal studies have indicated that chemicals, including amphetamines, that increase dopamine lead to stereotypic behavior similar to catatonia in humans.[8] Catatonic schizophrenia is characterized in part by bizarre, repetitive movements or by the ability to remain in whatever position one is placed for hours on end, called "waxy flexibility."[9] Similar behavior, such as constant pacing or rigidity, has been seen in animals given large doses of amphetamine.

To complete the parallel between schizophrenic behavior and the effects produced by excessive amounts of amphetamine, we find that drugs, such as the phenothiazines, which block dopamine receptors, reduce (or eliminate) the more dramatic symptoms of both schizophrenia and amphetamine psychosis. The similarity in symptoms and treatment of amphetamine psychosis and schizophrenia does not mean that they are the same disorder. Clearly, there are differences in the environmental triggers that set off psychosis in the two: an externally administered drug in the case of amphetamine psychosis and environmental stresses in the case of schizophrenia. In addition, the symptoms reported in an amphetamine psychosis primarily mimic paranoid and catatonic behavior and generally have little resemblance to social withdrawal, inappropriate or flat affect, ambivalence, and autism which play such an important role in schizophrenia. Nevertheless, the similarities between amphetamine psychosis and schizophrenia that do exist suggest that excessive brain dopamine may play a part in causing schizophrenia.

Another piece of evidence suggesting a biochemical involve-

8. Creese and Iversen, 1975; Ellinwood, Sudilovsky, and Nelson, 1973; Garver *et al.*, 1975; Randrup and Munkvard, 1970.
9. Bleuler, 1950; Kraepelin, 1917.

ment in schizophrenia are the side effects of antipsychotic and anti-Parkinsonism drugs.[10] Parkinson's disease is a neurological disorder in which the dopamine system in the brain is broken down. That is, there is a deficit of brain dopamine in the Parkinsonism patient. The treatment for Parkinson's disease is the drug L-Dopa, whose effect is to increase the amount of dopamine. Patients given large doses of L-Dopa, which results in larger than normal amounts of dopamine, sometimes exhibit psychotic behavior. As in the case of amphetamine psychosis, psychotic behavior has been associated with excess brain dopamine.

Conversely, the antipsychotic drugs used in treating schizophrenia lower the amounts of dopamine. The drugs that are most effective in treating psychotic symptoms also are most likely to produce side effects mimicking Parksinson's disease: tremors, "pill-rolling" movement of the fingers, shuffling gait, and a masklike facial expression. These findings regarding the side effects of antipsychotics and the anti-Parkinsonism drug L-Dopa suggest that excessively low levels of brain dopamine underlie Parkinson's disease and excessively high levels of brain dopamine underlie schizophrenia.

If there is a genetic component to schizophrenia, and if the interpretations of the drug studies are correct—namely, that excessive dopamine underlies schizophrenia—then we should find more brain dopamine in schizophrenics than in the general population or other psychiatric patients. While the question is simple—namely, do schizophrenics (or people with a predisposition for schizophrenia) have more brain dopamine than nonschizophrenics—getting the answer is very difficult. There are problems in the biochemical assay (measuring) techniques. In addition, many factors can be confounded in working with adult schizophrenics. There are unknown, possible long-term effects of medication (which decreases dopamine) and stress (which generally is associated with dopamine increases). If we do find differences, we cannot be sure if they are the result or the cause of schizophrenia. Thus, we must be careful in making

10. Meltzer and Stahl, 1976.

statements about what causes schizophrenia. Nonetheless, evidence is beginning to accumulate suggesting that some schizophrenics have a lower-than-normal level of an enzyme that breaks down dopamine.[11] This would result in an increased level of dopamine. These same studies, however, indicate that the enzyme deficiency may also be found in other psychoses—namely, manic-depression.

On the basis of both clinical observation and experimental study, excessive amounts of brain dopamine have come to be associated with psychotic behavior. The dramatic changes in behavior produced by greatly increasing dopamine largely manifest themselves as bizarre body movements and paranoid symptoms. We have concentrated on dopamine because it has received the most attention in recent research. Other neurotransmitters also are being investigated. Although we cannot precisely define a biochemical cause of schizophrenia yet, the evidence points to an important role of some biochemical process that leaves one susceptible to schizophrenia.

If a genetically transmitted biochemical imbalance causes schizophrenia, why, then, is someone with the imbalance not always psychotic? The answer is that the biochemical imbalance, by itself, is not sufficient for schizophrenia. Rather, the schizophrenic-prone individual, though having a higher-than-normal level of dopamine activity, requires further dopamine increases before exhibiting symptoms of psychosis. The added dopamine activity results from environmental stress, which is known to affect the activity of brain biochemicals and susceptibility to further stress.[12] We may compare the biochemical situation in the preschizophrenic person to a dam. The higher the water level (the genetically-set biochemical activity), the more strain on the dam. Continuous strain on the dam weakens its resistance. In response to a heavy rainfall (the environmental stress), the low-resistant, high-water-level dam will give way under less added stress than the more resistant dam holding back less water. If our analogy is appropriate, we would also expect to

11. Wyatt and Murphy, 1976.
12. Meltzer and Stahl, 1976.

find schizophrenics expending more energy in response to the environment than people who are not schizophrenic.

If we accept, for the moment, the idea that brain biochemistry is abnormal in schizophrenia, we must still find a way to link biochemistry and behavior. This link may well be found in the different ways in which schizophrenics perceive (or misperceive) the environment.

INFORMATION PROCESSING

Our ability to get along in the world is based in part on how we perceive external reality and respond to it. Subjective accounts of the schizophrenic experience repeatedly have emphasized a distortion of reality, an increased sensitivity to sights, sounds, and feelings, and in many cases the perception of phenomena having no external basis. It is reasonable, therefore, to seek the causes of schizophrenia in how schizophrenics perceive or process information from the environment.

The search for the information processing disorder in schizophrenia has ranged from a study of physiology to thinking. The thread that ties these studies together is the belief that the schizophrenic's inefficient processing of external reality eventually causes him to withdraw as much as possible from the environment. Buffeted about by excessive stimulation, unable to conceptually organize the world, and unable to shut out unnecessary information, the schizophrenic copes by shutting himself off from external stimulation. Rather than feel too much, the schizophrenic adapts by not feeling at all. This dampening of feelings is a very common response in all of us. After a traumatic event, either physical or psychological, people frequently describe themselves as if they could no longer feel any emotions. Indeed, this is probably true. For a time, the person simply cannot respond. This seems to serve as a psychological circuit breaker to avoid overloading the system. In the case of chronic, severe schizophrenia, this closing down of feelings and responding becomes a way of life.

The Arousal Model

Because the transmission of information along nerves is electrical, we can get an indirect measure of a person's responsiveness to the environment by measuring the body's electrical activity. This is done by placing harmless electrodes, small pieces of metal, on the scalp or hands. These electrodes pick up the body's electrical activity and pass it along wires to some recording device, which produces a graphic representation of the intensity of the electrical activity. Generally, researchers have concentrated on measuring the electrical activity from the scalp and the hands, the latter representing general body activity. While there is no simple, direct correlation between electrical activity and emotional responsiveness, it is usually the case that increased electrical activity reflects increased attention to and interaction with the environment. The more one withdraws from the external world, the less electrical activity is generated. The responsiveness of the body is typically referred to as *arousal*. If schizophrenics' subjective experience of the world is due to a higher-than-normal responsiveness, then schizophrenics should show a great deal of activity as measured physiologically.

The expected overarousal in schizophrenics has been reported by many investigators. Adult schizophrenics have been shown to give greater responses, take longer to recover from, and respond more similarly to different events than groups of nonschizophrenics or nonpsychiatric patients. However, other reports suggest that some schizophrenics show the predicted picture of overarousal, while other schizophrenics are under-aroused.[13] The latter finding is what one would expect from a schizophrenic who has shut out the world. These two types of

13. Buchsbaum, 1975, 1977; Maher, 1966; Silverman, Buchsbaum, and Henkin, 1969; Venables, 1977; Zahn, 1977.

schizophrenic response, namely over- and underarousal, suggest that a schizophrenic begins in an overresponsive state, then over the years gradually withdraws until he shows underresponsiveness. While this a reasonable theory, the change from over- to underarousal has not been demonstrated in any single schizophrenic.

Some recent research findings indicate that a person predisposed to schizophrenia may be both overaroused and underaroused.[14] Children of schizophrenics were found to have extreme physiological responses, both in the direction of underresponding and overresponding. While this work is still in the early stages, it does point to an absence of control, or modulation of response, rather than an absolute under- or overarousal.[15]

The Attention Model

One facet of schizophrenic behavior that has been studied extensively is that of *attention*.[16] Since schizophrenics frequently cite their inability to concentrate or to focus their attention as a serious problem, many investigators have pursued the idea that schizophrenia is caused by some basic defect in attention. Attention can be measured in many different ways.

There is, for example, an experimental procedure called a *reaction time task*. In a reaction time task, a person is required to respond (usually by lifting a finger from a timing device) as quickly as possible after a designated signal is perceived. For example, one might be asked to release a timing button as soon as one saw a brief flash of light on a screen, or heard a tone presented over earphones. The more attention one pays to the task and the designated target, the more quickly one can respond. The reaction time is, in other words, faster when paying attention than when not paying attention.

14. Itil, 1977; Itil *et al.*, 1974.
15. Epstein and Coleman, 1970.
16. McGhie, 1969.

On the basis of reaction time performance under many different conditions, it has been proposed that schizophrenics are less able than most people to maintain an optimal level of attention over long periods of time.[17] Schizophrenics are also more prone than other people to make perceptual errors. They more frequently will respond when nothing is presented and fail to respond when something is presented than most other groups of psychiatric or nonpsychiatric comparison groups. Schizophrenics also exhibit extremely variable attention. That is, they might attend and respond quickly on one occasion, and fail to respond in the same situation on a different occasion.

Another method for measuring attention has been to record one's eye movement when asked to follow a smoothly moving target.[18] Many schizophrenics have trouble tracking a smoothly moving target. Whereas normal visual tracking is characterized by continuously keeping on target, schizophrenics frequently either fall behind or jump ahead. This visual under- and overshooting of the target results in erratic, variable performance. The same erratic visual tracking has been reported in the first-degree relatives of schizophrenics. While there is evidence that deviant eye tracking may reflect general distractibility,[19] there is some suggestion of a perceptual deviation in those having a genetic high risk for schizophrenia, even in the absence of overt psychiatric disturbance. A warning is in order, however, since this is a recent finding and requires further investigation.

Finally, there is a very large body of evidence reflecting the schizophrenic's difficulty on tasks requiring problem solving, perceiving and categorizing meaningful material, and organizing one's thoughts. In other words, the schizophrenic has trouble attending as reflected in studies of thinking.[20] As one example, it has been found that schizophrenics tend to interpret words out of context. The word *pen*, for example, may refer to a writing instrument or to an enclosure for animals. How one interprets the word is determined by its use in a sentence. When

17. Cromwell, 1975; Shakow, 1963, 1971.
18. Holzman and Levy, 1977; Holzman *et al.*, 1974.
19. Brežinova and Kendell, 1977.
20. Chapman and Chapman, 1973.

asked to choose a synonym for *pen*, the most frequent response is to pick "a writing instrument." If, however, one is asked to choose a synonym for *pen* in the sentence "The pigs strayed out of their pen," one would designate "an enclosure." Giving the appropriate answer in the latter case requires attending to the overall meaning of the sentence and eliminating the most frequent association to *pen*—namely, writing instrument.

Schizophrenics seem to have trouble both in attending to precise meaning and to processing context. This is also reflected in their interpreting words literally when the words are intended as metaphors, as in proverbs, failing to precisely differentiate among different related concepts, and having trouble in organizing concepts in commonly accepted fashion. Sometimes schizophrenics do not discriminate enough, at other times too much. Thinking may, therefore, be described as narrower than usual as well as diffuse or disorganized.

As in the case of reaction time studies, eye tracking, and physiological arousal—indeed, as in most schizophrenic behavior—there is also great variability in schizophrenics' performance on these types of thinking tasks.[21] While in general, they perform poorly, there are many instances in which they do well, others in which they do not. Overall, the results of the study of schizophrenic thinking are consistent with a dysfunction in modulating one's reaction to and organization of the environment. The schizophrenic appears, in other words, to be responding to his environment in an extreme and erratic way.

A tremendous amount of energy has gone into studying the schizophrenic's perceptual and cognitive responses in search of the link between brain biochemistry and schizophrenic symptoms. An equal amount of energy has gone into exploring the childhood events that some theorists believe precipitate a schizophrenic breakdown. In these explanatory models genetics and biochemistry are downplayed or ignored entirely. Nevertheless, the findings of these researchers may have something to offer us as we attempt to fit all of the pieces of the puzzle together.

21. Wishner, 1964, 1971, 1977.

THE PSYCHODYNAMIC VIEW

Many schizophrenics describe themselves as unlovable, unworthy, disgusting, and poisonous. It is, therefore, not surprising that the schizophrenic is very sensitive to any threat, whether real or perceived, to his self-worth.[22] When we are feeling bad about ourselves, we become much more likely to interpret others' comments and behaviors as insults. It may be in this same way that extremely low self-esteem sensitizes the schizophrenic to potential challenges to his worthiness as a person. Whereas most people have areas in which they feel good and secure about themselves, the schizophrenic appears to expend much energy fending off feelings of worthlessness on many fronts.

Part of the sensitivity to criticism that the schizophrenic experiences is due to his faulty judgment of reality and an insecure sense of self. If, for example, someone criticizes us, we can evaluate the criticism in terms of our own past behavior, the motivations of the other person, and what others have told us. Because the schizophrenic both has not built up a firm, consistent idea of who he is (that is, he frequently must define himself in terms of how others respond to him) and feels inadequate about himself, the criticism becomes quite powerful. The schizophrenic acts as if he had not established the psychological boundaries that allow one to ascribe some feelings, thoughts, and actions to "I" and other behavior to external people. For the schizophrenic feeling, thinking, and acting take place in only one domain which does not distinguish between a self and others. Psychodynamic psychology, as first outlined by Sigmund Freud, attempts to describe how this state of nondifferentiation in schizophrenia comes about.

The psychodynamic view of human behavior explains mental disorder in terms of individual psychological energy.[23] Emphasis is placed upon human motivations, instinctual drives, and unconscious forces. Individual development requires moving from a state of uninhibited needs and an absence of distinction be-

22. Grinker and Holzman, 1973.
23. Cameron, 1963; Freud, 1952, 1965; Meyer, 1910; Sullivan, 1953.

tween self and others to one in which gratification can be post-
poned, basic drives such as sex and aggression are channeled
into socially acceptable forms, and a definition of one's self is
formed. Schizophrenia, in this kind of theoretical framework,
is explained as a return to a less developed state in which the
part of us that copes with reality is not functioning properly
and the person is overwhelmed with infantile thoughts, feelings,
and drives.

The infant is a bundle of wants and needs that require immediate fulfilling. Whether hungery, wet, or tired, the infant
responds to his unpleasant state with a totality rarely seen in
adults. The infant screams, squirms, and cries with every part
of his body and with all the energy at his disposal. His thinking
is untouched by external realities and control.

Although we cannot ask the infant about himself, it certainly
appears that he has little idea, if any, of who he is. He will play
with his toes or a parent's fingers in very much the same way.
Indeed, some psychologists have suggested that it is this very
form of playing with one's own limbs and objects in the environment that allows the young child to make the distinction
between self and others.[24] If I bite "my" toe, "I" feel pain,
whereas if I bite daddy's finger, I may hear a shout but feel no
pain. Through a series of trial-and-error manipulations of self
and environment, the child begins to form some idea of who
he is.

Much of what we eventually call self is thought to reflect the
ways in which parents have responded to these early demands.[25]
A child, for example, can learn to trust that his needs will be
taken care of or that one cannot trust the environment to satisfy
one's needs. If parents respond to the child with frustration and
dissatisfaction, the child may come to think of himself as unworthy and incapable of success. Conversely, if the child sees
that his parents are pleased with his actions, he may learn to
think of himself as a basically good, competent person.

The process of growing up requires controlling and directing

24. Piaget, 1952.
25. Cameron, 1963; Sullivan, 1953.

the uninhibited, diffuse energy with which the child is born, taking external reality into account, and differentiating oneself from others. Some psychological energy, of which it is claimed there is only a limited amount, must be expended to successfully pass through each of a number of stages of development. If, for some reason, a person has a great deal of conflict at some stage, more energy is required to get beyond that point. During times of stress in adulthood, a person may regress, or go back to an earlier stage in development. Like a tire with a weak spot, one may function quite adequately under favorable conditions. With increased pressure and a rocky terrain, however, one may give out at the point that had been the most difficult in growing up.

All of us regress to some extent when we are under pressure. Take, for example, the change in most of us regardless of our age when visiting parents. Many of the old conflicts and behaviors that had existed when we were children are relived. The need to get father's attention, old sibling rivalries, the renewed ambivalence between our wanting to depend on our parents and the need to be separate and independent are common conflicts that are renewed in the old family environment. We seem to go back to developmentally earlier ways of interacting.

A particularly important developmental period in relation to schizophrenia is adolescence. It is a time of turbulence, instability, the trying out of various roles, a breaking away from the family, and an attempt to discover one's true sense of self.[26] Loyalties that had formerly been concentrated in the family are transferred to people outside the family. Heroes are found in other peoples' families or in strangers, rarely in one's own family. The adolescent, in trying to establish an identity separate from the family, is caught in a bind between the desire for independence and dependence. That is, the adolescent seeks independence, individuality, and autonomy, yet seeks parental approval of his actions. Furthermore, the uncertainty about how to act as an adult makes him want advice at the same time that he strikes out on his own. The bravado and arrogance of the

26. *Ibid.*

adolescent frequently belie a frightened, unsure child. Getting through adolescence requires having successfully built up a pool of resources for dealing with the outside world. This includes intellectual growth, the ability to form social relationships, mastery over one's body, and the use of language to communicate with others in one's environment.

Schizophrenia is described as a state in which the differentiation between self and others is reduced or eliminated, thinking is overwhelmed by primitive fantasies, and testing of external reality is defective.[27] The loss of ability to compare one's internal productions with the outside world is thought to be a response to stress in which there is a regression to very early developmental stages, which are characterized by lack of boundaries between self and the rest of the world. That only some people respond to stress with schizophrenic regression is explained by assuming that people disposed to schizophrenia have inadequate psychological resources. They never developed a basic trust at a time when an important person had to provide for them.[28] Adolescence is particularly important since it is a time when a person's sense of self and ability to successfully cope with the outside world are most severely tested. Two major issues of adolescence, self-identity and the conflict between dependence and independence, play a central role in schizophrenia. It is not surprising, therefore, to find that many schizophrenics break down at this time in their lives.

While the psychodynamic viewpoint paints a vivid picture of schizophrenia, it is difficult to test the psychodynamic theories of schizophrenia and impossible to predict who will become schizophrenic on the basis of a psychodynamic interpretation.[29] There is little doubt, however, that the issues, conflicts, and events described by psychodynamic psychology are of major importance to understanding the adjustment issues that must be addressed in the treatment of the schizophrenic individual.

27. Cameron, 1963; Werner, 1948.
28. Erikson, 1950.
29. Maher, 1966.

THE FAMILY-THEORY PERSPECTIVE

Psychodynamic theory is not the only model in which the biological basis of schizophrenia is ignored. There are several explanations of schizophrenia, falling under the general name of family theory, that shift attention from the schizophrenic individual to the family system as the unit under study.[30] From the family-theory perspective, schizophrenia is not just a disorder of the individual but rather a manifestation of deviant family interactions. Family theorists have explained the designation of an individual family member as schizophrenic in three ways.[31] First, the schizophrenic may serve to keep together a family that is so full of hidden interpersonal conflict that it would not otherwise survive. The schizophrenic in this situation is the common enemy against which the rest of the family unites. Second, the schizophrenic may be adaptively responding to deviant parental communication. Finally, there may be such a strong family identity, that the schizophrenic, in trying to break loose, is labeled as deviant.

The idea that the schizophrenic serves to draw off family conflict is captured best by the term *scapegoating*.[32] In other words, one person is designated by the family to play out conflicts among other family members. One might find, for example, that two parents who show little affection toward one another, are united in their concern for a child they perceive as not being affectionate. By directing their attention to the child's problem they can avoid their own conflict. As long as the child remains the problem, the family can remain intact. If the child begins to function successfully, the family is faced either with disintegration or with choosing a new sick member.

A related view of the family causation of schizophrenia emphasizes the adoption of a dominant spouse's deviance by the passive spouse. This is reflected in normal family interaction by

30. Bateson, 1972; Bowen, 1960; Erikson and Hogan, 1972; Foley, 1974; Haley, 1969; Lidz, 1958; Wynne *et al.*, 1958.
31. Maher, 1966.
32. Haley, 1959.

the "father knows best" philosophy in which the father's views, decisions, and actions are adopted by the mother and used as the standard in dealing with her children. A deviant form of this family pattern might be one spouse's supporting the other spouse's irrational fears that someone is out to poison them. This complicity of one spouse with another in preserving some deviant behavior has been termed "marital skew."[33] This unified front of deviant behavior serves as a model of pathological responding for the child.

An early view of the type of family that caused schizophrenia was that of a dominant, cold, distant, aloof, and rejecting mother, the "schizophrenogenic mother."[34] The father in this family was described as irrational, passive, withdrawn, unsure of his masculinity, and in need of his wife's admiration. The schizophrenic's poor self-image, inability to relate appropriately to other people, and general psychological immaturity were presumed to be a function of inadequate rearing by the schizophrenogenic mother and passive father. The schizophrenogenic mother was thought to foster extreme dependency and emotional expression toward her, yet repel open displays of affection. The father in this family played a minor, quiet role, failing to exert the expected authority from the father figure.

Schizophrenia in an offspring also has been attributed to deviant communication by the parents. One of the most frequently researched communication deviances has been the "double bind."[35] The double-bind theory views schizophrenia as an appropriate response to mixed messages. The contradictory messages occur at two different levels of communication.

The classical example of the "double bind" is that of the parent who criticizes a child for not showing affection, then involuntarily withdraws physically or fails to respond when the child tries to sit on the parent's lap. On the verbal level, the parent is asking for a show of affection, but behaviorally is saying stay away. It is impossible for a child to act correctly in such a situation. No matter which approach the child takes, he

33. Lidz, Fleck, and Cornelison, 1965; Lidz, 1958; Lidz *et al.*, 1957.
34. Arieti, 1959; Fromm-Reichmann, 1948.
35. Bateson, 1972; Bateson *et al.*, 1968.

must go against one of the two expressed parental demands. Schizophrenia, according to this theory, is an attempt to avoid this inevitable failure in meeting social (or parental) expectations by withdrawing from social interactions, becoming confused, or attempting to follow each message literally.[36] While all families express some messages of a double-bind nature, it is the frequency and emotional intensity of the double bind that characterizes the schizophrenic family.

Finally, schizophrenia has been described as a general problem of family identity. Part of our self-image includes our family roles. The family identity, which is greater than the sum of its individual members, may provide a very strong sense of identity and membership. For example, families may identify themselves as "never quarreling," "liberal," or "persecuted." Whatever one's sense of family identification, there is also room for establishing oneself as an individual outside the family. In schizophrenic families, however, the family identity is thought to be so pervasive and powerful that the individual cannot break free. There is no identity other than the family. The phenomenon of family boundaries expanding to discourage all attempts at establishing individuality has been called the "rubber fence."[37]

The potential ubiquity of the family tie is captured in a contemporary comic strip in which the son's every attempt to form relationships outside the sphere of his mother's influence is sabotaged. The son's own mental representation of his mother is just as great an obstacle as mother herself. In one episode, for example, Francis asks his mother: "Oh, Momma, mind if I skip this evening with you and see my *girl* instead? I mean, is there any *reason* why I couldn't?" To which Momma replies: "One very simple reason: I am your MOTHER." Francis, unable to consider any alternatives, says to his sibs: "You know, I think 'MOTHERHOOD' was invented by clever ladies to gain control over the rest of us."[38] Clearly, for this character, the power of the mother-dominated family precludes any action that does not conform to the family rules.

36. Foley, 1974.
37. Wynne *et al.*, 1958.
38. Lazarus, 1977.

While family theories of schizophrenia have provided valuable descriptions of family interactions, there is *no evidence* that parental personality style, communication deviance, or inability to break family boundaries causes schizophrenia.[39] Indeed, it has not even been established that any of the family patterns described above are specific to schizophrenia.[40] Many families, with and without a disordered member, give contradictory messages, have one dominant parent, and have family members who find it hard to disengage from the family sphere. Further, many families having a schizophrenic member show none of the deviations and styles of interaction that had been thought to characterize the schizophrenic family.[41]

The early hopes of family theorists to isolate the types of family systems that cause schizophrenia have not been fulfilled. These unfulfilled expectations may have led, in part, to the passing of the traditional family study of schizophrenia.[42] Nevertheless, in recent longitudinal studies of schizophrenics' children, the relationship between family interaction and the development of the child's social and intellectual skills are reexamined.[43] While the early family theories of schizophrenia have proven untenable, it is reasonable that family conflict and interactions may act as a *general stress* in the schizophrenic's life. But the evidence does not support the myth that families directly cause schizophrenia through their feelings, thoughts, and actions. To believe that the family does cause schizophrenia only places an undue burden upon the families of schizophrenics.

SCHIZOPHRENIA—THE PUZZLE

We have covered many areas in describing the possible causes of schizophrenia. Schizophrenia has been explained in terms

39. Jacob, 1975; Riskin and Faunce, 1972; Schuham, 1967.
40. Foley, 1974; Goldstein and Rodnick, 1975; Maher, 1966.
41. Arieti, 1974.
42. Goldstein and Rodnick, 1975.
43. Hirsch and Leff, 1971; Wynne *et al.,* 1975.

ranging from biochemicals to family interaction. It is not always apparent how the various explanations of schizophrenia relate to one another. However, we must pursue the causes of schizophrenia on many fronts if we are eventually to understand its origins.

A reasonable causal theory of schizophrenia, consistent with available data, is that genes transmit a particular biochemical state which leads to erratic, unmodulated behavior. The potential schizophrenic develops a poor self-image, fails to develop adequate social and work skills, and withdraws from society in an attempt to avoid failure. Environmental stress, such as that reflected in family conflict and in meeting developmental crises, may serve in an as yet unknown way to push the predisposed individual into schizophrenic psychosis.

There is one crucial piece of the picture that we have not discussed up to now—namely, that we have based our theories of schizophrenia predominantly on work with adults. Studying adults in order to generate hypotheses about causes is not satisfactory. Unless we can demonstrate that some event or behavior occurred *before* the onset of schizophrenia, we cannot be sure whether a given phenomenon is a cause or effect of schizophrenia.[44] We can take, as an example, the attempts to link poor intellectual development with schizophrenia.[45]

Some studies have suggested that adult schizophrenics are inferior to people without psychiatric problems on various tests of intellectual functioning. We may interpret this difference either as an indication that low intelligence predisposes one to schizophrenia or that schizophrenic disorganization interferes with intellectual functioning as measured by test performance. In order to make a causal statement, it is necessary to determine what the person's level of intellectual function was *before* the onset of schizophrenia. If we could demonstrate that the person's performance was much higher before psychosis, we could infer that schizophrenia was interfering with test taking. If, in contrast, the schizophrenic's test performance was poor long

44. Garmezy, 1974(a); Mednick and McNeil, 1968.
45. Chapman and Chapman, 1973.

before the presence of schizophrenic disorganization, then we could infer that low intelligence may be one condition for the development of schizophrenia. Even this interpretation, however, is provisional in that many more people of low intelligence do *not* develop schizophrenia than those who do. We must actually observe the prepsychotic behavior of the adult psychiatric patient if we are to make any statements about events that cause schizophrenia. Ideally, then, we would like to be able to follow the lifetime development of the individual who is eventually diagnosed as schizophrenic.

The Development of Schizophrenia

Three methods have been used to provide this needed link between childhood behavior and adult schizophrenia: follow-back, follow-up, and high-risk studies.[46] The follow-back strategy requires tracking down the childhood school or child guidance records of people who are diagnosed schizophrenic as adults. In follow-up studies, young people already diagnosed as having serious behavioral or emotional disorders are followed to find who among them become schizophrenic. By studying a wide range of variables it is hoped that some will be isolated that will distinguish between those disturbed children who become schizophrenic and those who do not. Finally, the high-risk strategy involves identifying a group of children at higher risk for schizophrenia than the general population. By studying the development of these high risk children through the age of risk for schizophrenia, we attempt to determine what causes some children to become schizophrenic while others at risk do not.

Although we may define risk on the basis of genetics, behavioral disturbance, social-class membership, or presence of birth complications, by far most researchers use genetic risk, or being biologically related to a schizophrenic, as their criterion for choosing children to study.[47]

46. Garmezy, 1974(b). Garmezy and Streitman, 1974; Mednick and McNeil, 1968, Ricks, 1970.
47. Garmezy and Streitman, 1974.

Biochemical, Neurological, and Physiological Factors

As we have indicated previously, there is some very early and tentative evidence suggesting a biochemical imbalance among the offspring of schizophrenics. There is at this point no corroborating evidence, so we must accept these findings as interesting leads.

There have been several reports indicating delayed neurological development and birth complications among children who have serious schizophrenic disorganization as adults.[48] Preschizophrenics have been reported to be slower in attaining developmental milestones such as walking and talking and to have poorer motor coordination.

It seems probable, however, that any type of physical deficit interacts with other factors such as genetic predisposition and family environment in leading to schizophrenia. One investigator, for example, has presented the case histories of three male infants who were at risk for schizophrenia on the basis of their slow and uneven development during infancy.[49] When the children, whose family environments differed widely, were evaluated nine years later, all three children had different outcomes. One child, whose schizophrenic mother had trouble caring for him and whose father was actively hostile toward him, was diagnosed as having childhood schizophrenia. The second child was judged to be neurotic, but moderately well adjusted. This child had a mother who was "sensitive, responsive, intelligent, fragile, and lonely." The third child had been placed in various foster homes following his mother's psychotic breakdown. He was described as being "more psychopathic than schizophrenic."[50]

Finally, some investigators have reported evidence of unmodulated physiological responding in schizophrenics' offsprings.[51] That is, some schizophrenic offspring both over- and underrespond to the environment. Overall, these early biochemical,

48. Fish, 1957, 1960; Fish and Hagin, 1973; Mednick, 1970; Mednick *et al.*, 1973; Sameroff and Zax, 1972; Pollin and Stabenau, 1968.
49. Fish *et al.*, 1966; Fish, 1971; Fish and Hagin, 1973.
50. Garmezy and Streitman, 1974, p. 19.
51. Mednick, 1970; Garmezy and Streitman, 1974.

neurological, and physiological findings are consistent with the view that people disposed toward schizophrenia are more susceptible to external stimulation.

Patterns of Childhood Behavior

One of the most striking findings to emerge from longitudinal studies is that the childhood behavior of those eventually diagnosed schizophrenic takes many forms. In contrast to the shy, quiet, withdrawn stereotype, male schizophrenics frequently are reported to be aggressive, antisocial, and to direct their hostility against the environment.[52] The antisocial boys who eventually become schizophrenic men are distinguished from antisocial boys who become antisocial adults by their isolation from peer groups. The preschizophrenic boys are, in other words, alone and not part of a group, though hostile in their behavior. Girls who eventually are diagnosed schizophrenic, in contrast to the boys, frequently do conform to the passive, quiet, withdrawn image one has of the person who is disposed toward schizophrenia.[53]

Other researchers have suggested two adolescent behavior styles that are associated with severe adult psychiatric disorder, including schizophrenia.[54] Based on only a small number (twenty-four) of children, it has been concluded that "the most vulnerable (to schizophrenia) adolescents appear to be those caught up in active family conflict, and those who are excessively dependent on their parents and withdrawn, passive, and isolated in their relationships with others."[55] Another group of children directs its antisocial, hostile behavior toward the community rather than the family, and also appears to be at risk for future disorder, though not necessarily schizophrenia. Thus, while hostility and aggression seem to be part of the early development of the schizophrenic, the brunt of the preschizo-

52. Ricks and Berry, 1970; Robins, 1966; Watt, 1972.
53. Watt, 1972.
54. Goldstein *et al.*, 1968.
55. Garmezy and Streitman, 1974, p. 22.

phrenic's aggression is the family. At the same time, the child eventually diagnosed schizophrenic appears to lack a peer group with whom he can identify.

As further evidence of the inappropriateness of the shy-child myth, we can point to a study in which the incidence of adult schizophrenia was examined in a group of fifty-four people seen in child guidance clinics because of shyness and withdrawal.[56] Only two (or 4 percent) of the shy children were judged to be mentally ill as adults.

Other reported behaviors exhibited by children eventually diagnosed schizophrenic include "more eating and sleeping disturbances, more tics and mannerisms, fears and phobias, and feelings of depression and chronic unhappiness" than problem children not developing schizophrenia as adults.[57] Overall, the childhood development of people destined to become schizophrenic adults may be marked by a wide range of disturbances. It is not yet clear, however, what the causes and what the effects are. Overdependency on parents, for example, may be an expression of schizophrenic dysfunction rather than a causal agent. Future developmental research will have the difficult task of separating the signs from the etiology of disorder.

Family Factors

There is some evidence that parental loss, either in the form of parental death or parental separation and divorce, occurs more frequently during the schizophrenic's childhood than the normal's.[58] Similarly, "emotional divorce," or a family in which the spouses have little to do with one another emotionally, seems to occur often in the families of eventual schizophrenics.[59] Both findings suggest the importance of the parents' emotional presence in the development of the child. Indeed, this may be said for the healthy development of any child. In general, the early

56. Morris, Soroker, and Burruss, 1954.
57. Garmezy and Streitman; 1974; p. 43.
58. Robins, 1966; Garmezy and Streitman, 1974; Watt *et al.,* 1970.
59. Ricks and Berry, 1970.

results of family studies indicate the presence of conflict or disorganization in the families of those children who go on to become schizophrenic.[60]

It is clear from the developmental studies that many of the children eventually diagnosed as schizophrenic show signs of disorder long before they receive a diagnostic label. Clearly, there can be no effects of "labeling" in the case of these pre-schizophrenic children. Indeed, clinicians generally prefer not to label childhood disorders for fear of stigmatizing the child. There is, therefore, no basis for the contention that labeling itself causes schizophrenia.

The diathesis-stress model suggests that schizophrenia is the result of a complex interaction between a genetic predisposition and environmental influences. Evidence from a number of different areas of research lend support to the model. The work of geneticists indicates that schizophrenia has a genetic component. Biochemists have suggested that an excess of the neurotransmitter dopamine may be implicated in the development of the disorder. Other researchers have attempted to provide the link between brain biochemistry and behavior in their studies of schizophrenic attentional and thinking processes. Psychodynamic and family studies may provide clues to what sorts of environmental stresses contribute to the development of clinical symptoms. Finally, developmental studies are now aimed at distinguishing between cause and effect in schizophrenia. While we are certainly far from having all the answers, we expect to become more precise and confident in our understanding of schizophrenia as we continue to follow up the leads generated by these research efforts.

60. Nameche, Waring, and Ricks, 1964; Gardner, 1967; Rosenthal, 1962; Rutter, 1966.

6

TREATING THE SCHIZOPHRENIC INDIVIDUAL

The development of a comprehensive treatment plan for an individual who suffers from schizophrenia can be a time-comsuming and, at times, frustrating endeavor. Such a plan might include medication, an attempt at restructuring the immediate environment, counseling the individual and the family with respect to the nature of the disorder and its implications, and the readjustment of both short- and long-term personal goals. In addition, many clinicians would add individual or group psychotherapy to the plan, hoping to help the individual to gain or regain needed social skills as well as insight into the nature of his or her feelings, conflicts, and behaviors. In this chapter, we will acquaint the reader with the various treatment methods that are currently used with schizophrenic individuals, exploring each one with respect to its positive and negative aspects. In subsequent chapters we will explore the role of family and social institution in the rehabilitation of schizophrenics, concluding with guidelines for an optimum treatment plan which we believe could usefully be followed with each newly diagnosed schizophrenic.

MEDICATION

The most widely and successfully used treatment modality, antipsychotic medication, serves to reduce disordered thinking, to calm runaway feelings, and to return to the individual vol-

123

untary control over behavior.[1] Numerous studies have indicated that patients taking medication are more likely to be discharged from the hospital and spend fewer total days in the hospital than nonmedicated patients.[2] The rehospitalization rate for medicated patients is approximately one half that of nonmedicated patients.[3] Thus, the new drugs have enabled patients who would otherwise have been institutionalized for long periods of time to live and work in the community. In addition, they have altered the milieu within hospitals so that rehabilitation and psychotherapy can be effectively undertaken. By contrast, psychotherapy alone is rarely, if ever, effective for chronic schizophrenic patients.[4]

As often happens in medicine, the specific antipsychotic effects of these medicines were discovered almost by accident. In the early 1950s chlorpromazine (Thorazine®) was being used in France as an aid to clinical anesthesia. By chance, some of the patients on whom the drug was being tested were mental patients. It was noticed that a number of these patients improved dramatically. Subsequent research indicated that the drug provided symptomatic relief of agitation and anxiety and, in addition, had a beneficial effect on psychotic processes with apparently diverse symptomatologies. Shortly after the drug was released for marketing in the United States in 1955, its widespread usefulness in the treatment of psychotic disorders became apparent. Since that time, the number of antipsychotic medications has increased dramatically. At present, close to two dozen such drugs are available (see Table 6:1).

While there appear to be individual reactions to the different medications, there is no evidence that one is consistently better than another,[5] although they seem to differ in the amount of initial sedation that they induce and in the frequency and

1. Spohn *et al.*, 1977; National Institute of Mental Health, 1964.
2. Cole and Davis, 1969; Efron, 1968; Engelhardt, 1974; Gittelman-Klein and Klein, 1968; Klein and Davis, 1969; Hogarty *et al.*, 1974.
3. Engelhardt *et al.*, 1967; Hogarty, Goldberg, and The Collaborative Study Group, 1973; Pasamanick, Scarpitti, and Dinitz, 1967; Serban and Thomas, 1974.
4. Feinsilver and Gunderson, 1971; May *et al.*, 1976(a).
5. National Institute of Mental Health, 1964.

TABLE 6:1

Antipsychotic Drugs

GENERIC NAME	TRADE NAME
Chlorpromazine	Thorazine
Promazine	Sparine
Triflupromazine	Vesprin
Thioridazine	Mellaril
Mesoridazine	Serentil
Piperaietazine	Quide
Prochlorperazine	Compazine
Trifluoperazine	Stelazine
Butaperazine	Repoise
Perphenazine	Trilafon
Fluphenazine	Prolixin
Acetophenazine	Tindal
Carphenazine	Proketazine
Haloperidol	Haldol
Droperidol	Inapsine
Chlorprothizene	Taractan
Thiothizene	Navane
Molindone	Moban
Loxapine	Loxitane

strength of the side effects that they produce. Since there are so many medications, each physician usually chooses a few with which to become most familiar. However, if a patient has had a good response to a particular medication in the past, that same medication typically will be prescribed again if the illness worsens. In other cases, the first drug to be tried is usually chosen on the basis of the physician's intuitions and previous experiences with similar patients or on the basis of the amount of sedative effect that would be optimal.

We ought to point out that these medicines are not beneficial to *all* schizophrenics. A substantial minority appear not to respond positively to their effects.[6] We do not know why this is so. Recent research indicates that medication may be most val-

6. Klein and Davis, 1969.

uable for low-competence, hospital-prone patients,[7] but much work needs to be done before we can predict which individuals will respond to psychotropic medicine. In addition, these same drugs are sometimes used, at low dosages, with nonpsychotic people who are anxious and agitated. So, not all people who receive these medications are diagnosed as having schizophrenia.

Therapeutic Effects of Medication

Antipsychotic medications may be prescribed in tablet form, liquid form, or injected into a muscle. They are usually taken one, two, or three times a day, although there is now a long-acting, injectible form of one of them, Prolixin, that is given weekly or biweekly.

When a person first begins to take the medication, regardless of its form, he will generally experience initial sedating effects within forty-eight hours. The primary effect of the medication at this time is to help control acute anxiety and panic, decrease the intensity or frequency of hallucinations and delusions, and inhibit aggressive behavior. The patient's responses to external stimuli are slowed down, as are physical responses. In addition, the person will usually experience an emotional quieting, finding it easier to sleep well and to remain calm.

These effects are not typically accompanied by a change in the state of waking or consciousness or of intellectual functioning. There is little incoordination, and the patient may be easily aroused. It is clear, however, that the sedative effects are not, themselves, responsible for the noted improvement. Quiet, withdrawn, lethargic patients may be also helped by medication, becoming more active, more motivated, and more in touch with reality. That is, the medication seems to return the thinking and emotional processes to a more normal level rather than simply sedating the patient. Further, the sedative effects, when they do

7. Saenger, 1970; Evans *et al.*, 1972; Engelhardt and Freedman, 1965; Rosen, Klein, and Gittelman-Klein, 1971.

occur, are short-lived and tend to decrease or disappear within a few weeks' time. However, the antipsychotic effects are long lasting with benefits accruing over many months or even years.

When treatment is continued over a number of weeks, as it almost invariably is, there is usually a marked positive effect on disturbed thinking. Hallucinations may disappear or become less intrusive, less frightening. Delusional thinking tends to subside and along with it the panic (and the euphoria) of the false ideas. Thoughts that previously raced out of control slow down and regain their attachment to reality. Bizarre behavior that was provoked by psychotic ideas diminishes in frequency. Fear, withdrawal, and negativism gradually subside. In some people these changes occur abruptly while in others they occur more gradually. Generally, in responsive individuals, these improvements appear to occur and stabilize within the first three months of treatment, although there is wide individual variation.

The antipsychotic medications are not psychologically addicting. They do not produce a euphoria or "high" and so do not produce a craving for the drug. Occasionally, patients may complain of difficulty sleeping, muscular discomfort, and increase in psychotic symptoms if the medication is stopped abruptly.[8] It is not clear whether these symptoms represent a recurrence of the psychosis or some degree of physical dependence.

In some cases, medication eliminates virtually all of the dramatic signs of schizophrenia. However, most people continue to exhibit psychological and interpersonal vulnerabilities long after the more acute symptoms have been controlled. Among these vulnerabilities are the tendency for thinking to become disorganized under stress, a fragile sense of self-concept and self-esteem, and difficulty in establishing satisfying interpersonal relationships. Thus, medication is often only the first step in the treatment process. It brings the patient back into contact with reality so that he can learn to maximize his adaptive capacities with respect to these on-going problems.

While there are some patients who can stop using medication

8. Detre and Jarecki, 1971.

without an increase in psychotic symptoms, many, perhaps the majority, need to continue to take it for many years, if not for a lifetime. In one ten-year follow-up study, for example, 62 percent of the patients were taking medication at the time of the follow-up. Of the patients who were rated as fully recovered, 39 percent had taken medication continuously for over five years while 45 percent had discontinued medication within ten months of discharge from the hospital.[9] At present, there is no way of telling whether a specific person can safely discontinue medication at a specific time. Thus, it is necessary to interrupt drug treatment and observe the person for signs of mental deterioration. Since symptoms may recur in as short a time as a week or as long as six months, withdrawal should be accomplished slowly and with intensive professional supervision. The fact that so many patients experience a relapse if medication is discontinued[10] indicates that schizophrenic symptoms are controlled, rather than removed, by medication. That is, the symptoms are gone but the underlying disorder is still there. This situation is analogous to the use of insulin in the treatment of diabetes. As insulin controls the symptoms of diabetes but does not remove the underlying cause, antipsychotic medicines generally control the florid schizophrenic symptoms but do not eliminate the intra- and interpersonal vulnerabilities.

Often, schizophrenics (and their families) are upset by the prospect of long-term medication, fearing that the patient will become a drug addict. Again, insulin, rather than heroin, is the appropriate analogy. The antipsychotic medicines are useful in controlling the symptoms of an illness. They are not taken to achieve a "high" or to avoid dealing with life's problems. Quite the opposite, they may enhance the ability to cope with interpersonal and vocational demands.

Side Effects of Medication

One of the most frustrating aspects of the use of antipsychotic medications is the wide range of side effects that may occur.

9. Bland, Parker, and Orn, 1976.
10. Olson and Peterson, 1960; Prien, Cole, and Belkin, 1969.

Many of these effects are short-lasting and only annoying as opposed to prolonged and dangerous, but the medication regimen must be followed closely by a physician, particularly during the first few months of therapy.

Occasionally, patients will have an allergic reaction to medication, including jaundice, skin reactions, and blood disorders. However, these problems occur rarely and are apparent early in therapy. If they do occur, the drug is discontinued and a different drug is tried.

Another troublesome side effect that may occur early in treatment is a drop in blood pressure. However, tolerance to this effect usually develops, and it tends to disappear after the first few days of treatment. Other early side effects include faintness, palpitation, nasal stuffiness, dry mouth, slight constipation, and a mild elevation in temperature. Again, these effects, if they occur at all, tend to disappear over the first few weeks of therapy.

A wide range of muscular disturbances can occur as a result of treatment with antipsychotic medication. It is estimated that approximately 39 percent of patients will experience at least one of the muscular problems at some time during treatment.[11] The most common of these is a feeling of restlessness. Patients may have difficulty sitting still and may feel a strong urge to move around. This uncomfortable symptom, known as akathisia, occurs in approximately 21 percent of medicated patients,[12] and may be mistaken for psychotic agitation or nervousness by the untrained observer.

Another set of muscular symptoms resembles those seen in Parkinson's disease and is, therefore, labeled Parkinsonian syndrome. The patient experiences motor retardation and rigidity. It may be difficult to move the facial muscles, resulting in a masklike expression. Difficulty controlling other muscles results in a shuffling gait and hand tremors. These symptoms occur in about 15 percent of medicated patients.[13] Patients with these symptoms have *not* developed Parkinson's disease, but

11. Ayd, 1961.
12. *Ibid.*
13. *Ibid.*

rather are experiencing motor problems *similar* to those seen in patients with Parkinson's disease.

Finally, a very small number (approximately 3 percent) of medicated patients will experience dystonia.[14] This commonly appears as extreme rigidity of the neck, head, and face muscles. Sometimes the patient's eyes will turn upward and he will be unable to bring them down again. While this last symptom, called oculogyric crisis, can be extremely frightening to the patient and family, it is quickly and easily treated by an injection, which brings relief in a matter of minutes. The episode, once it is over, has no residual effects of any kind.

All of these muscular effects tend to be of short duration and are completely reversible. Patients who experience them can be treated by either a reduction in the dosage of antipsychotic medication or by adding an additional medication, usually Cogentin, Artane, or Benedryl, which counteracts the side effects. Typically, the additional medication can be withdrawn after a few weeks or months with no return of side-effect symptoms.

An effect of relatively high doses of medication, particularly Thorazine, is the tendency of some patients to get severely sunburned easily. This complication can be prevented by insuring that the patient is well covered when exposed to sunlight or by switching to a different medication.

While impotence, frigidity, and decline in sexual interest are rarely reported as side effects, large doses of Mellaril may interfere with the ability to maintain an erection or to ejaculate in some male patients.[15] Again, substitution of a different medication is sufficient to alleviate the problem.

Some of the phenothiazines induce increased appetite so that the patient gains weight. This can be problematic when the weight gain negatively affects the patient's body image and self-esteem. In patients for whom this problem is likely to arise— for example, young female patients—one of the less-appetite-enhancing medications may be prescribed.

There is one apparently irreversible side effect that may occur with prolonged and heavy use of antipsychotic medication, al-

14. *Ibid.*
15. Detre and Jarecki, 1971; Taubel, 1962.

though usually only after a number of years. It is called tardive dyskinesia and is estimated to occur in 3 to 6 percent of the psychiatric population and in up to 40 percent of elderly, chronically institutionalized patients.[16] The syndrome involves involuntary mouth and head movements, often appearing as smacking or licking of the lips, chewing motion, tongue protrusion, and grimacing. Tardive dyskinesia is particularly worrisome, not only because it is irreversible, but because it may not appear until the antipsychotic medication has been discontinued and is, therefore, difficult to detect. Recent concern over this symptom has increased the likelihood that physicians will interrupt drug treatment occasionally as a diagnostic and preventative measure. This long-term effect occurs only infrequently and typically only after prolonged administration of medicine at high doses. Thus, the risk of its occurrence must be weighed against the value that the medication has for the patient.

Perhaps the most troublesome side effect of medication is the marked diminution of creativity and spontaneity of which many patients complain during recovery from an acute episode. It is not clear whether the drugs themselves produce feelings of emptiness, boredom, and lethargy, or whether they merely allow these feelings to resurface. In any case, this effect is far more upsetting to patients themselves than any other. Often schizophrenic patients who stop taking their medicine cite this symptom as the most intolerable. Additionally, there is some research evidence that patients who refuse or discontinue medication tend to develop symptoms of grandiosity and feelings of power when they are ill,[17] thus increasing the felt discrepancy between the medicated and unmedicated state.

For this group of patients who experience some gratification from the symptoms of their illness, treatment can be a rude awakening. Few of these people are adequately prepared by their physician for this outcome. Such a patient may agree to take a medicine that will "make you feel better" and may find, to his dismay, that he feels unstimulated and unmotivated. He may respond by feeling betrayed, angry, and defeated at the

16. Kobayashi, 1977.
17. Van Putten, 1976.

hands of his "helpers." Were such a person counseled that the medication would help him regain control over his thoughts and behavior, although possibly at the expense of feeling intense emotions, it is likely that he would be in a better position to work with the treatment team toward his rehabilitation rather than against the team.

While it may not be possible early in treatment to make the patient fully aware of the likely outcome, it becomes not only possible but also necessary as the medications begin to work. If the patient is told that he is getting better as he feels himself to be getting worse, he must necessarily become confused and distrustful. If, however, the ways in which he is better, like increased control and more appropriate behavior, are specified and the complaints he voices of feeling unspontaneous and empty are acknowledged as real, he is more able to trust his "helpers" and develop with them a set of priorities and rehabilitation strategies. He will be able to acknowledge the positive effects of the medication as his doctor and family are able to acknowledge the negative effects, and both can then work to maximize the benefit to the patient.

While medication side effects are certainly troubling to the patients who experience them, there is no evidence that antipsychotic medications taken by pregnant women will have harmful effects on their offspring. Variables such as congenital malformations, mortality rate, birth weight, and intelligence have been studied and no significant differences between offspring of medicated and nonmedicated women have been found.[18] In addition, fatal accidental or purposeful overdoses are extremely rare.[19] The amount necessary to overdose is very much greater than the therapeutic dose, making the antipsychotic medications quite safe in this respect.

Antipsychotic medications generally have been shown to be of significant value for both acutely ill and chronically ill schizophrenics. They reduce psychotic symptoms and result in decreased frequency and length of hospitalization. While all the

18. Spohn *et al.*, 1977.
19. Detre and Jarecki, 1971.

drugs are approximately equal in therapeutic value, individual patients tend to respond better to one than to another, and finding the best medication can be a time-consuming trial-and-error process. The exact mechanism by which these medications exert their beneficial effect is presently unknown, although it is likely that they do so by blocking dopamine receptors in the brain. This would reduce the dopamine available for synaptic transmission, thereby compensating for the hypothesized dopamine excess. For the great majority of patients who respond to antipsychotic medication, the eventual benefits in terms of increased ability to function far outweigh any discomfort they may experience early in therapy.

ELECTROCONVULSIVE THERAPY

Before the advent of antipsychotic medicines, electroconvulsive therapy (ECT) was commonly employed with schizophrenic patients. This method, which was invented in 1938 and has since been refined, involves producing convulsions in the patient by passing an electrical current through the brain.

As it is presently done, the patient, dressed in loose clothing, lies on a bed. His shoulders and arms are held down lightly so that he does not injure himself during the convulsion. Electrodes are attached, one to each side of the forehead, and a shock is given. The patient has a seizure that lasts less than one minute. Since the patient is unconscious from the moment the current begins, there is no feeling or memory of a shock. The experience is not physically painful. After the convulsion, the patient remains unconscious for about five minutes and then arouses during the next five to ten minutes. There usually follows a period of confusion that lasts about an hour. Many patients sleep during this period. Since the most common complications of ECT are fractures that occur during the seizure, many physicians prefer to put the patient to sleep and then give a medication that briefly paralyzes the muscles in order to reduce the risk of broken bones.

Treatments are usually given two or three times a week, but may be given as often as twice a day, every day. Most patients receive twenty five to thirty treatments. Patients may receive ECT in the hospital or as outpatients.

While ECT typically produces confusion and immediate memory loss, studies indicate that memory gradually returns with full recovery being complete within a few weeks.[20] It produces no intellectual impairment, and the physical risk is extremely low except in patients with brain disease. Death associated with ECT is estimated to occur once in every 28,000 treatments.[21]

Electroconvulsive therapy has been shown to be quite effective in reducing depressive symptoms, but is not generally as valuable for schizophrenics as is antipsychotic medication. In one study, for example, ECT produced symptomatic improvement in 79 percent of the patients, while medication reduced the symptoms of 96 percent.[22] ECT is rarely valuable for those patients whose illness develops slowly and gradually. Nor does it decrease the major cognitive symptoms of schizophrenia.[23] It is most likely to be of use for patients in whom acute emotional disruption, particularly depression, is prominent. For these patients the calming effect, however short-lived, decreases the risk of suicide and provides time for medication to exert its effect.

PSYCHOSURGERY

In 1935, a Portuguese neurologist developed a surgical procedure in which the connection between two adjacent sections of the brain, the frontal lobes and the thalamus, could be severed. Patients who underwent the operation were often less tense and more manageable as a result. Preoccupation with

20. Kolb, 1973; Squire and Chace, 1975.
21. Barker and Baker, 1959.
22. May *et al.*, 1976(b).
23. Kolb, 1973.

symptoms, hallucinations, and delusions appeared to diminish. However, symptoms such as isolation and withdrawal were not decreased. Further, the operation often impaired the patient's sense of responsibility and feeling for others. Typically, the patient exhibited a lack of self-criticism and restraint after surgery.

The advent of antipsychotic medication abruptly diverted the attention that was once paid to psychosurgical procedures. The effectiveness of surgery in substantially and permanently reducing psychotic symptoms has never been demonstrated.[24] It is almost never undertaken now and is considered only for patients who have been unsuccessfully treated for two years, who cannot be managed in any other way, and who require constant isolation or restraint even in the hospital setting.[25] With the treatment methods that are presently available, such patients are extremely rare.

VITAMIN THERAPY

Recently, the attempt to treat schizophrenia and numerous other emotional and physical disorders with large doses of various vitamins has received wide publicity. The assumption underlying this strategy is that schizophrenics convert epinephrine, one of the neurotransmitters, into toxic substances that produce hallucinations.[26] This abnormal process is presumed to be due to the presence of a certain protein ingredient, called taraxein, which is thought to sensitize the schizophrenic's brain to the hallucinogenic substances.[27] Some researchers believe that vitamin B_3, known as niacin, or nicotinic acid, blocks the production of taraxein, thereby alleviating the symptoms. Other vitamins, such as vitamin C and vitamin E, are thought to further

24. McKenzie and Kaczanowski, 1964; Detre and Jarecki, 1971.
25. Detre and Jarecki, 1971.
26. Hoffer and Osmond, 1959.
27. Heath *et al.*, 1957.

suppress the schizophrenic's production of hallucinogenic substances.[28] Therapy consists of administration of massive doses
of vitamins. For patients who do not respond, a four-day period
of fasting precedes a second trial, on the assumption that many
schizophrenics may be highly allergic to substances found in
many foods.[29]

While this treatment strategy has become almost a fad among
large sections of the public, evidence for its efficacy is based
largely on theoretical speculations and personal testimonials
rather than on controlled clinical studies. In fact, controlled
studies by independent investigators have failed to validate
either the model[30] or the treatment.[31] Further, since most vi-
tamin-therapy proponents also use antipsychotic medication and
other treatment methods along with vitamins, any positive therapeutic outcome is difficult to evaluate. At present, the value of
massive doses of vitamins in the treatment of schizophrenia
must be considered doubtful. Its use, *instead* of antipsychotic
medication, is risky in the sense that a highly speculative, un-
proven treatment is being substituted for one whose positive
effects have been well documented.

However, one point often raised by proponents of vitamin
therapy deserves emphasis. Numerous metabolic disorders—for
example, low blood sugar—can produce symptoms similar to
those seen in schizophrenia. Thus, a careful medical assessment
must be made before a diagnosis of schizophrenia can be accepted with some degree of confidence. Misdiagnoses sometimes do occur due to the overlap of schizophrenic symptoms
with those of other physical and emotional disorders.

SUPPORTIVE PSYCHOTHERAPY

While antipsychotic medication is an extremely important,
possibly necessary, part of the treatment plan, it is rarely the

28. Hoffer, 1974.
29. *Ibid.*
30. Axelrod, Perlin, and Szara, 1958; Holland *et al.*, 1958.
31. Ban and Lehman, 1975.

only method of value. Psychotherapy is often a valuable adjunct. This is not surprising in view of the vulnerabilities to disorganization, lowered self-esteem, and personal and vocational deficits, which we discussed above. A therapist may prove invaluable in helping the individual re-establish ties with reality, set appropriate expectations and goals, regain a measure of self-confidence, and develop much needed social skills. Most importantly, the therapist can be supportive during the arduous rehabilitation process. Thus, while medication is generally effective in controlling the immediately troubling psychotic behavior, additional help is often necessary with respect to issues of self-esteem and interpersonal competence.[32] The latter task, while more difficult, may prove more valuable in enhancing the quality of life for the schizophrenic individual.

Family members often feel that they ought to perform these functions themselves. While their patience and understanding can be of tremendous value to the patient, they are almost always unable to maintain the objectivity necessary to do the therapist's job. Understandably, they have many feelings about the patient's past behavior and its effect on them, and they have certain expectations and aspirations for the patient's future. In addition, they lack the experience and training that allows the therapist to help the patient understand, adapt, and change. Thus, the need for a therapist should not be viewed as a failure on the family's part, but rather as a useful addition to the help they have to offer.

There are many kinds of psychotherapy. Each shares with the others the assumption that talking about oneself, with insight and suggestions offered by a trained and competent therapist, can increase one's ability to adjust successfully to life's demands. Thus, psychotherapies involve talking with a therapist at regular intervals. However, psychotherapy with a schizophrenic individual is usually quite different in both form and content from psychotherapy with people who are not schizophrenic. In general, schizophrenic people are best treated with *supportive psychotherapy,* while most nonschizophrenic people are best treated with *expressive psychotherapy* (see Table 6:2).

32. Engelhardt and Rosen, 1976; Keith *et al.*, 1976.

TABLE 6:2

A Comparison of Supportive and Expressive Psychotherapy

	SUPPORTIVE PSYCHOTHERAPY	EXPRESSIVE PSYCHOTHERAPY
Goal	To help the client learn new skills; separate reality from fantasy	To unearth unconscious conflicts that guide behavior
Focus	Behavior	Feelings
Time orientation	Largely present	Largely past
Therapist behavior	Active, directive, teaching	Passive, nondirective, reflective, and interpretive

Expressive psychotherapy is designed to facilitate the exploration of feelings by the client. The assumption is that awareness of one's feelings and understanding of the effects of feelings on perception and behavior help the client to become more competent in dealing with the realities of his or her life. The therapist attempts to provide a link to unconscious conflicts, often based on childhood experiences, which interfere with the client's ability to function efficiently. In order to help the client explore feelings, the therapist is often quite passive and the client carries responsibility for structuring the sessions. In psychoanalytic psychotherapy, one kind of expressive therapy, the client may lie on a couch, facing away from the therapist, in order to minimize the distractions that impede awareness of internal processes. When the expressive therapist comments, it is usually by way of reflecting or interpreting what the client is feeling.

Supportive psychotherapy is quite different. Here, the goal is to help the client cope with the real requirements of the present situation by learning or relearning certain skills. The focus is largely on behavior rather than on the exploration of feelings. Thus, the supportive psychotherapist provides a link to reality rather than a link to the unconscious. In order to do so, he or she is active, structuring, personally engaging, and instructive. Supportive psychotherapy more nearly resembles a two-way conversation than expressive psychotherapy, in which the client does most of the talking and the therapist does most of the listening.

In general, the cornerstones of any therapeutic endeavor with a schizophrenic patient are *support* and *structure*. Such a strategy is the natural outcome of our understanding of the schizophrenic deficit. The difficulty lies in modulating behavior, thoughts, and feelings rather than in coping with conflicting desires. This is not to say that schizophrenics do not have conflicts like the rest of us, only that such conflicts do not lie at the center of the problems that they experience.

Therapeutic Objectives

The first and most important therapeutic task is to develop a supportive relationship. Since the patient often may be withdrawn, frightened, and suspicious, this may take many months. This goal will be accomplished successfully insofar as the therapist is able to communicate that he or she (1) understands what the patient is experiencing, (2) values the patient as a person, and (3) is genuinely committed to helping the patient achieve maximum recovery. As a result of experiencing both the subjective and objective symptoms, the schizophrenic individual may find it extremely difficult to trust another person. Establishing a relationship of trust is the first order of business and must be accomplished if the therapist and patient are to function as "partners" in the rehabilitation process.

Once a trusting relationship is established, the therapist generally fulfills a number of functions. Of primary importance is an ability to help the individual test reality. During the recovery period, which may take many months, schizophrenics often retain a number of irrational ideas. They may be unable to accurately judge the meaning of others' behavior. Typical of these ideas are the thoughts of a young man that people are staring at him or of a young woman that someone she knows possesses magical powers. When these ideas are shared with a trusted therapist, they can be checked against reality more effectively. Often, they will then disappear, but at minimum, they will become less intrusive and less disorienting.

The recovering schizophrenic may be unable to accurately judge the social appropriateness of his own behavior. He may wonder if the way he expresses feelings of anger or affection are appropriate to the situation. He may wonder whether he sounded stupid or crazy during a conversation. Here, again, the therapist helps the individual learn to test himself against reality. By comparing his behavior with that of other people and by learning to realistically assess the requirements of situations, the individual becomes increasingly more able to evaluate his skills and his weaknesses. Since the therapist, unlike the patient's family and friends, is not personally affected by the patient's behavior, he or she is often in a unique position to appraise the patient's behavior without communicating negative feelings.

Another important function of the therapist is that of a teacher. Through role playing, modeling, homework assignments, and other forms of practice, the therapist can help the patient learn social skills that he may have never acquired or relearn skills with which the illness has interfered. Consider the patient who has difficulty in making social conversation. The therapist may well begin by engaging in such conversations with the patient, both modeling the skill and encouraging the patient to practice and to evaluate his own performance. When the patient feels ready, he may take on the assignment of initiating one or more such conversations in his outside life. He then discusses these experiences with the therapist, evaluating the outcome and practicing in the areas in which he still feels deficient.

The therapist also teaches the patient about schizophrenia. This has several ramifications. The therapist may choose to discuss the probable genetic predisposition for schizophrenia with the patient. In addition to preparing the individual for possible future decisions about having children, such a discussion helps the patient understand that his difficulties in achieving goals may be in large part, the result of processes outside of his control rather than the result of laziness, lack of intelligence, or poor will power. While this realization may at first be upsetting and depressing, its end result is often an increase in the patient's self-esteem and determination. Typically, the patient's self-concept has been contaminated by his illness for quite a while. For instance, if he has been physically agressive while acutely ill, he may be tremendously relieved to trade the dangerous, hateful, and murderous images he has of himself for a self-image in which he sees himself as a basically good person with an illness. In this way, he may become able to accept anger while still rejecting aggressive behavior. He will not have to reject "himself" in the process. As a function of these discussions the patient develops a clearer understanding about the aspects of his functioning over which he *does* have control as well as those over which he does not.

The therapist also engages with the patient in exploring his limitations. For many patients, the acute phase of schizophrenia (if it occurs) is only the beginning of the conflict. There are many repercussions to being diagnosed as, treated for, or hospitalized for schizophrenia. Even after the acute effects of the illness have passed, the person may not be able to accomplish what he used to or what he hopes to accomplish. His short-term goals, like immediately returning to college, will almost certainly have to be revised, and even his long-term goals, like becoming a lawyer, may turn out to be unattainable. The process of setting appropriate goals within the limitations of the schizophrenic experience is often an extremely difficult and upsetting task for the patient, who may feel tremendous pressure from family and society, as well as from within, to set goals consistent with his background but not with his illness.

The therapist and client may also spend time discussing the possibility of future periods of worsening symptoms. Ideally, the client learns from reviewing his own experience which early signs indicate symptom onset. For some patients insomnia or agitation precede more severe symptoms while for others the presence of obsessive thoughts about a particular subject can function as a clue that the illness may be worsening. Throughout the recovery phase, the therapist helps the patient to learn to distinguish between normal responses to stressful episodes and prepsychotic symptoms. Further, they discuss strategies for handling renewed symptoms if they should occur, including whom to contact and at what point.

In addition to learning how to cope with increasing mental disorganization, the patient learns, with the therapist's help, what he can do to prevent such recurrences by exploring the sorts of situations that cause stress in him. Since stress seems to make schizophrenia worse, the patient is helped by becoming aware of those things, people, tasks, or circumstances that tax his emotional strength. Some of these stresses he may learn to handle better, others he may learn to avoid. He may learn, for instance, to monitor his thinking when he is under pressure and to "back off" if he becomes confused or overloaded. Often, simply withdrawing from the stressful situation for a while will be helpful. He may be able to use such strategies as making lists and structuring tasks in order to decrease the experienced overload.

Intimate relationships can be particularly stressful. One young woman who experiences significant disorganization in her thinking when under much stress has come to look for predictability and stability in her personal relationships. She systematically avoids relationships that are confusing and full of conflict, preferring those in which she "knows what's expected." While she sacrifices a certain amount of intensity—for example, the feeling of being "in love"—she does so willingly in the interest of her comfort and continued high level of functioning.

Among the most common stressful situations that the patient will encounter is his relationship with the family. The schizophrenic individual may need the support of the family more than other people. Nonetheless, he often feels the same pressure to become independent that we all experience. The therapy situation is one in which the individual can explore such decisions as whether or not to live with family, how often he should see them, and what sort of support he should request of them.

We have found it useful, in this context, to describe schizophrenia to patients and their families as one way in which a person's body responds to stress. Just as some people develop ulcers or headaches when stressed, schizophrenics develop problems in thinking when stressed. In each of these cases, medicine that increases the body's resistance to symptoms, combined with a better strategy for dealing with stress, can produce a positive outcome.

In sum, supportive psychotherapy is often a useful adjunct to medical treatment of schizophrenia. It provides a safe, supportive, and instructive relationship in the context of which the individual can try out new, and often more productive, ways of coping with the realities of life. While early in the rehabilitation process the therapy relationship may be the only one in which the patient feels comfortable and valued, it becomes, after a time, one of a number of supportive alliances that the patient maintains.

GROUP THERAPY

The schizophrenic often has deficient social skills. This person tends to be frightened of interpersonal relationships and lacks confidence in the ability to interact with others. Often, group therapy can help with these problems once the psychotic episode has abated somewhat and the individual has regained a sense of his physical boundaries.

The group usually meets at regular intervals and is composed of one or more therapists and some number of patients (usually between four and ten). Topics of conversation include problems that members may be encountering outside of the group situation, as well as the effect that each participant's behavior has on the other members. The leaders may give advice, suggest exercises, or make observations about what any member or the group as a whole is doing.

Through the group experience the patient can accomplish a number of goals. First, he can be helped to realize that there are other people with similar difficulties—that is, he is not alone. Typically, patients experience great relief in finding that others have had similar thoughts and exhibited similar behavior. Communicating with others about oneself often relieves feelings of tension, guilt, and loneliness.

In addition, the therapists attempt to provide a relatively safe milieu in which each person can practice social skills and gain confidence. Through structured communication exercises, role playing, and discussion, each group member can test the effects of his social behavior on others within the supportive environment provided by the therapists. He can, for example, practice asking for a date or going on a job interview and can expect to get helpful feedback from his peers on how his behavior has been perceived. Further, the patient can use the group, much like he uses an individual therapist, to test reality. He can voice, without fear of censure, his thoughts and feelings, his plans and dreams, again receiving supportive feedback as to their appropriateness.

Finally, the group situation may be a useful stimulus to the frightened, withdrawn patient who observes other patients learning and practicing social skills. In effect, less disturbed patients model appropriate behavior for more disturbed patients. As is true of individual psychotherapy, support and structure are the important ingredients for successful group therapy.

ACTIVITIES THERAPY

It is rarely possible for the schizophrenic patient to derive significant benefit from individual or group psychotherapy while he is acutely psychotic. Rather, these treatment strategies generally are begun after the patient's contact with reality has been re-established, his concentration has improved sufficiently, and his agitation is reduced. In addition to medication, another possible therapeutic intervention for the acutely ill patient is activity therapy, including occupational and vocational therapy. The activities therapist is trained to assess the patient's level of functioning in many areas, including activities of daily living, motor skills, ability to concentrate and follow instructions, work tolerance and work habits, impulse control, perceptual defects, memory, and reality-testing ability. Once the assessment has been made, and the patient's strengths and weaknesses have been noted, the therapist develops a specific set of activities designed to reduce the particular deficits and enhance the particular strengths of the patient.

For example, if the patient experiences significant difficulty in following directions, the therapist may develop a graded program of specific tasks. The therapist may demonstrate each step of the first task for the patient. The patient need only imitate the therapist's movements at this stage. When the patient is able to follow the therapist's example consistently, the therapist may introduce the steps for the next task verbally, although still one step at a time. When the patient appears competent at following instructions in this way, the therapist begins to give directions for a number of steps at once. This procedure, which may take days, weeks, or even months, depending on the patient, is continued until the patient is able to follow complex verbal directions.

Activities therapy is valuable, not only for the acutely ill schizophrenic patient, but for the recovering patient as well. As psychotherapy is basically teaching by talking, activities therapy is teaching by doing. The recovering schizophrenic may need help in preparing to hold a job or to take care of his living quarters. In addition to helping the patient acquire needed skills, activities therapy helps raise the patient's self-esteem as tasks are tackled and accomplished in a systematic way. It is clear that medication does not, in itself, insure the social and vocational rehabilitation of the schizophrenic patient. Programs designed to build specific skills and enhance personal strengths are essential.[33]

Schizophrenia, while not presently a curable condition, does respond to treatment. A representative study indicates that 75 percent of patients followed for ten years after hospitalization (1963 to 1974) had two or fewer than two readmissions during

33. Engelhardt and Rosen, 1976.

that time. Over half were rated as fully recovered; they were able to think clearly, to experience emotional and social stability and to earn a living. Another 25 percent had periodic or mild psychological problems. The majority of patients in this study survived for most of the ten years outside of the hospital, making an adequate adjustment.[34]

Some of the factors that affect recovery are within the individual's control. Of utmost importance is the willingness to accept continuing treatment. It is almost always necessary to continue to take medication for many months or even years after initial recovery has been achieved. Changes in dosage should always be monitored by a physician. Therefore, regular meetings with a doctor are important. One of the most likely reasons for relapses is the discontinuance of medication against medical advice.

In addition, patients often have significant control over the amount of stress they will face. For example, a patient who has great difficulty concentrating ought not to go to medical school. A patient whose family is in constant conflict ought not to return home to live. These are situations in which stress and failure are likely and the threat of disorganization and confusion high.

Finally, the patient has a great deal of control over how much he is willing to use available resources to aid and maintain recovery. Extended individual or group psychotherapy, vocational training programs, and recreational activities are examples of the sorts of activities that might prove valuable.

34. Bland, Parker, and Orn, 1976.

7

THE FAMILY'S ROLE IN TREATMENT AND RECOVERY

In *I Never Promised You a Rose Garden*, a novel about a young woman with schizophrenia, the patient's mother speaks with the doctor for the first time:

> You see—all these days. . . all these days we've been thinking and thinking how and why this could have happened. She was so much loved! They tell me that these illnesses are caused by a person's past and childhood. So all these days we've been thinking about the past. I've looked, and Jacob has looked, and the whole family has thought and wondered, and after all of it we just can't see any reason for it. It's without a cause, you see, and that's what's so frightening.[1]

Schizophrenia affects all of us, either directly as members of a family with a schizophrenic, or indirectly as members of a society that must bear the psychological and economic burden of schizophrenia. The scene depicted above is one that frequently occurs. Often confused, angry, and in need of help, the family is sometimes too embroiled in conflict and guilt to ask and receive answers to some basic questions about schizophrenia. At the same time, with the discovery of antipsychotic medication and the subsequent decrease in long-term hospitalizations, family members have become the real primary care givers

1. Green, 1964, p. 34.

for many schizophrenic individuals. The majority of treated schizophrenics return to a family environment. Many more remain in significant contact with family members even though they may reside elsewhere. The maintenance of a schizophrenic person within a family context can present very real problems for relatives, who must learn to cope with difficult behavior through trial and error, often with a minimum of external support and understanding.

In this chapter, we attempt to provide some information and advice which may help such family members to become more comfortable and more efficient in their attempts to provide for each other.

IS THE FAMILY AT FAULT?

When a child becomes emotionally or psychologically impaired, that child's parents will spend much time and energy attempting to cope with guilt. They will review in endless detail the child's history, condemning their own behavior at each turn. Father will blame himself for being absent much of the time during the child's formative years, for being unable to express his affection fully, for losing his temper, for refusing certain of the child's requests, and for granting others. Mother will blame herself for occasionally resenting her child, for slapping the child in anger, for being preoccupied, for being overprotective. Both parents will blame themselves and each other for being overbearing or underinvolved, too rigid or too lax, too punitive or too protective. They will have catalogued a hundred ways in which they failed to be the perfect parents they would have liked to have been. They will feel that they are ultimately responsible for the disturbance in their offspring.

If they have been unlucky in their search for help, parents of schizophrenic children will find the burden of professional opinion added to their already heavy load of guilt. They may be told, more or less directly, that unresolved marital problems are being acted out in the child's disturbance. Struggling in their attempt to cope with the disruption of their lives, they may find the inconsistencies and inadequacies of their behavior pointed out to them with maddening regularity. Often, the guilt they experience fuels resentment. They may find themselves angry at the disturbed family member and furious at the professionals who appear to have no appreciation for what their lives have been like. Ultimately, some families withdraw their support entirely in frustration and hopelessness.

Pinpointing the family's role in the development of a schizophrenic illness is a most difficult task. While certain patterns appear frequently in families with a schizophrenic member— for example, an overinvolved mother and a passive, withdrawn father—these same patterns occur frequently in families without a schizophrenic member as well.[2] Further, the "pathological" behaviors that we often see in such families may well be a result of attempts to cope with a disturbed member. We do know that there are similarities in behaviors between families with emotionally ill members and families with physically ill members.[3] We do not know whether the disturbed behavior of families of schizophrenics predated the illness, nor whether the family members played a causal role in the development of the illness. The only statement we can make with any assurance is that inconsistent, confusing, or stressful family interactions do interfere with maximal recovery. Let us observe a few minutes of the behavior of one fairly typical family to illustrate our point.

J.P. is twenty years old. He has been diagnosed as schizophrenic since age sixteen. In the therapist's office he discusses with his parents a proposed trip to a nearby city which he intends to make alone.

FATHER: You can't go. I forbid it. You're not going.
J.P.:   I am going. You can't stop me.
FATHER: You're right. I can't stop you. Go if you want to.
THERAPIST: Mr. P., how would J. have to behave to convince you that he was responsible enough to go?

2. Frank, 1965.
3. McAndrew, 1976.

FATHER: No way. He's not ready. (*To J.*) If you go, you can expect to find your stereo gone when you get back. Maybe your records won't be there either.

MOTHER: (*To therapist*) He already bought the ticket. I told him not to buy the ticket. (*To J.*) Why did you go ahead and buy the ticket when I told you to wait?

J.P.:   They only had a few left. I told you they would sell out. Don't bother me. I'm going.

THERAPIST: J., why do you suppose your father is worried about your going to B—— by yourself?

J.P.:   Aw, I'm not gonna get sick. I don't feel good. I'm tired. Can I get a cup of coffee?

THERAPIST: Did you get sick the last time you went on a trip alone?

MOTHER: (*To father*) Don't you think if he does everything he's supposed to this week . . . He already bought his ticket.

FATHER: No way. He's not going.

J.P.:   Shut up. I am going!

FATHER: So go. I can't stop you.

This interaction is clearly disturbed and disturbing. Father is inconsistent, stubborn, and makes idle threats that he has no intention of acting upon. Mother changes the topic and undercuts father's authority. J.P. is hostile, belligerent, and unable to understand his parents' concerns. However, consider the background against which this conversation takes place.

J.P. has a history of aggressive behavior. He has, in the past, attacked both parents and even now hits his mother when he doesn't get his way. He spits and breaks furniture as well. He is extremely demanding, requesting money, rides, and other favors dozens of times each day. He doesn't take "no" for an answer and often follows his mother into the bathroom to press his point. If she locks the door, he punches a hole through it. Even though J.P. has spent time in a hospital, there has been little, if any, attempt to help the family cope with, understand, and modify J.P.'s disturbed behavior.

J.P. has gone out of town alone on three occasions. Once he

got picked up by the police and his parents had to come for him at three o'clock in the morning. On the way home, he vomited all over his mother. Once he took LSD and ended up in a hospital out of town. Once he got drunk and again called his parents to come for him in the middle of the night. On each of these occasions, he has gone without their permission. They cannot bodily nor legally restrain him. Nor can they stop bailing him out. He is their son, and they are aware that he is ill.

Seen in this context, J.P.'s parents' behavior becomes understandable. Father knows that he cannot control J.P.'s behavior, but he continues to try, however ineffectually. Mother knows too well where arguments lead. She has had many bruises by which to remember, so she tries to prevent another one.

We don't know whether J.P.'s parents have always behaved in this inconsistent, ineffective way, but we suspect that they haven't. They have a healthy daughter with whom they behave quite rationally. We can see that their behavior with J.P. is not useful, but we do not believe that they have caused his illness. Rather, they are responding to it, without help, in the only way they know how.

Families do not cause schizophrenia simply by mistreating their child (or sibling or spouse). They may have transmitted genes that have made the individual vulnerable to schizophrenia. Surely, this was not intended. They may have been unable to protect the individual from the stresses of growing up. But what family could, or would, isolate a child from the world? They may have added to these stresses in innumerable ways. But has any of us found our families to be completely free from conflict, mixed messages, and stress?

SEEKING HELP

While, so far as we know, families do not cause schizophrenia, they usually carry the burden for bringing their disturbed member into treatment. Parents of schizophrenics often feel intensely guilty about failing to understand the implications of the early signs of the disorder. They feel that if only they had been more vigilant, more knowledgeable, more responsible, the illness could have been averted. But, as we have seen, schizophrenia often develops slowly and gradually over many months. Further, it typically begins during adolescence, which is a troubled and confusing time for most young people and their parents. Many adolescents become moody, withdrawn, uncommunicative to family, and rebellious during this period. Usually, family members do not become concerned enough to seek professional help unless there has been an abrupt and inexplicable change in behavior or until the young person shows clear signs of deteriorated functioning.

Among the early warning signs of schizophrenia are social withdrawal, evidence of decreased interest in the environment, decreased motivation to engage in normal activities, and confusing or bizarre behavior. While these signs do not necessarily indicate the presence of schizophrenia, if they occur, particularly in an individual who has a family history of mental illness, professional consultation to the family ought to be obtained. A family doctor, a mental-health center, a psychiatrist, or a psychologist can often make a preliminary assessment and give the family some advice on how to proceed.

It often happens that the individual who is showing symptoms is unwilling to see a mental-health professional due to the fear and stigma surrounding mental and emotional problems. In these cases, it may be useful for the family as a whole to visit the family physician to discuss the problem. This is particularly true when the disturbed person has a trusting relationship with the doctor. Family physicians differ widely with respect to their training and experience in dealing with mental illness, but at minimum, they are able to smooth the way into treatment by referring the family to a competent mental-health professional.

In some cases it may be necessary to cajole, implore, or insist that the person see a physician. In other cases, where the individual flatly refuses to seek help, the family faces a real dilemma. Many communities now have mobile psychiatric emergency teams capable of offering crisis intervention and psychiatric evaluation in the home. The National Institute of Mental Health publishes a national directory of emergency mental-health services. In addition, most cities have a mental-health "hotline" telephone service which can provide direction and suggestions to families in need of help. Finally, when such resources are not available, the family retains the option of calling the police and requesting assistance. The police will usually take the disturbed individual to a mental hospital where the process of *civil commitment* may be set in motion. At present, civil commitment is the only legal strategy available for insisting that a person submit to psychiatric assessment and treatment.

Few people question society's right to incarcerate people who have committed a crime, whether in a prison or mental hospital. However, there is much disagreement about society's right to infringe upon the liberties of a citizen who has not committed a crime. Civil commitment is designed to protect society from a person who is considered to be a *potential* danger, and to provide treatment to those who are incompetent to consent to or to refuse care. Thus, involuntary commitment serves two purposes - to protect society and to rehabilitate the individual.

The current trend is a decline in the number of involuntary commitments as more and more procedural safeguards are erected by the courts to protect the rights of individuals. Statutes vary from state to state, with one or more of three primary criteria generally enforced: (1) the need for care or treatment, (2) dangerousness, (3) the welfare of self or others.[4] The first criterion is usually equated with "having a mental illness" despite the confusion surrounding this concept and despite the uncertain relationship between labels and treatment prospects. The second criterion is impossible to predict with a degree of accuracy which is useful for the individual case. That is, since very few people are actually dangerous, even a test that predicts dangerousness with 90-percent accuracy would still label a large number of people as dangerous who were not. This constitutes a serious infringement upon the civil liberties of many nondan-

4. Stone, 1976.

gerous persons. Statistically, we would mislabel fewer people if we predicted that no one is dangerous. The third criterion is so ambiguous as to function as a wastebasket category, with all the attendant dangers of abuse.

In most states, exhibiting symptoms of mental illness is not sufficient cause for involuntary commitment. Generally, it must be shown that the individual presents an immediate physical danger to himself or to others or that he is gravely disabled and unable to care for himself.

As a result of these guidelines, and of procedural safeguards, such as the right to a hearing, civil commitment is often an arduous process. Frequently, families are left to care for markedly psychotic and sometimes assaultive members because of the legal morass. While there can be no doubt that the civil commitment procedure has been abused and can still be abused, leading to unjustified incarceration, in many instances the pendulum has swung too far.

Even if a person is involuntarily committed to a hospital, he may be considered competent to refuse any or all treatments. He may even have the right to resist psychological or psychiatric tests which are necessary in order to propose a treatment plan. Unless one takes an extreme position such as "the doctor always knows best" or that any patient, no matter how deluded, has the absolute right to refuse any therapy, the question of when a patient should be allowed to refuse treatment becomes very difficult to answer. Ethical problems such as whether the patient has the "right" to be mad or whether the physician has the "right" to perform mind altering procedures form a network of complex and highly charged issues. Of major importance are the issues involving when a patient is competent to choose and what constitutes an appropriate explanation of the risks and benefits of treatment. Practically speaking, what this means is that safeguards that are *legally* in the patient's interests may not be *therapeutically* in the patient's interests. Families who attempt to secure treatment for the disturbed member, but find that their attempts consitute an infringement on his civil liberties, are caught, most painfully, on the horns of this dilemma.

PROBLEMS FAMILIES FACE

Let us suppose that the family has been successful in bringing in a schizophrenic person for treatment. This step is by no means a permanent solution to their problems. As we have seen, recovery from schizophrenia is a prolonged process. Many schizophrenics show residual symptoms and vulnerabilities for many months or years.

What sorts of problems are likely to arise? A recent survey of families of eighty diagnosed and treated schizophrenics provides some answers.[5] Social withdrawal was cited as the most common problematic behavior exhibited by the schizophrenic person. Three quarters of the families reported that the schizophrenic individual was withdrawn and seclusive. Most of these patients were also described as markedly or somewhat underactive, making little conversation, and having very few leisure interests. Many families felt confused about how to deal with these problems. They were uncertain as to whether they should push the person to interact more, to do chores around the house, to attend social or family gatherings. They were concerned lest the patient become more withdrawn without their prodding, yet worried that they might push too hard and upset the patient. They felt embarrassed by the response of acquaintances to the schizophrenic's behavior and at a loss about how they could explain it. A common complaint was that if they spoke about these and other concerns to a professional, they were given no guidelines about how to behave.

Approximately one third of the patients sometimes had delusional ideas of various kinds—for example, that a family member was plotting against them or that poison gas was leaking into the house. The verbalization of these ideas as well as the behaviors associated with them, like refusing to eat a meal cooked by a particular person, were most frustrating for families. Again, they were unsure of how to behave. Should they passively accept the idea, or would this cause the patient to retreat further from reality? Should they tell him it was all in

5. Creer and Wing, 1975.

his imagination, or would this cause him to become upset, distrustful, and even more withdrawn?

One third of the patients engaged in odd behavior like laughing inappropriately or talking to hallucinatory voices. Approximately the same number tended to neglect their appearance. Such behaviors were acutely embarrassing to relatives when they occurred in the presence of others. Coping with them was apparently quite stressful.

Families in the survey cited other difficulties that did not stem directly from the patient's behavior. Among these were concerns about when and how to hospitalize the schizophrenic individual if he became acutely disturbed, the lack of supportive community facilities, the administration of medicine, the strain within the family, and the sense of shame and need for explanation outside of the family.

Fear and Aggression

Among the most difficult problems with which families must cope is the possibility of aggressive behavior. In Chapter One, we addressed the myth that schizophrenics are invariably dangerous. On the contrary, they are much more frequently passive and withdrawn. Nonetheless, schizophrenics do sometimes become violent.

Like many of us, schizophrenics are most likely to become aggressive when they are severely frightened and can see no way to escape a pressured situation. However, unlike the rest of us, they may perceive themselves to be cornered or surrounded by hostile and dangerous forces when they are, in reality, quite safe. For example, a schizophrenic may believe that his family members and friends are engaged in a conspiracy to poison him, and he may use violence to protect himself from the perceived threat. He may believe that someone is attempting to gain control of his mind and will attempt to physically ward off the invasion. Thus, as a rule, those schizophrenics who are paranoid, who falsely believe themselves to be persecuted by others, are most likely to become aggressive.

In other cases, aggressive behavior may occur in response to auditory hallucinations, voices that instruct the individual to assault another person. Usually, such hallucinations occur in the context of the kind of delusional thinking we have described. In addition, since rational thought, which often serves as a mediator between feelings and behavior, is impaired in schizophrenia, the schizophrenic individual may be more likely to directly and immediately discharge angry feelings through explosive behavior. Thus, in the acutely ill state, when emotions may be intense and volatile, the schizophrenic is at heightened risk for aggressive behavior.

Are there any warning signs? Sometimes an individual will signal his agitated state by accusing others of intent to harm him or by becoming suspicious and withdrawn. He is likely to appear both angry and frightened either simultaneously or in quick succession. He may behave erratically and strangely when approached. These signs of distress may be a prelude to aggressive behavior. In other cases, the individual may be so frightened that he conceals his delusional ideas and feelings. In such instances, no warning may be given.

When a schizophrenic person does become agitated and begins to signal aggressive intent, it is probably best not to approach him or her physically since such an approach is likely to increase the feeling of panic. Our personal space becomes even more important to us when we feel ourselves to be in danger. Similarly, it is probably not useful to attempt to argue with an agitated person about his delusional ideas. The interchange itself is stressful and will tend to exacerbate the emotional state. It is wise, although not always possible, to avoid becoming overtly distressed oneself when dealing with such a person. Since the individual may be frightened by his own aggressive impulses as well as by the perceived external threat, a calm attitude may help quiet his feelings. Keeping in mind that the person is probably frightened can help to guide our behavior. Additionally, since the tendency toward assaultive behavior is significantly lowered by antipsychotic medication, it is important to bring the assaultive patient into treatment as quickly as possible or, if he is already in treatment, to bring his behavior to the attention of the mental-health worker.

To summarize, while schizophrenics are capable of becoming aggressive because they are simply angry, they are much more likely to lose control of their behavior when they are feeling panicked by a perceived threat. Thus, their violent behavior is usually a function of fear rather than anger. Further, most schizophrenics do not ever behave aggressively. Those who become confused and disoriented tend simply to withdraw. Generally, only those who have a fairly coherent, fixed set of delusional ideas are likely to become assaultive. They can be helped by adopting a calm attitude and by securing treatment.

Suicide and Accidental Death

Another worry is that the rate of suicide among schizophrenics is twelve times higher than the rate of the population as a whole.[6] For some patients, disturbed thinking includes suicidal or self-mutilatory elements. These often take the form of hallucinatory voices that instruct the patient to engage in self-destructive behavior like sitting on railroad tracks, ceasing to eat, or jumping off a bridge. The voices may be attributed to God or to a close relative, but their admonitions are usually perceived as compelling by the patient. Suicidal behavior resulting from hallucinatory experiences is usually encountered in the acutely ill, highly agitated schizophrenic.

Self-destructive behavior can also occur paradoxically as a result of the grandiose feelings that sometimes appear in acute episodes. Schizophrenics may believe that they have acquired special powers that allow them to fly, withstand the elements, or walk on water. They may feel invulnerable, taking dangerous risks and ignoring precautions. In these instances, suicidal intent is absent, but the risk for injury or death is increased.

Sometimes the capacity for goal-directed thinking is so impaired that risks and precautions are simply not considered. For example, a young man who sets off to visit friends in a neigh-

6. Pokorny, 1964; Temoche, Pugh, and MacMahon, 1964.

boring state rides his bicycle with no lights at night on an expressway. He has no money and is improperly dressed. He does not wish to die, nor does he have grandiose ideas. He is simply incapable, at that time, of considering the possible consequences of his behavior.

Finally, despair is often associated with schizophrenia, both in the acutely ill and in the recovery phases. Individuals who despair of achieving their personal goals, who envisage a lifetime of suffering, may be candidates for suicide. This holds true, not only for schizophrenics, but for persons suffering from a variety of emotional and physical problems. Often the recovering schizophrenic experiences substantial depression as he begins to face his vulnerability for breakdown, to re-evaluate his goals, to feel ashamed of his psychotic behaviors, and to cope with the stigma attached to mental illness that is communicated by his society, family, and peers. This depression not only interferes with mobilizing the energy required for continued improvement, but may provide an impetus for self-destructive behavior.

How can the risk of suicide in schizophrenia be minimized? During an acute episode, a suicidal patient may need close supervision and physical protection until the thinking disorder has abated somewhat and behavioral control has returned. Since suicidal attempts during these periods are primarily a function of disturbed thinking, they are best treated by medications that lessen disorganization and by environmental controls, such as restricting the person's freedom or removing dangerous objects, that prevent dangerous behavior.

Treating the depression that may occur during recovery presents a more difficult problem. Antidepressant medications appear not to be of substantial benefit. Providing the patient with success experiences is probably most valuable. By setting a series of personal, social, and vocational goals that are attainable, and by protecting the individual from continuous failures, one can help the recovering schizophrenic achieve a sense of optimism and personal competence. Further, giving the individual the opportunity to discuss the issues underlying the depression and taking the feelings seriously rather than glossing over them may help the individual to feel less alone. Support and structure are the keystones of a successful program to alleviate depression and despair in a recovering schizophrenic.

WHAT CAN THE FAMILY DO TO HELP?

Not all families are faced with all of the problems we have discussed. However, most are faced with at least some. If the family environment is accepting and outside sources of support exist, many of these difficulties can be expected to decrease with time.

J.P.'s family, for example, has learned to tolerate much undesirable behavior. While most of their own behavior has become ineffectual, they have not institutionalized him nor given up on him. They protect him, take care of him, tolerate him, love him. At great personal expense, they have provided a life for him which has some satisfactions. They have developed some ways of minimizing his adverse impact on them so that they are able to continue to care for him and for each other. They have not done too badly, all things considered. Some families are able to do more, some less.

What are some of the factors in rehabilitation that the family can control? First, the family can provide a structured, tolerant environment. We have emphasized how important external structure can be to an individual whose thinking is easily confused. The family can be of assistance in setting clear expectations for behavior and in developing a patterned way of living for the recovering schizophrenic. Regular mealtimes, scheduled family events, and daily chores can all be used to help the individual settle into a comfortable routine. While it may be frustrating to watch the schizophrenic family member do chores extremely slowly or somewhat incompetently or only after much coaxing, it is probably of value, if expectations are realistic. As is true with all of us, developing some "rewards" for expected behavior is more effective than nagging or cajoling.

The family can explore ways of stimulating the individual without stressing him. Participating in projects, like planting a garden, structured recreational activities, like sports or going to the movies, visiting friends, and similar events may well enhance recovery, but only if they are of interest to the person and if they are within his ability to function acceptably. It is difficult to know how much any particular individual can be pushed toward activity without significant resistance. Some relatives are able to gauge the response of the patient quite well, while others continue to press for increased activity until the patient becomes confused or angry. No hard and fast rules apply. Learning how far to go is a trial-and-error process.

While setting realistic expectations is important, creating a tolerant, noncritical environment is also of high priority. Feeling themselves to be failures, schizophrenics tend to be unusually stressed by criticism or anger. Patients who return to families with high expressed emotion fare more poorly than those who return to a more accepting home. Thus, it is useful for families to learn to expect and tolerate some degree of deviant behavior. Those who can share their frustration with each other, with a trusted friend, or with a professional will generally provide a better environment than those who become angry with the patient or who withdraw themselves.

Often, the patient's deviant behavior will decrease if he is told, in a nonemotional way, that the behavior is inappropriate to the setting. Some families have been able to convince their schizophrenic member not to respond to hallucinatory voices in public. The same nonaccusatory tone is useful when responding to delusional verbalizations. If handled with a minimum of attention and emotion, they will often subside. In general, cross-currents of strong feelings will agitate the schizophrenic individual, increasing the disorder of his thoughts and decreasing his self-control. In avoiding becoming overinvolved and over-invested in change, family members can help the schizophrenic person achieve maximum recovery.

The family can also help by exploring and making use of medical or social facilities outside of the home when the individual is unwilling or unable to make these contacts for himself. This is important not only for the patient, but for family members who may be making substantial personal sacrifices to care for the patient. Sometimes, community mental-health centers will have day or evening programs that afford the patient the opportunity to practice socialization skills while giving family members some time off. Church groups or athletic clubs can be used in the same way. Many communities have some sort of sheltered work environment where individuals who are unable to manage a full time job can function comfortably and effectively.

The issue of time off from caretaking responsibilities needs particular emphasis. Living with a schizophrenic person can be very disruptive to relatives' own goals and lifestyles. Each family member has his own life to lead and must attempt not to become so committed to fulfilling the patient's needs that his own needs remain largely unmet. When this does happen, the end result is usually that the patient achieves less independence than he is capable of and the supporting family member finds his own reserves of strength and the capacity to give depleted.

Recovery from schizophrenia is a function of the individual and his environment. An optimum environment is one in which realistic expectations about behavior are set within an accepting, nonemotional climate. Social stimulation is available but not forced on the individual to the point at which he becomes disorganized. Outside resources are called upon to add to what the family can provide.

Perhaps the most disconcerting reality is the uncertainty of the future. We cannot predict how well a specific individual will recover, how long it will take, or whether he will become seriously disturbed again. Thus, families of schizophrenics need to live in the present more than most of us since the future is so uncertain. This is not to say that plans and dreams must be abandoned, but only that they must be put in a realistic perspective with some understanding of the impairments and vulnerabilities that are associated with schizophrenia.

FAMILY THERAPY

Most of the suggestions we have made so far have been general statements, rather than solutions to specific problems. This is so because each patient is different and each family is different. What works well in one situation may not work well in another. Thus, it is not necessary to view the family as a *cause* of the patient's problems in order to see the value of family therapy. Typically, the families with a schizophrenic member have been under severe stress for many months, if not years. They may have developed a pattern of interacting with the individual that had served protective purposes in the past but that may not be conducive to rehabilitation. For instance, they may have found it necessary to buy the patient's clothes, structure the patient's days, and in other ways take over decision-making functions. While these behaviors may have been expedient and appropriate during the patient's illness, they may slow the process of recovery. By way of further example, families may have learned to tolerate a high degree of deviant behavior on the patient's part, behavior that he may, during recovery, be able to control or modify.

Family members may, themselves, feel confused and guilty. Typically, parents are more than willing to accept the responsibility for having somehow caused the disordered behavior in their child. Likewise, spouses of acutely ill individuals may feel at fault in causing or provoking the breakdown. They may have many questions about their role in the sick member's past and in his future. They want to know what to expect and what they can do to help. They want to know if they have been at fault and if so in what ways. The stress imposed by their thoughts and feelings interfere with the family's own adaptive functioning, making them less able to offer support to the sick member.

Family therapy is aimed at re-establishing appropriate modes of communication in the family where these have been disrupted throughout the course of the illness, as well as helping the family to understand the nature of the illness and its effects, develop realistic expectations for the future, and learn how to support the patient's recovery. Often, of course, these two goals are merged as the therapists, family members, and patient struggle together to understand the past and plan for the future.

Family therapy may be conducted with the patient present or absent, with all or part of the family involved, and with one or more therapists. Meetings typically occur on a regular basis, usually weekly, at first, and may continue for many months. During the first few meetings, the family and therapists get to know one another and jointly establish a set of goals that the family would like to reach. These goals may include, among others, understanding how their behavior affects the schizophrenic member and vice versa, reaching agreement about what are appropriate functional expectations for the patient, deciding how much responsibility they ought to take for the patient, and what they should do if the patient becomes ill again. During subsequent meetings, these issues will be discussed by the family, with the therapists providing support, suggestions, or exercises designed to help the family achieve their goals.

The needs of these families for personal support and involvement in the treatment plan are understandable. However, families have often been criticized, if not ostracized, by members of the helping professions. One mother, for example, described repeatedly attempting to share information with the treatment team at the hospital where her schizophrenic son was a patient. She was seen only once, when he was admitted, and was never asked to return for an interview. Her calls were not returned by the staff psychiatrist, and when her son was discharged, she was given no guidelines about what to expect or what she should do. Not surprisingly, her impression was that the psychiatrist believed she and her husband were responsible for their son's illness. After similar treatment from a number of different hospitals off and on for over five years, she finally learned not to attempt to make contact. As she withdrew, her interactions with her son became less supportive and more hostile. Her story is by no means unusual. Despite the diversity of views about schizophrenia, such a strategy toward dealing with the family can only serve to catch the patient "in the middle" and to deprive him of valuable sources of support.

This mother's plight can be contrasted with the eventual outcome for J.P. and his parents. At the time of this writing, J.P.'s parents have been participating in therapy, as a couple, for about six months. During that time J.P. has successfully moved into his own apartment, and his aggressive and demanding behaviors toward his parents have almost disappeared. As they began to discuss and overcome their guilt about his illness, the P's have been able to set appropriate expectations and to teach their son to live more independently. While their work is not yet finished, they report that they are significantly calmer and happier. At the same time, J.P. has improved dramatically. When families know what to expect and are supportively taught and encouraged to develop patterns of behavior that enhance the patient's recovery, their own strengths are bolstered and their capacity to be of help is increased.

Families of schizophrenics are typically burdened by guilt and a need for secrecy due to the stigma associated with mental illness. In addition to the problems they encounter in securing treatment, they are frequently faced with problems after the patient has been treated. However, these problems are often surmountable. Many families effectively provide for their members, schizophrenic and nonschizophrenic alike. Many more families could do so if they received competent professional support and advice. There are numerous social institutions that families can call upon for help in the rehabilitation process. We turn now to a description of mental-health facilities.

8

HOSPITALS AND
OTHER SOCIAL AGENCIES

In the past, treatment for schizophrenia often involved consignment to a mental hospital for many months or years and frequently for a lifetime. Volumes have been written on the antitherapeutic effects of such a long stay in a hospital.[1] The most important of these effects is the passivity, lethargy, and dependency fostered by prolonged hospitalization. Because schizophrenia was thought to be a progressively deteriorating condition, patients were given largely custodial care by a hospital staff who did not expect that patients would or could improve significantly. These negative expectations were communicated to patients, who then accepted the role of sick, incompetent individuals who could not care for themselves. Often, functional behaviors, like taking care of personal hygiene, which were still intact upon admission would gradually deteriorate over the course of hospitalization as the need for these behaviors did not exist within the hospital setting.

The behavior of the long-stay patient is characterized by lack of interest in surroundings, lack of attention to personal grooming, social withdrawal, and reliance upon others to make decisions and to provide for one's needs. Thus, the hospital environment works against the goal of preparing the patient for reentry into the community.

Another antitherapeutic effect occurs because hospitalization removes the individual from the normal social context, thus

1. See, for example, Goffman, 1961.

fostering a sense of alienation. While a short period of withdrawal from the problems of everyday life can be extremely valuable, a prolonged hospital stay often has the effect of diminishing motivation to cope with those problems. Since the majority of the people with whom the person interacts in the hospital are also disturbed, he has few models from whom to learn about appropriate, functional behavior. In many ways, learning to be a good hospital patient is antithetical to the goals of community re-entry. In addition, the general public is being made more aware of the possible infringement on civil liberties resulting from involuntary hospitalization as well as the potential for the abuse of hospitals in terms of confining political or social critics.

BRIEF HOSPITALIZATION

The present trend is to hospitalize the schizophrenic person only as a last resort, and even then for the briefest possible period. Such an approach has been made possible by the impact of the antipsychotic medicines, which allow the patient to exert greater control over behavior, and by the proliferation, at least in theory, of community-based facilities designed to support the maintenance of the recovering individual in the community. Nonetheless, despite the potential for abuse and despite the possible harmful effects, hospitalization remains a necessary and, at times, highly useful adjunct to outpatient treatment.

Perhaps it would be useful to elaborate on each of these points. First, let us examine some of the indications for hospitalization. The course of schizophrenia is uneven, with periods of stress-related worsening of symptoms interspersed with periods of relatively good functioning. Among these environmental stresses are change in situation, like job loss or transfer, reduction in support through death or relocation of a family member or close friend, and conflict-laden situations of all kinds. Even without stress, worsening of symptoms is a risk whenever the individual, for one reason or another, stops taking antipsychotic medication. During such times the individual may find himself unable to function adequately. He becomes confused, disorganized, frightened, and incompetent. A brief period of hospitalization may serve to hasten the recovery process. First, the individual is temporarily removed from the stressful situation. He can gain a measure of objectivity and can strengthen his defenses. In addition, he is likely to benefit from the routine, the structure, and the clear-cut set of expectations that the hospital regime provides. During this period, when his thinking is disorganized, he is insulated from the pressure of having to make decisions and the stress of having to respond appropriately to a variety of unstructured interpersonal situations. In this way, he may be protected from perhaps losing his job or alienating important sources of support. The primary purpose of hospitalization is not to "incarcerate" in the sense of protecting society at the expense of the individual's freedom, but rather to provide an environment in which stress is reduced and structure is provided. Indeed, the great majority of schizophrenics are hospitalized voluntarily.

When exacerbation of symptoms includes suicidal or aggressive ideas or behaviors, the indication for hospitalization becomes even more apparent. At such a time, when the individual is unable to exert adequate control over his behavior, such control may have to be provided externally. Typically, a hospital offers more protection than is possible elsewhere.

Hospitalization can also be used (and, indeed, is used in Europe) to provide a brief respite for the individuals in the community, usually family members, who are providing support to the patient. This is particularly true when the patient's maximum level of functioning is still not enough to allow him to be financially and personally independent. Providing for such a person, like having an aged parent in one's home, can be quite stressful for the family. This stress can be minimized through the use of occasional brief respites during which time the patient is hospitalized. Such respites often help the family to continue to provide long-term support, and thus obviate the need for prolonged hospital care. Such a strategy is used not simply to get rid of the disturbed individual, but rather to respond to the very real need for relief from the burdens of caring for another that is experienced by family members.

When such a resource is not made available, the family members may experience such intense distress that their own reserves of strength are sapped. They may themselves become withdrawn and uncaring, or they may become hostile toward the disturbed member. Such a situation, if prolonged, may provoke the family to refuse further involvement. It is conceivable that, in the future, community resources could be marshaled so that the use of hospitals for this purpose will become unnecessary.

Hospital Procedures

Hospitalization can be a trying experience for both the schizophrenic individual and the family. The patient, who is often confused and frightened, is removed from the normal environment and set down, after much paperwork and questioning, among strangers. The members of the family, who have tried very hard to maintain the disturbed individual at home, perceive hospitalization as a reflection of their own failure. Often caring deeply about this patient, they may be dismayed at the casual, seemingly callous, way in which the hospital staff goes about the intake process. The family may have frightening fantasies about mental hospitals and mental patients. In this section, we attempt to allay some of these fears by providing a realistic description of what occurs during hospitalization.

A person may enter the hospital voluntarily or as a result of a court commitment. In either case, the procedures and treatments will be generally the same, with the exception that the involuntary patient's civil rights will be more closely guarded since he is not at liberty to leave if he is unsatisfied with his care. For instance, medicating an involuntary patient without his consent will usually require a court order. His case may be reviewed more frequently than the voluntary patient's.

Most mental hospitals and mental-health sections in general hospitals are divided into units, each of which houses from ten to thirty patients. Depending on the particular hospital, patients may be placed in single rooms, double rooms, four-bedded rooms, or wards which house a larger number of patients. Each unit generally has its own nursing staff and its own therapeutic staff, including psychiatrists, psychologists, social workers, and activities therapists.

The newly admitted patient will generally be interviewed by one of the therapeutic staff, usually a psychiatrist, either immediately preceding or immediately following admission. At this time, a tentative diagnosis is made, and a short-term treatment plan is begun. The patient may be restricted is some way initially. For instance, the unit may be locked. Certain possessions, like penknives or matches, may be removed. These restrictions are designed to protect the patient, and others, if he appears highly confused, agitated, or assaultive. Many patients feel calmer knowing that they are in a secure place, although some are dismayed at the infringement on their personal liberty. Keeping the patient on the unit also gives staff members maximal opportunity to observe and interact with the patient. The information they gain in this way is used in the development of the treatment plan.

As a result of the first interview, the schizophrenic patient is usually prescribed some antipsychotic medication, is assigned a primary therapist, which may be a psychiatrist or some other staff member, and is scheduled for a number of activities to occur over the next few days. These activities may include a medical examination, an interview with the social worker, a visit to the occupational-therapy area, and assignment to a therapy group.

The family as well as the patient should be involved at this early stage. Often some member of the treatment staff will request a meeting with one or more members of the family. At this meeting, the staff member will try to get information about the patient's illness and will attempt to answer any questions the family may have about the treatment plan. Often, the family will be encouraged to visit with the patient frequently. However, if the patient's recent behavior has created turmoil in the household, or if the patient is particularly angry with or frightened by some members of the family, they may be advised not to visit until both he and the family are calmer. In the latter case, the family members may benefit as much as the patient from some time away from each other. Such a recommendation does *not* mean that the family is at fault, but only that they would all do better with some time off.

Sometimes, a patient will refuse to see some or all of his family. He may be angry at them, either for good reason or because he has psychotic ideas about them. Often, his refusal to see them is an attempt to protect the family. He may feel guilty about his behavior toward them or even his thoughts about them. He may feel that he is dangerous or contaminated with evil. It may be that such a refusal reflects the patient's disturbance and agitation rather than represents a real rejection of the family.

After a day or two, an attempt is made to involve the patient in a structured, scheduled, daily routine. This constitutes the short-term treatment plan. Occupational and recreational therapy activities often occur on a daily basis. The patient meets with his therapist at regular intervals, which may be as often as every day. He may be involved in group therapy once or more often each week. He receives medication daily.

During this time, the staff is evaluating the patient's progress and is beginning to make plans for discharge and for follow-up care. Often, the family remains involved. They may take the patient home for weekend visits. They may meet with the treatment staff to discuss problems that remain, discharge plans, and strategies that will aid in the rehabilitation process.

Since the effects of long-term hospitalization are thought to be countertherapeutic, every effort is made to discharge the patient as soon as possible. Usually the idea of discharge is entertained as soon as the patient's response to medication is stabilized, his thought processes regain contact with reality, plans have been made for follow-up services, and he has a supportive environment to which to return. In general, both the patient and his family will collaborate with the treatment staff to develop a follow-up plan. Decisions will be made concerning where the patient will live, how he will spend his time, and what sorts of continuing services he will receive. Referrals will be made to agencies like the community mental-health center for follow-up medication and psychotherapy, or vocational rehabilitation services for occupational training. When these decisions have been reached and the appropriate referrals have been made, the patient can be discharged from the hospital. The duration of hospitalization can vary from a week to many months depending on the patient's rate of recovery and the quality of the environment to which he returns.

THE ROLE OF COMMUNITY-BASED AGENCIES

So far, our discussion has focused on brief hospitalization. Are there any indications for prolonged hospitalization? In principle, the answer is probably "no," but in practice, at the present time, the answer is "yes." Let us consider why this is so. The extent to which different schizophrenic people respond to appropriate treatment is highly variable. While some people become quite functional and are able to pick up their lives and carry on successfully, many others continue to need various amounts of structure and support. Far too often, programs having these qualities are not available in the community to which the patient attempts to return.

At present, publicly funded community mental-health centers, located throughout the country, are mandated to provide aftercare services for discharged mental patients. Such services may include prescribing and monitoring medication, offering group, individual, and family therapy, and referral to other community agencies for additional needed services. In principle, a newly discharged patient is referred by the hospital to the nearest community mental-health center, which then provides all of the needed follow-up services. In reality, however, community mental-health centers are often overcrowded and understaffed. They may have a waiting list, which either delays discharge or makes the transition to aftercare more difficult. In many instances, patients see a physician once every six weeks for fifteen minutes. While some people can maintain themselves adequately on such minimal contact, many others cannot.

Lack of staff time and money frequently prevents the community mental-health center from providing much needed service. Outreach services like home visits, for example, are often crucial in bringing withdrawn, frightened patients into follow-up treatment. Without such services, many newly discharged patients do not get to the community mental health center at all. In addition, even if the community mental-health center does develop a comprehensive treatment plan, the services and facilities necessary to carry out the plan are often not available in the community. Two of the most important rehabilitation needs are met by occupational services and residential services.

Occupational Services

There can be little doubt that schizophrenia is an occupationally disabling disorder in that it impairs concentration and goal-directed thinking. Some re-evaluation of occupational expectations is necessary in almost all cases. However, the extent of recovery from schizophrenia is an extremely variable, individual, and unpredictable matter. Some people recover so completely that they can function as well as they had done before their illness. They appear capable of coping with significant stress in an adaptive way and are full participants in the business of life. Others appear unresponsive to treatment and are so incapacitated that they are unable to provide for themselves outside of a highly structured, institutional setting. The great majority of schizophrenic individuals fall somewhere in between. They may be unable to fully use their intellectual and occupational resources, but are capable of some level of productive work. It is estimated that from 15 to 40 percent of schizophrenics fully support themselves.[2] Of the approximately $15 billion spent annually to care for the country's two to three million diagnosed schizophrenics, only $3 billion, or one -fifth,

2. Roberts, 1978.

goes to treatment. Two thirds of the total, or $10 billion, is lost due to patients' lack of productivity.[3] Thus, it is economically, as well as therapeutically, wise to provide services that increase schizophrenics' ability to be self-supporting.

Part of the recovery process involves reaching toward occupational goals in stepwise fashion, first by following simple instructions, then a series of instructions, then self-initiated instructions, and so on. For some individuals, a sheltered, structured work situation will be necessary, while others will be able to function successfully with little external structure and much responsibility. A community-based network of occupational services would enhance vocational recovery and would decrease society's financial burden considerably. One of the components of such a network, the *sheltered workshop*, exists in some communities. The workshop receives contracts from local businesses to produce a certain amount of work. Jobs may include stuffing envelopes, collating papers or objects, assembling small products, and other simple tasks. Disabled individuals, including schizophrenic persons, retarded persons, and others, are trained and supervised to do the work on a part- or full-time basis. They usually receive some salary, although the major benefit lies in the improvement in work habits and concentration that they experience. Far fewer sheltered workshops exist than are needed. Many patients who function well in the hospital, where they are involved in a predictable daily routine and are capable of productive work, decompensate when they enter a community that offers no opportunities in this area. Another component of the network would be training in a particular vocational skill. Again, some communities have such programs, although their quality varies widely.

While diverse occupational opportunities, which vary in the amount of structure and support they provide, would enhance the schizophrenic person's chances of being at least partially self-supporting, few communities have all of the necessary components. Some hospital-based day activities centers and free-

3. *Ibid.*

standing workshops do exist, but many more innovative community-based programs are needed.

Residential Services

While many recovering schizophrenics return to a supportive family environment, many others are in need of a residential placement. Some people are able to live independently, in apartments. Others may need various amounts of supervision. Far too often, high quality, supervised living arrangements are not readily available. For many patients, the only alternative is a boarding home, which often offers less social stimulation and fewer productive activities than the hospital did. Often, people in these settings are unable to structure their own time and end by becoming more withdrawn, lethargic, and dysfunctional. Indeed, many of them return to the hospital. Burdened by the stigma of failure and the fear of isolation, they become more resistive to discharge. If the community were to provide an array of structured group living situations, both rehospitalization and prolonged hospitalization would certainly decrease.

Among the best alternatives, available in some communities, is the *halfway house* in which a number of recovering patients live together and share household duties, usually with some professional supervision. After a time in the halfway house, they may move to apartment settings in which they function more independently with less intensive supervision.

SOCIETAL BARRIERS TO RECOVERY

There can be little doubt that mental hospitals are filled with people who do not need, and are indeed being damaged by, total institutional care. However, simply discharging these people to a nonsupportive community is not the answer. There is continuing evidence of a growing "revolving door" syndrome in which patients are discharged from hospitals without serious consideration of these issues, only to quickly return, more frightened, more alienated, and more dysfunctional than before.

Ironically, one of the most serious threats to quality care and treatment for schizophrenic individuals, arises from recent judicial attempts to safeguard the health, well-being, and civil liberties of mental patients.

PROBLEMS HOSPITALS FACE

While patients may refuse treatment, the first criterion for involuntary civil commitment, need for care or treatment, implies that treatment is available and will be given. In the past, mental hospitals, chronically understaffed and overutilized, have functioned in large measure as custodial institutions. Recent court actions have begun to set minimum standards in terms of privacy, physical plant, staff-patient ratios, and treatment programs for mental-hospital settings.[4] While, in principle, reasonable standards for care ought certainly to be enforced, in fact such standards, since they are general rules, often interfere with the goals they are intended to reach. For example, in one large East Coast hospital the following changes occurred.

Treatment teams were required to interview and revise treatment plans for each patient on a monthly basis. No doubt, such a standard is appropriate for vigorously treated patients whose status is expected to change. However, in one building, which housed a mixture of active young adults and older, chronically ill patients, the result was a loss of over fifty hours a week of treatment time. The treatment team, which had met formally for two hours weekly, began to meet for ten hours weekly. The treatment of active patients suffered as a result of the necessity

4. Stone, 1976.

for formal interviewing of patients whose mental status had not changed in years. It should be noted that these older patients were being seen by staff members in group, recreational, and often occupational therapy weekly, by a psychiatrist monthly, and by ward staff daily so that their status was known.

Each patient was allotted a certain amount of living space, in the interest of privacy and adequate living conditions. As a result, private rooms, which had been much in demand but were slightly smaller than the required allowance, became storage spaces.

A patient peonage law was enacted, which prevents patients from working without adequate monetary compensation. While such a law is clearly intended to prevent the forcing of patients into unpaid, nontherapeutic labor, the result was that patients could no longer work in the patient store (where they learned short-order cooking, waiting on tables, and how to work a cash register) nor as assistant to the staff beauticians. Patients who were competent and willing to make a voluntary decision to work without pay were prevented from doing so. Numerous letters were sent by patients to state officials protesting this new law.

The right to treatment standards combined with the right to refuse treatment statutes have placed mental hospitals in a most difficult position. Hospitals must provide treatment, but patients may refuse any or all of it. It is no wonder that treatment plans often consist of "milieu therapy" (the patient lives in a ward with other patients), and "relationship therapy" (the staff interacts with the patient in the ward). Ironically, this situation occurs at a time when treatment for schizophrenia is increasingly successful.

In addition to judicial attempts to right past abuses, a number of monetary damage claims have been secured against mental-health professionals and hospitals for negligence, false imprisonment, and denial of treatment.[5] The possibility of such suits has had a most unfortunate and paradoxical result:

5. *Ibid.*

> The pattern of discharging the chronic mentally ill
> from total institutions without adequate alternatives
> and refusing to commit because of new standards is
> becoming a familiar pattern all over the United
> States. . . . The result is to place an intolerable burden
> on the welfare system. . . . Thus, the adequacy of treat-
> ment deteriorates where it once existed, and there are
> large numbers getting no treatment—all this in the
> name of civil rights and the right to treatment.[6]

Where mental hospitals once functioned as warehouses for
society's misfits, welfare rolls and boarding homes presently
serve the same purpose. While large hospitals were no doubt
degrading and dehumanizing, the present facilities are often no
less so. It may well be that some massive total institutions have
provided little in the way of treatment, often fostering the dependence and degradation they were designed to alleviate.
However, the practical result of the right-to-treatment actions
is that many patients now inhabit the impersonal inner-city,
unsupervised and untreated. The trend toward deinstitutionalization provoked by the new civil commitment standards and
the right-to-treatment decisions presently amounts to abandon-
ment. Reversing this outcome will necessitate financial commitment either through providing the financial and legal resources
to transform institutions from custodial to treatment facilities or
through making the community mental-health dream a reality.

There is some evidence that the federal government is aware
of this problem. In early 1977 the General Accounting Office
released a report on deinstitutionalization that cited numerous
failures by federal agencies to provide for the needs of the
chronically mentally ill. In response, the National Institute of
Mental Health has appropriated some federal funds to pilot a
new comprehensive community support system initiative, which
will, hopefully, stimulate state and local governments to develop
a more realistic set of priorities for funding decisions.[7]

6. *Ibid.*, p. 93.
7. Roberts, 1978.

THE EFFECTS OF SOCIAL STIGMA

Social stigma, while more subtle in its effects than judicial sanctions without economic support, is equally detrimental to recovery from schizophrenia. For example, most of the vocational training programs available to ex-mental patients are publicly funded. Private industry, which could, in principle, provide highly valuable programs, is rarely involved. One of the reasons for the lack of private involvement is the stigma associated with mental illness.[8] There can be no doubt that attitudes toward people labeled mentally ill are extremely negative. Those who are so stigmatized are seen as relatively worthless, frightening, unpredictable, insincere, and incompetent by virtually everybody in the general population, regardless of income, age, sex, religion, or locale. Further, the most negative attitudes are reserved for those persons labeled as "psychotic" or "insane."[9] These preconceptions make it difficult for a schizophrenic person to secure training and employment. In addition, they may make it more difficult for the individual to function well if he does succeed in getting a position.

One illustrative study indicates that normal people who believe that they are perceived as being mentally ill show defective social skills.[10] In a companion study, ex-patients who believed that others knew of their psychiatric history performed poorer, both vocationally and socially, than those who believed that others had no knowledge of their background.[11] Thus, social stigma can cause people to modify their behavior in a dysfunctional direction. In addition, the stress of coping with stigma can, in itself, foster decompensation in a schizophrenic individual. Not surprisingly, the expectation of failure by the schizophrenic and those around him often results in a self-fulfilling prophecy.

Another example of the impact of social stigma is in the area

8. Landy and Griffith, 1958; Farina, Felner, and Boudreau, 1973.
9. Nunnally, 1961.
10. Farina, Allen, and Saul, 1968.
11. Farina et al., 1971.

of community-based living facilities for recovering mental patients. Community groups, while assenting to the need for such facilities, consistently lobby for their placement in some other community. This lobbying stems from a number of fears, most of them irrational. It is feared that ex-mental patients are dangerous. Parents fear for their children's safety, and for their own. In reality, ex-mental patients, as a group, are more likely to be withdrawn and passive and present very little threat to the community.

It is argued that property values plummet. But this argument is circular and is only true if homeowners act in a way that makes it come true. While such a result has occurred in some communities, it has been prevented by persistent groups who feel strongly that the community should be involved. It is feared that schizophrenics are "drug addicts" because of their reliance on medication and that they will be a bad influence on youth in the neighborhood. This is no more true of schizophrenics than it is true of diabetics.

Recovered schizophrenics can be very good neighbors. As a group they tend to be quiet, peaceful, and nonintrusive. In many cases, they are capable of making substantial contributions to the community.

Our understanding of the factors involved in recovery from schizophrenia has progressed dramatically in recent years. However, more than understanding is needed. Rapid return of schizophrenic patients to the community will not be wholly successful until the community provides the support and structure so crucial to successful rehabilitation.

A GENERAL TREATMENT STRATEGY

Figure 8:1 is an outline of the major considerations in the treatment of schizophrenia. When an individual begins to behave in ways that may be indicative of schizophrenia, the first order of business is to establish the diagnosis. This process will typically include a medical examination to rule out or treat other physical disorders, a psychological examination, and a review of the history of the development of the symptoms. Data obtained through observing the individual and hearing about his behavior from his family and friends are considered. The diagnosis should be viewed as a working hypothesis that can be modified at any point where additional data warrants a change.

The decision must then be made as to whether a period of hospitalization is appropriate. This will depend on a number of factors, including the nature and severity of the presenting symptoms, the capacity of the environment (often the family) to support the individual and to cooperate with the treatment plan, and the availability of community resources that can be called upon to provide the individual and his family with the needed support and structure. Often, a period of brief hospitalization allows the family time to strengthen its own adaptive capabilities, while providing a convenient milieu in which to institute various therapeutic strategies. Whether or not hospitalization is used, the initial treatment plan would optimally include chemotherapy, instituting a supportive therapeutic relationship with the patient and the family, structuring the environment so that expectations about behavior are clear and attainable, and the planning of a global rehabilitation strategy.

Through all of this, it should be kept in mind that recovery from schizophrenia is rarely an all-or-none process. Since symptom remission usually occurs gradually, the rehabilitation process should proceed in stepwise fashion, during which time external support and structure are to be gradually decreased as the patient improves. Further, since the symptoms of schizophrenia wax and wane in response to stress, a long—perhaps indefinite—plan for follow-up should offer the recovered patient, and the significant people in his environment, continued support and guidance.

In summary, recovering from schizophrenia can be a long and arduous process for both the disturbed individual and for

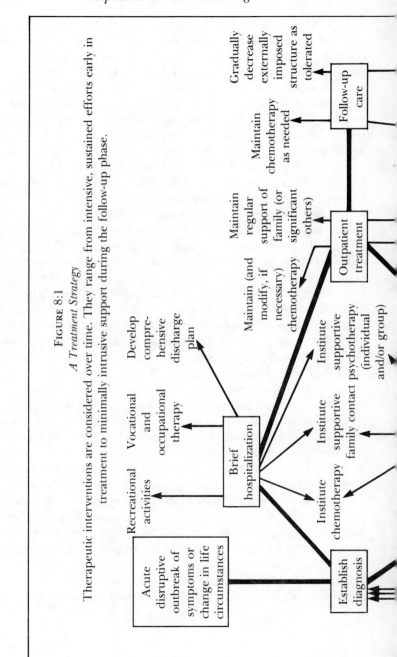

FIGURE 8:1
A Treatment Strategy

Therapeutic interventions are considered over time. They range from intensive, sustained efforts early in treatment to minimally intrusive support during the follow-up phase.

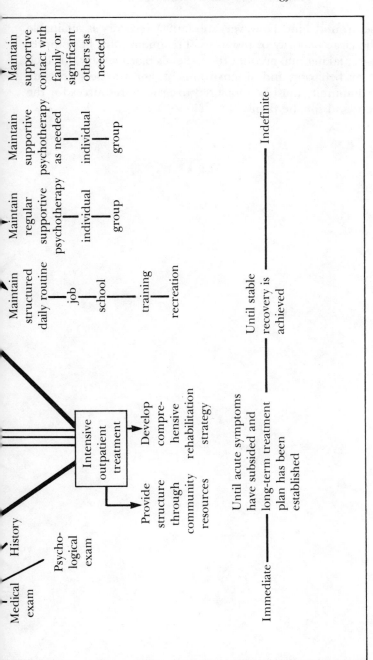

those around him. However, substantial recovery is attainable in the large majority of instances. Treatment must be comprehensive, taking into account the patient's biochemistry, his feelings, his behavior, and his environment. For it to be successful, the community must be mobilized to provide resources for the patient and for the family.

9

PREDICTORS OF RECOVERY

A schizophrenic illness can have many different outcomes. While some patients recover so completely that they can function quite competently, with little or no risk of further episodes of disorganization, others appear never to attain a successful, independent mode of functioning. Some researchers have focused on discovering what variables influence the extent to which a particular person will recover. The findings of these studies can be illustrated through the following two case histories.

A CASE WITH A POOR OUTCOME

Since present events color one's perceptions and memories of the past, it is hard to know what actually took place in John's childhood.[1] Nonetheless, all the available life history indicates that John had always been a bit different, peculiar, and odd. All his relatives agree that he had never really been a member of the family. John rarely showed any enthusiasm for family activities and managed to spend most of his childhood on the psychological perimeter of personal involvement. It is also true

1. Both case histories, based on clinical experience, published accounts of schizophrenia, and informal discussions with colleagues, are fictitious. To the authors' knowledge, neither the events nor the people depict any known individual.

that being a member of his family was difficult. Mother was always going away on "family trips." Sometime around the fifth grade, John overheard a group of neighborhood children talking about his mother and her being in the hospital because she was crazy. About the same time, John noticed that his mind seemed to be floating out of his body to a quiet place. Frightening at first, this special magical power became increasingly comforting and provided a safe place to which he could retreat.

School was fine as long as John did not feel pressured. When rushed, as when taking a test, he often had to reread each question carefully and slowly. If John tried to hurry, all the letters or numbers began to stand out as individual elements. Words lost their usual meanings and became strings of unrelated letters. The other students never really gave John trouble; they just tended to ignore him. The few times John tried to break in, to become a part of the group, his attempts were interpreted negatively by the other children. Once John was too pushy, another time too standoffish. He never did gain acceptance by peers. The one or two people John knew also were social outcasts.

In contrast to school, which seemed to continuously demand performance, home was a refuge. Mother had never really had any authority, and father had chosen long ago to do the odd jobs around the house they originally had tried to give John. It was so much easier to take out the garbage or do the dishes oneself rather than watch John perform these tasks at an infuriatingly slow pace. Thus, John never assumed the youthful responsibilities that lay the groundwork for later participation in the social system outside the family. The feelings of oddness, not belonging, and worthlessness were merely gnawing at the edge of John's consciousness. He continued in this suspended state until high school, when increased demands for social and academic skills made John feel more withdrawn and less adept than ever before.

One cannot point to a dramatic event, a family problem, or personal tragedy as a reason for John's failure to mature socially. It was clear, however, that being a member of a group, belonging to anything or anyone, was simply not to be for him. John became the person who, in gym class, always turned right when everyone else turned left, who ate alone at a small corner of a large cafeteria table, and who made people laugh when being serious and was taken seriously when joking. John found it hard to concentrate and much more pleasant to use the magic of escape.

John's withdrawal from reality had become more elaborate over the years. His fantasy world was inhabited by superhumans who spoke a special language, the significance of which was known only to John. This powerful, make-believe world held increasingly more meaning for him than the world of school and family. Although physically present both at home and at school, John spent less and less time with teachers, students, and family.

Without anyone really noticing, John stepped over the boundary from the world of external social interaction into that of the imagination. John had tried out this new world bit by bit over the years, then one day simply had not returned. It was some time before his family noticed that John now not only failed in his responsibility to the family, but also in those to himself. This time, he had gone too far. Not doing little jobs around the house was tolerable, but not washing for weeks without being reminded was unacceptable. They tried to reason, cajole, push, and beg John to show some concern for his personal hygiene. Finally, when they could take it no longer, they called the hospital. John was sixteen at the time.

John was in and out of the hospital six times during the next ten years. At first, there had been much hope. Both therapists and family felt John could be cured, to return home functioning at a higher level than he had attained before hospitalization. Indeed, for a brief period their goals for him seemed within reach. Medication helped John to concentrate. Occupational, recreational, group, and individual therapies were focused on teaching him skills he had never learned. Discharged in remission, John returned home. Soon, however, he began taking less care of himself, experienced the old feelings of worthlessness and loneliness, and eventually gave in to the call of the fantasy world. He returned to the hospital, worse off for having failed the first "cure."

With each succeeding admission, discharge, and readmission, John lost a little more self-confidence and the strength to try living outside the hospital. Over the years, John's family tired of the burden of having to care for their adult child. The pain, frustration, anger, and guilt they felt after one of his visits home was too much to bear. They still had much of their own lives to lead.

Today, John shuttles back and forth between the state hospital and a comunity halfway house, where the old family conflicts are replayed. The halfway house members are tolerant of John until he requires close, constant supervision. Then, John is sent to the hospital. Treated then released, he may continue in this way until the halfway house refuses to accept his return. If so, John could become a permanent resident of a state psychiatric hospital or manage to survive by himself on the edge of society.

A CASE WITH A GOOD OUTCOME

It is unlikely that anyone would have predicted that Sam would one day be hospitalized, diagnosed, and treated for schizophrenia. There is nothing unusual in Sam's background that one could point to as a predictor of his future schizophrenic episode.

His family was, from all indications, stable and supportive. His parents got married in their early twenties. After working for several years, his mother assumed primary responsibility for rearing their first child. His father, meanwhile, directed much of his energy toward establishing himself in a local company.

Sam was the second of three children. Healthy as an infant, he grew into a lively, engaging child. Sam enthusiastically took part in frequent family outings. His parents expected Sam as well as their other children, to take on a share of the family chores as their child grew older. Although he grumbled, as children frequently will, Sam usually finished chores on time.

He did well throughout school, generally bringing home A's and B's at report-card time. Liked by both teachers and peers, Sam had a circle of friends who always did things together. Although one or two children were always moving into or out of the group, Sam maintained close contact with this core group of friends.

In high school, Sam began discovering new areas of interest and seemed to enjoy the expanding network of social and academic relationships. Emerging as a leader in school, Sam was chosen as editor of the school paper during his senior year. He took the job quite seriously. Sam spent many hours writing stories, editing, and planning the layout of the paper. A perfectionist in his work, he would revise and reorganize an issue until it was just right.

During this time, Sam's social life had also widened to include both casual and serious relationships. In contrast, his home life seemed to be one of frequent conflict, as occurs between all adolescents, seeking to establish their identities, and their parents. However, under the friction and Sam's testing of parental limits, a warm stability maintained the family.

Toward the end of senior year, Sam began making plans to attend a large college well known for its journalism department. After a summer of work, play, and anticipation, he went away to school. At first, Sam was a little homesick. The work was harder than in high school, and he found it more difficult to meet people. Although Sam occasionally worried about this, college life was too hectic to allow much time for self-pity. Overall, he seemed to be adjusting as well as anyone, until the first exam period.

Although Sam studied diligently, he failed the first exam. Since Sam had never failed an exam before, the F did not seem real. Over the next few days, Sam found it harder and harder to concentrate. He began to believe that college was society's attempt to brainwash its young people by forcing them to think alike and that it used grades to reinforce this conformity. It became clear to him that the school was keeping a detailed record of his activities because those in authority realized his potential power to overthrow the system. He stopped studying and began burning all his notebooks and records so that they would have no written evidence of his work. Sam also started keeping irregular hours so that no one could follow his movements, thereby avoiding any traps. He began cooking his own meals. In every issue of the college paper, he found more coded and symbolic evidence that the school authorities considered him to be a major threat to their plans. On more than one occasion, he thought that he decoded a message transmitted during a local radio show.

In an attempt to alert others, Sam tried to describe the brainwashing plot to his friends. Although he was not always well received, he continued dodging the traps of the school authorities and talking to others. He became very excited and began making plans for exposing the school's plot. This might have gone on for some time had Sam not shown up at a local television station demanding free time to broadcast a general warning about public education. When denied, Sam became very angry, threw furniture, and eventually had to be subdued by the police.

Referred for psychiatric evaluation by the court, Sam spent several weeks in a psychiatric hospital. Treated first with medication, he finally calmed down. Since Sam could not recall the events preceding hospitalization, it was necessary to rely on family and friends to provide an explanation of what had happened. After several months of outpatient therapy, he was able to return to school.

Even now, Sam occasionally has fleeting moments when he wonders if the school authorities really were out to get him. However, these thoughts have been quite brief. Accepting any sort of failure still is a problem for Sam, though he has learned what to expect of himself during periods of stress. Whenever he feels he has failed to perform adequately, he experiences the old thoughts that others are plotting against him. He has learned, however, to arrange much of his life so that he can avoid too much unexpected stress. Overall, Sam has used his psychotic experience to learn something about himself and to cope more effectively with life's unexpected setbacks. Since he knows that failing is so stressful for him, he has lowered his expectations somewhat to ensure more frequent success. He has decided to accept the assurance of lower-level success in place of the chance of bigger victories but potentially bigger losses.

SCHIZOPHRENIC OUTCOME: A CHANGING OUTLOOK

Both John and Sam went through periods when their thinking had little correspondence to external reality. Alone during their crises, they lived in worlds created by their own imaginations. The strain of performing was an important element in both their disorganizations, though John apparently tolerated far less stress than Sam. John's life reflects a long, slow development of schizophrenia. John had not developed many social or work skills before his hospitalization. As a result, he had little to fall back on during his therapy. In contrast, Sam had achieved a high level of adjustment before his rapidly developing psychotic episode. He was able to use his personal resources in learning to cope with his vulnerability to disorganization. Finally, John and Sam represent two extreme outcomes. On the one hand is John, who wages a life-long struggle to find a place in society where he can survive. On the other hand is Sam who has managed to successfully deal with his vulnerabilities.

The prevailing view of schizophrenic outcome emerges from a history of pessimism. When dementia praecox was first formulated as a single disease concept by Kraepelin, about 4 percent of all patients were observed to recover.[2] People diagnosed as having dementia praecox were expected to deteriorate progressively until they could no longer care for themselves, much like John. Because outcome was the primary basis for diagnos-

2. Bleuler, 1950; Garmezy, 1970; Pollack, Levenstein, and Klein, 1968.

ing dementia praecox, if someone recovered, it was assumed that the original diagnosis had been incorrect. In contrast, later observations indicated that as many as 50 percent of schizophrenics recovered.[3] Today, professional opinion and research statistics reflect this historical conflict between schizophrenia as a disorder from which one may recover and as one that invariably leads to total disorganization of the person. It has been estimated informally that anywhere from 10 percent to 50 percent of diagnosed schizophrenics have a single psychotic episode in their lives.[4]

One important factor contributing to the difference in observed recovery rate is a change in diagnostic practices. Many clinicians and researchers, especially in the United States, have moved from a very narrow view of schizophrenia as a severe, progressively deteriorating disease marked by a dulling of emotions, to a broader one including personality style and emotional expression. There is, for example, evidence that many schizophrenics in the United States would be diagnosed as having an affective disorder in Great Britain.[5] From the broad view, the presence of depression or excitement with schizophrenic thought disorder would be interpreted as a different subtype of schizophrenia from that in which little emotion is displayed. We can contrast, for example, Sam's excitement and John's emotional blandness. From the narrow view, emotional expressions indicate a person may not be schizophrenic. The distinction between the presence and absence of emotion in schizophrenia is an important one since it helps distinguish schizophrenics with good outcomes from those with poor outcomes. One interpretation, then, of the shift in schizophrenic outcome is a broadening of our definition of schizophrenia.

A second, recent important development in altering the course of schizophrenia has been the regular use of antipsychotic medication. Our increased ability to control the more immediate, disruptive symptoms of schizophrenia may have some impact on long-term outcome by reducing the passivity

3. Bleuler, 1950; Pollack, Levenstein, and Klein, 1968.
4. Vaillant, personal communication, 1976.
5. Professional Staff, 1974.

and lethargy that often result from lengthy hospitalization. At worst, the antipsychotics help change outcome by reducing the intensity of or eliminating schizophrenic symptoms. Schizophrenic outcome has been changed, in part, by more effective treatment than has been previously available.

Since the initial description of dementia praecox, there has been a move toward a more optimistic outlook for schizophrenia. While disagreement continues about the percent of schizophrenics who recover, we generally no longer view schizophrenics as doomed. The recognition that all schizophrenics do *not* have the same psychiatrically fatal outcome has had two major impacts. One is a change in the clinician's hope for influencing the course of schizophrenia and a possible effect of expectation on outcome. For example, the cure rate at a well-known state hospital doubled from a period when schizophrenia was viewed as incurable to a time when schizophrenia was viewed as capable of cure.[6] Though one might argue that this simply represents a shift in the reporting of cure rates to match current theoretical views, we do know that one's expectations and values are powerful determinants of human behavior.[7] Therefore, there is reason to believe that changes in expectations may have a real effect on schizophrenic outcome.

The second important result of separating diagnosis from outcome has been an attempt to predict which schizophrenics will recover and which will not. During the last twenty years, we have amassed a body of information relating outcome to prepsychotic levels of development, demographic variables, and variations in the development and course of schizophrenia. The increasing ability to describe schizophrenics with potentially "good" or "poor" outcomes has important implications for theories of causation, choosing an optimum therapy, and testing the effectiveness of therapy.[8] A review of the predictors of schizophrenic outcome and their relevance to cause and treatment make up the remainder of this chapter.

6. Phillips, 1953.

7. Bruner and Goodman, 1947; Freeman and Simmons, 1963; Orne, 1965; Rosenhan, 1973; Zilboorg, 1941.

8. Pollack, Levenstein, and Klein, 1968; Strauss, 1975.

SCHIZOPHRENIA AS A DEVELOPMENTAL PROCESS

It is sometimes easy to forget that any individual, at any given time, is both the object of past development and the subject of future development. This seems especially true when considering schizophrenic psychosis, since this human event can be so dramatic that it stands apart from everyday life. It is important, therefore, to emphasize that all of us face the same social conflicts and demands in the process of growing up.

Early in a child's life, social demands are based on culturally determined family expectations. A child is expected to be weaned by the end of the first year. Toilet training is the primary developmental task from about one to two years of age. Obedience to parents and the child's awareness of the power of "no" predominates during the transition from infancy to childhood. All the while the child generally is expected to think, feel, and act like a child.

Once in school, however, the child must take on the role of student. The student role requires academic and interpersonal skills in order to both learn and adapt to the social system called "school." Not only must the child learn to sit still, study, and concentrate, but he or she also must learn to share with, tolerate, and work with other children.

Adolescence brings the first attempt to form close relationships with someone outside the immediate family and the urgency of finding out who one is. During young adulthood, people begin to develop and test their work skills in preparation for finding their niche in society. Though sex roles have changed dramatically since World War II, there is still a cultural pressure for men to be the workers and women to be the mothers and housewives. Around this time, social demands on the two sexes begin to diverge as men and women are expected to fulfill their respective roles.

An important part of development has been the establishment of families through which the accumulated experience of the now maturing adult can be transmitted. In the past, this has been literal—namely, nuclear biological families carried the culture of past generations. This process also occurs in the work field as the older, established person helps, teaches, and advises younger workers. At each stage of life, a person must develop new, more complex, yet more flexible roles to meet the expectations of society.[9]

The manner in which one has interacted with family members often serves as a model for social interactions in general. The consequences of failing to develop work skills during young adult years may last a lifetime.[10] It is clear, in John's case, that a lifetime of avoiding responsibility and the practice of basic social and work skills made it more difficult for him to benefit from therapy than would be the case for someone like Sam. While a psychotic period is a dramatic event in a schizophrenic's life, it is but one aspect of a person's ongoing development.

PROCESS AND REACTIVE SCHIZOPHRENIA

The concepts of process and reactive schizophrenia emerge from both the consideration of schizophrenia as a developmental process and a recognition of differences in schizophrenic outcome. They are the concepts by which we predict schizophrenic outcome.

Process schizophrenics, like John, are those who have slowly developing symptoms with little or no apparent external stress. Their thinking disturbance is not accompanied by extreme emotionality. They are presumed to have a relatively high genetic predisposition for schizophrenia. Process schizophrenics tend to have poor postpsychotic adjustments.

Reactive schizophrenics, like Sam, have rapidly emerging symptoms, with marked emotionality, during periods of observable stress. They are presumed to have a lower genetic predisposition toward schizophrenia. In general, reactive schizophren-

9. Erikson, 1950; Phillips, 1953; Sheehy, 1974; Higgins, 1964; Sullivan, 1953; Williams, 1977.
10. Keith *et al.*, 1976.

ics have better postpsychotic outcomes than process schizophrenics.[11] Though originally conceived as representing two separate types of schizophrenia, more recent evidence suggests that process and reactive schizophrenics are two opposite ends of a single dimension. The observed differences between process and reactive schizophrenics serve as the basis for the developmental view of schizophrenia.

The development of schizophrenia can be considered in four phases.[12] The first, a premorbid phase, spans birth to young adulthood. During this time the person develops personal characteristics and capabilities that will be relevant to how he copes with the later disorganization. Following this is a precipitant stage, during which individual predispositions and external events begin to interact, resulting in what eventually becomes the psychotic episode or the onset of psychosis. Third, there is the morbid phase, during which the schizophrenic exhibits severely disrupting symptoms. Finally, the crisis stage subsides into the outcome phase. It is this postpsychotic, or postmorbid, phase to which we generally refer when we ask if the schizophrenic will recover. Although clinicians and researchers sometimes are inclined to think in narrow outcome terms such as length, duration, and number of hospitalizations, outcome may be measured in many different ways.[13]

We have been referring to outcome up to this point as if it were a single phenomenon. Simple consideration, however, will reveal the problem in not defining outcome. For example, consider a patient who has six hospital admissions of two months each versus one who has a single, year-long admission. Do the two patients have the same outcome? Let us compare one patient who has rather vivid schizophrenic symptoms yet maintains a job (a not unusual situation) to another who has minimal symptoms in hospital, but is unable to care for himself in the community. Once again, who has the better outcome? Finally, to what extent are we willing to attribute good outcome to a schizophrenic who leaves the hospital, manages to maintain a

11. Garmezy, 1970; Phillips, 1953; Sullivan, 1953.
12. Garmezy, 1970.
13. Phillips, 1953; Strauss, 1975.

job, but has virtually no social relationships? Clearly, outcome can have many different meanings. Among the outcome measures used in the study of schizophrenia are level of social relationships, degree of work functioning, intensity of symptoms, length, duration, and number of hospitalizations, need for outpatient therapy, and assessment of global adjustment.

In view of the four stages of development—premorbid, precipitant, morbid, and outcome—the case of John illustrates how process schizophrenics may be described as having inadequately met early social demands, showing a slow development of psychosis in the absence of any obvious environmental trauma, and having poor outcomes in many aspects of postpsychotic life. In contrast, reactives like Sam have had generally adequate premorbid adjustments, exhibit a quick onset of symptoms often in response to some external event, and have good outcomes.

The importance of outcome studies of schizophrenia lies in our ability to identify, at some point before the postmorbid phase, variables that predict how well a person will fare in response to schizophrenia. It may be too late to study adult schizophrenics who have passed through several morbid and outcome phases, since "patients with established chronicity or failure can be predicted to continue to fail."[14] If we are to have major impact on schizophrenia outcome, we must be able to predict a person's potential coping ability before a pattern of failure is established.

PREMORBID DEVELOPMENT

The best indication of how well the schizophrenic will respond to a psychosis, treatment, and re-entry into the community is the degree to which the person has coped in the past. Indeed, this statement may be equally true of anyone's response to disorder of many forms. Premorbid social competence describes

14. Keith *et al.*, 1976, p. 517.

the extent of one's fulfilling of age- and sex-appropriate social demands before the identified onset of psychosis.[15] In our examples, Sam had achieved a much higher level of competence before his illness than had John.

The most commonly used measure of premorbid social competence are total years of education, intelligence, occupation, employment history, marital status, and age at first hospital admission. Education and intelligence reflect both a person's intellectual ability and the successful application of this skill to school demands. A person who finished high school is judged to have met social demands better than a person of equal intelligence who leaves before graduating. Jobs can be rated in terms of their salaries, prestige, and type of work. In our culture, better jobs, generally associated with supervisory, nonmanual work and high salaries, have been taken as signs of a person's work skills and ability to deal with people. Poor work skills or a severe inability to get along with people usually result in no job or a job below that which one would expect, given a person's intelligence. Similarly, a long history of frequent jobs of short duration reflects an inability to meet either work or interpersonal demands.

Marital status—whether one is single, divorced, widowed, married without children, or married with children—has been the most frequently used measure of a person's ability to interact with other people. While marital status has been useful in predicting schizophrenic outcome, especially in males, we must caution against continued reliance on this measure as marriage norms shift.[16] That is, marriage is currently not as common as in past years, and it is much more socially acceptable to live one's life as a single person. Therefore, being single in the future may not have the same social meaning as it did in the past.

Finally, age at first hospital admission may be taken as the amount of time one has had before psychosis in which to develop social competence. The longer one stays out of the hospital, the more chances there are for practicing social and work

15. Phillips, 1953.
16. Williams, 1977.

skills and establishing a social support system. The person hospitalized for the first time at age forty is more likely to have built up social, financial, and work resources to help cope with hospitalization and discharge than the person hospitalized for the first time at age twenty. The older person, quite simply, has lived longer. Another interpretation is that the more severe a disorder is, the earlier a person will require treatment. Both views are reasonable and next to impossible to distinguish from each other in practice.

Schizophrenics can be divided into "good" or "poor" premorbid development groups on the basis of a single score combining all of the six premorbid measures. In other words, we distinguish between those schizophrenics, such as Sam, whose past behavior indicates good adjustment, and those, such as John, whose prepsychotic adjustment has been poor. Comparing the outcomes in good and poor premorbid schizophrenics reveals that poor premorbid schizophrenics generally have more frequent and longer hospitalizations and lower levels of postpsychotic adjustment in the community.

The ability to predict outcome in schizophrenia varies somewhat with different schizophrenia diagnostic criteria, measures of premorbid competence, and type of outcome. For example, premorbid social competence based on interpersonal skills predicts length of hospitalization better than it predicts employment outcome. Similarly, premorbid social competence predicts most outcome measures better for broadly defined than narrowly defined schizophrenia. Recent evidence also suggests specificity between measures of premorbid behavior and outcome. In a study assessing the two-year outcome of a group of schizophrenics, hospitalization duration, interpersonal functioning, and employment at the time of the outcome evaluation were best predicted by *previous* hospitalization, *premorbid* level of social relationships, and *past* employment, respectively.[17] It appears, then, that the best estimate of a particular behavior after psychosis is the quality or quantity of that behavior before psychosis. Despite the evidence for specificity between predictor and out-

17. Strauss, 1975.

come measures, hospitalization duration, level of interpersonal relationships, and work ability all emerge as consistent predictors of outcome.[18]

Other efforts to identify adult premorbid predictors of schizophrenic outcome have focused on personality or life style rather than developmental level of adjustment. "Schizoid" personality is the premorbid personality type most frequently associated with a poor schizophrenic outcome. The schizoid person is withdrawn, "shut in," has few, if any, social contacts, and generally lives on isolated existence. The premorbid presence of this schizoid type of life style has been associated with long hospitalization, poor social functioning, and poor work functioning.[19] In contrast, the absence of an asocial, or withdrawn, premorbid personality has been associated with short hospitalizations, good work functioning, including maintaining a household, and independence from one's family or origin.[20] Both of these reports are consistent with the general good and poor premorbid social competence position that suggests that some people have developed more social support and work systems before psychosis than others.

While some disagreement exists about the relative abilities of various premorbid measures to predict outcome, it is frequently the case that one's development before the appearance of the signs of schizophrenia is a good indication of one's ability to cope. The more social relations, work skills, and resources one has prior to psychosis, the better one's chances for a successful outcome.

TIMING OF PSYCHOSIS

Four aspects of schizophrenic onset have been examined in predicting outcome. The first aspect is the presence or absence

18. *Ibid.;* Strauss and Carpenter, 1974.
19. Gittelman-Klein and Klein, 1969.
20. Stephens, 1970; Vaillant, 1963; 1964.

of any recent events that may have triggered the psychosis. The second is the schizophrenic's age at first psychiatric hospital admission or psychiatric contact. The third, course of symptom development, has been described. Do symptoms suddenly appear, as in the case of Sam, or do they have a long, unremarkable history in a person's life, as they did for John? Fourth, the type and severity of symptoms have been assessed in an attempt to link symptom picture with eventual outcome. A good outcome generally is indicated when there is an event that is judged to have precipitated psychosis in older first-admission schizophrenics who exhibit mood or emotional disruption as well as thought disorder during psychosis.

One difficulty in measuring these various features of onset is determining when onset of schizophrenic psychosis occurs. In the case of John, for example, we cannot confidently pinpoint the beginning of psychosis since it seems to have developed slowly. The use of hospitalization as the point of onset is as much an indication of the family's behavior as it is of John's. In contrast, Sam quickly developed psychotic symptoms resulting in behavior that clearly deviated from Sam's norm. How do we equate both types of onset? How can we look for environmental stresses triggering psychosis in schizophrenics like John, if we cannot say for certain when John became psychotic? The answer in research has been to use hospitalization as the marking point. Presumably, some change has occurred in a pre-existing equilibrium between schizophrenic and environment to require hospitalization. We note, in warning, however, that it is not always clear whether this change occurred in the individual, or in the individual's social environment.

Schizophrenics like Sam, for whom there seems to have occurred a dramatic life change prior to hospitalization, tend to have better outcome than those like John, who have a long history of disturbance without easily identified stress.[21] Although events threatening to self-esteem, such as job changes, loss of a close relationship, and academic failure, seem to precede the onset of some schizophrenic episodes, there is no established

21. Garmezy, 1970; 1974(b); Vaillant, 1963; 1964.

relationship between type of stress and outcome.[22] Precipitating events might just as well be positive, such as job promotions or birth of a child, as negative, such as loss of a job or death in the family. The factor that predicts a good outcome does not appear to be the type of stress, but rather that some objectively stressful event preceded psychosis.

The older one is when first hospitalized for schizophrenia, the better one's posthospital adaptation is likely to be. A three-year posthospital follow-up study of schizophrenics divided by age at first admission showed that those hospitalized between the ages of sixteen and nineteen had poorer outcomes than two older groups, twenty to twenty-nine years and thirty to fifty-seven years at first hospitalization. Outcome was measured by the number of rehospitalizations, the length of rehospitalizations, need for outpatient psychiatric treatment, employment status, financial independence, social relationships, and an over-all evaluation of adjustment.[23] The younger one is when hospitalized for schizophrenia the poorer the posthospital outcome in many areas of life.

The course and duration of symptoms prior to hospitalization also give some clue about the person's posthospital career. As in John's case, a person may have been psychotic or withdrawn from reality for a long time before hospitalization. For such a person, hospitalization is merely another step in a long history of the schizophrenic's inability to fend for himself. Posthospital adaptation is not likely to be much better. If however, symptoms are of short prehospitalization duration, reflect emotional involvement, and represent a dramatic departure from usual levels of thinking, feeling, and behaving, then the outlook is optimistic.[24] In contrast to this picture, recent evidence suggests little relationship between narrowly defined thought-disorder symptoms and outcome.[25]

For example, one cannot predict by means of the presence or absence of hallucinations whether a person will successfully

22. Brown *et al.*, 1966; Grinker and Holzman, 1973.
23. Pollack, Levenstein, and Klein, 1968.
24. Garmezy, 1970; Vaillant, 1963; 1964.
25. Strauss, 1975; Strauss and Carpenter, 1974.

function in a job. There are schizophrenics who can work despite hearing voices. They have either learned to ignore them or not to speak to them in public. This suggests to us that level of interpersonal attachment, development of social and work skills, and duration of disorder are important in predicting schizophrenic outcome.

It would simplify our understanding of the schizophrenic process if we could say that the person who was first hospitalized for schizophrenia at a young age showed little emotion, had a long history of slowly developing symptoms, had poor work skills and resource, and always had poor outcomes in the absence of treatment. Conversely, we would like to be able to say that the older schizophrenic has an abrupt onset of psychosis, shows good premorbid development, exhibits intense emotional symptoms during psychosis, and invariably has a good outcome. This would be ideal since we could then point to two different types of schizophrenia, each with its specifiable characteristics and, most likely, its own causes. We could predict accurately and, more importantly, focus upon the factors important to improving outcome in each group. Real life does not, however, always fit ideals. A single schizophrenic may show a mix of characteristics, while some seem to defy our predictions altogether. For now, we can say that presence or absence of precipitating events, age at first hospital admission or psychiatric contact, presence or absence of emotional symptoms, the course of symptom development, and duration of symptoms give us some clues to future behavior.

TREATMENT AND OUTCOME

So far we have tried to identify factors occurring in the natural—i.e., uninterrupted—development of schizophrenia that will predict outcome. In the process, we have looked at the schizophrenic's premorbid development, searched for environmental events that may have precipitated psychosis, and described symptom history and expression at hospitalization. That hospitalization duration is related in some way to future psychiatric career is evident from its ability to predict outcome in several different areas. Another important event in the schizophrenic's life at this point is therapy. We would expect therapy to predict outcome to the extent that it effectively treats schizophrenia. In other words, if therapy were always successful, however we might define that, we could predict with 100 percent accuracy that every schizophrenic given appropriate therapy would have a good outcome. Unfortunately, this is far from the case.

Chemotherapy, seems to be the best single therapy for combating the overt symptoms of schizophrenia, but it does not work for every schizophrenic. Currently, there are studies under way to determine if some types of schizophrenia or certain characteristics in different schizophrenics predict which schizophrenics will respond best to medication. Some early findings even suggest that certain schizophrenics should not be given any medication. However, these findings are very recent, experimental, have not been repeated by many investigators, and are, therefore, not appropriately generalized to clinical situations. This type of research, however, eventually may allow us to be precise in prescribing antipsychotics to those schizophrenics who will benefit most by them.[26]

We must also take into account psychotherapy in all its forms in the attempt to predict outcome. There are two questions of importance in examining the relationship between psychotherapy and outcome. First, can we predict who will benefit most from therapy? Second, can we predict a schizophrenic's outcome if we know the type and frequency of psychotherapy that person has received?

Regarding who is most likely to benefit from therapy, we can say that those schizophrenics showing the most adequate functioning before hospitalization or therapy, will be the ones to benefit the most from psychotherapy. Another way of saying this is that process schizophrenics like John will benefit the least

26. Goldstein *et al.*, 1968; Rappaport *et al.*, 1971; Phillips, 1953.

from psychotherapy; reactive schizophrenics like Sam will benefit the most from psychotherapy.[27] This is reasonable when we consider that more skillful, better educated, more resourceful people will both better understand the nature of psychotherapy and apply it to their lives than the less skillful, less educated, and less resourceful. This is not to say that psychotherapy is not useful for this latter type of person, but only that it may be more effective with the former. This may explain, in part, the generally accepted superiority of supportive therapy over more traditional psychotherapy with many schizophrenics.

Schizophrenia frequently has been associated with an interference in developing optimal levels of interpersonal and work functioning, including education. Therefore, many schizophrenics may be ill equipped to effectively use psychotherapies primarily evolving from work with less disturbed, more premorbidly competent patients. While this interpretation is open to empirical testing, it does illustrate how studies of psychotherapies and schizophrenia eventually may lead us in the same direction as studies of individual differences in responding to phenothiazines. This direction is toward specifying different therapies to best meet the needs of different schizophrenics.

CONTINUING STRESSES AND OUTCOME

A final group of factors that bear upon the schizophrenic's outcome after hospitalization is the type of environment to which the schizophrenic returns. A majority of the work in this area has focused upon the relationship between the schizophrenic and his family. In a study that followed the posthospital adjustment of schizophrenics, it was found that the former patients' ability to meet family and community responsibilities was related to their families' expectations. Those schizophrenics who were performing at the highest levels were living with

27. Luborsky *et al.*, 1971; Phillips, 1953; Stephens and Astrup, 1963.

families who expected the most. This is not to say that family expectation necessarily *causes* the schizophrenic to succeed or fail in meeting their social demands. It may have been that families' expectations accurately reflected schizophrenics' levels of ability. The two interpretations are equally plausible and likely. Furthermore, the schizophrenics' rehospitalization, if it occurred during the study period, was not related to their ability to perform in outside or family work. Thus, level of functioning, or performance, and rehospitalization may be separate issues in the life of the schizophrenic. Rehospitalization, most frequently initiated by the family, the patient, or some social agent, occurred most frequently when the former patient was reported to have become excessively nervous, dazed, or withdrawn from people.[28]

Finally, there has been a series of studies indicating that the quality of the relationship between schizophrenic and family is a predictor of recurrence of schizophrenic symptoms over approximately a one-year follow-up.[29] Psychiatric interviews have been used to assess the number of critical comments expressed by family members about the schizophrenic, the degree of hostility between family and schizophrenic, and the extent of parental overinvolvement in the schizophrenic's life. Critical comments are judged on the basis of tone of voice. Hostility indicates either rejecting or generalizing the criticism—for example, "he is the most unsociable person we've ever known." Overinvolvement is generally reflected by marked concern for trivial aspects of the schizophrenic's life, such as which clothes to wear, what to eat, and when to come home. Critical comments, hostility, and overinvolvement are combined into a single measure of "expressed emotion." High expressed emotion in the schizophrenic's family would indicate many critical comments and the presence of hostility, rejection, and overinvolvement. Low expressed emotion indicates few critical comments, and little, if any hostility, rejection, or overinvolvement.

Schizophrenics returning to homes in which there is a high

28. Freeman and Simmons, 1963.
29. Brown, Birley, and Wing, 1972; Brown and Rutter, 1966; Leff, 1976; Rutter and Brown, 1966; Vaughn and Leff, 1976; Wing, 1977.

level of expressed emotion were much more likely at the follow-up interview either to show symptoms when there had been none at hospital discharge, or to show an increase in symptoms over discharge level, than schizophrenics returning to families in which there was low expressed emotion. Schizophrenics from families in which there was high expressed emotion were, however, protected from relapse in two ways: use of antipsychotic medication and reduced face-to-face contact with family members. A combination of medication and reduced contact with the family resulted in the lowest relapse rates of those from families in which there was high expressed emotion.

All schizophrenics from families in which there was low expressed emotion had about the same rate of relapse, about 15 percent, regardless of medication and the amount of time spent in face-to-face contact with the family. Schizophrenics from families in which there was low expressed emotion, and schizophrenics on medication who were spending little time with their family, in which there was a high level of expressed emotion, had similar relapse rates.

By far, the highest rate (about 92 percent) of symptom relapse was for schizophrenics who were not on medication and who were spending much time with their family, in which there was a high level of expressed emotion. This result did not seem to be a function of either differences in the severity of the schizophrenics' symptoms or degree of overall functioning. These studies clearly suggest that medication and outcome in schizophrenia are not simply related. Once again, attention to individual differences among schizophrenics and their environments leads to more precise statements about outcome and, ultimately, about how best to treat each individual schizophrenic.

Can families prevent the recurrence of schizophrenic psychosis by not being critical of, avoiding too much contact with, and not being overly involved with their vulnerable member? At this point, there is no simple answer to this question. Nevertheless, fostering a supportive, yet independent home atmosphere must prove beneficial, if only in reducing the level of day-to-day tension. Allowing the schizophrenic family member his freedom within a supportive context, while living one's own

TABLE 9:1

Predictors of Good and Poor Outcome

	GOOD OUTCOME	POOR OUTCOME
Premorbid functioning	Good educational history; good work history; married	Poor educational history; poor work history; single
Symptom development	Late onset; rapid symptom development; clear precipitating event; emotional upheaval	Early onset; slowly developing symptoms; no apparent precipitant; emotional dullness
Response to treatment	Positive; short hospital stay	Unresponsive; long hospital stay
Continuing stresses	Low expressed emotion in family or medication and reduced contact; available community services	High expressed emotion in family; no medication; few services available

life is not easy. It is, however, a goal toward which the entire family might strive.

Table 9:1 provides a summary of outcome predictors. Level of premorbid development, onset and duration of symptoms, treatment, family and social expectations, and quality of family environment all provide somewhat different perspectives of the outcome picture. The study of outcome, following major changes in professional thinking about the definition and nature of schizophrenia, is a new area in schizophrenia research. We are really only beginning to identify with any consistency and precision some of the predictors of schizophrenic outcome.

SCHIZOPHRENIA AS A GROWTH EXPERIENCE

Some clinicians and researchers suggest that schizophrenic disorganization may be the first step in an adaptive process with potentially beneficial effects. This is consistent with some auto-biographical reports of schizophrenics in which the postpsychotic personality of the schizophrenic is stronger, more en-riched, and generally better integrated than before psychosis.[30] In this view the conflict and pain experienced by the schizophrenic is not denied, but rather the potential personal growth available to the schizophrenic is emphasized. The general view is that once the schizophrenic experiences total disorganization and despair, the way is open for reorganizing the personality. One very important condition for this to take place is the presence of a supportive atmosphere in which the schizophrenic may fully experience psychosis. Most people who take this view discourage use of medication. They claim it inhibits working through the psychosis.

Not using medication for schizophrenia, as proposed by many in favor of therapeutic communities, represents, at this point, more of a philosophical, political statement than a practical, proven means of coping with schizophrenia. While one day it may be possible to identify those schizophrenics who do better without than with medication, this cannot yet be done. In face of the overwhelming evidence showing the general effectiveness of the antipsychotic medications in reducing or preventing psychotic symptoms, the use of medication must remain the preferred initial treatment. That schizophrenics—indeed, any person—should be treated with dignity and respect is an ideal toward which all can strive.

There have been many attempts to establish *therapeutic communities.* The staff in these settings is either nonprofessional or, if professional, avoids taking on the traditional professional role of therapist. Instead, the nonpsychotic members of the community are perceived as facilitators who provide guidance for getting through a psychosis. Medication is discouraged, and schizophrenics are encouraged to fully experience their psychosis. Ideally, one leaves such a therapeutic community having used the disorganization of psychosis as the basis of a better functioning personality. Much of the information we have regarding the effectiveness of such an approach is based on tes-

30. Barnes, 1971; Epstein, 1973; 1975; Jefferson, 1948; Kaplan, 1964; Laing, 1965; Sechehaye, 1950; Vonnegut, 1975.

timonials of former residents.[31] Nevertheless, recent attempts have been made to rigorously compare the effectiveness of this form of supportive, nontraditional therapy to more traditional therapy.[32] While it is much too early to judge the value of such studies, it is hoped that this sort of research will tell us something about the characteristics of the social environment in which schizophrenics optimally cope.

To take a lesson from other areas of outcome research, we can predict that schizophrenics will differ in their response to this form of therapy. Specifically, we can expect that premorbid levels of adaptation will relate to how well an individual schizophrenic can make use of a therapeutic community. Overall, the recent application of rigorous research methods to the study of therapeutic community effectiveness is a welcome trend.

IMPLICATIONS OF OUTCOME RESEARCH

Since the study of outcome is a recent development in schizophrenia research, there have been only a few attempts to integrate the findings relating premorbid, precipitant, morbid, and posthospital events to outcome. Nevertheless, such attempts will eventually prove valuable in furthering the understanding of the causes of and effective treatments of schizophrenia. A case in point is the process-reactive conception of schizophrenia.

Recall that the process and reactive distinctions largely originated from the clinical and research observations that some schizophrenics progressively deteriorated while others recovered. While there is individual variability, the process schizophrenic generally has poor prepsychotic adjustment, a long duration of symptoms, a slow onset of identified disorder in the absence of obvious environmental stress, and generally unfavorable overall outcome. For some, this picture implies that the development and course of schizophrenia in the process indi-

31. Boyers and Orrill, 1971; Barnes, 1971; Laing, 1965.
32. Mosher, 1972; Mosher, Menn, and Matthews, 1975.

vidual, in contrast to the reactive individual, are strongly determined by potent biological factors. In terms of the diathesis-stress model, the process schizophrenic has a very high genetic predisposition for schizophrenia. As biological elements take precedence, greater environmental and psychological intervention is required to counteract the disruptive effect of schizophrenia. The reactive schizophrenic would be viewed from the diathesis-stress model as having relatively little genetic predisposition for schizophrenia, but responding to environmental stress with schizophrenic disorganization. Thus, the observation of differences in outcome led to attempts to define the characteristics predicting outcome, the delineation of different forms of schizophrenia, and, ultimately, hypotheses about differences in cause. Of course, we must realize that this is not the final answer and that science does not always proceed along a smooth, logical path. That differences in schizophrenic outcome have been associated with a rethinking of schizophrenia, however, is clear.

We must also be sensitive to outcome differences in our attempts to formulate effective treatment programs. Not all treatments have the same effect on all schizophrenics. For example, medication was found to reduce the rate of symptom relapse among schizophrenics returning to homes in which families expressed criticism and hostility and were overinvolved. In contrast, medication made little difference in the relapse rate among schizophrenics returning to homes with little expressed emotion. This type of difference not only suggested that treatment is multifaceted, but also that we must consider family, social, and individual differences among schizophrenics in determining the least intrusive, but most effective therapy.

Finally, in any study of therapy effectiveness, comparison groups must be equated on variables known to be associated with outcome.[33] To compare, for example, the effectiveness of a nontraditional form of community therapy with schizophrenics all of whom are like Sam and individual psychotherapy with patients all of whom are like John is meaningless. Sam would

33. Feinstein, 1967; Strauss and Carpenter, 1974.

be predicted to have a better outcome than John in the absence
of any therapy. To claim that community therapy is better than
individual psychotherapy in such a case is unwarranted. To test
one form of therapy versus another would require giving different therapies to two groups alike in their outcome predictions. Then, any differences in outcome could be attributed to
the effect of therapy. This sort of research sophistication is not
possible without an appreciation of the fact that schizophrenics
are not all alike and do not all have similar outcomes.

Schizophrenia can have many outcomes. At one extreme, the
course of disorder is slow and long, marked by an inability to
survive on one's own. At the other extreme, some schizophrenics
have a single psychotic episode and then recover. There is every
possible outcome between these two extremes. Also, outcome
may take many forms. Outcome may be measured by symptoms,
hospitalization, need for outpatient treatment, level of interpersonal functioning, ability to work, and individual growth. Thus,
when we ask "What will be the outcome for schizophrenics?"
the answer is "Which outcome?" Recognition of these various
aspects of both pre- and postpsychotic functioning results in a
complex collage. Many areas overlap. Some stand alone. Yet,
somehow, when we stand off a bit, it all makes a single picture.
Though we continue to reach for better predictors of schizophrenic outcome, we can say with some assurance that the more
competence, social supports, and human resources before psychosis, the better one's chances after psychosis.

10

A LOOK TOWARD THE FUTURE

THE RESEARCHER'S VIEW

The picture of schizophrenia has changed dramatically since the end of the nineteenth century, when Kraepelin described it as an inevitably deteriorating condition. The natural course of the disorder itself is actually highly variable. In addition, we have developed biochemical and psychosocial treatment strategies that are helpful in controlling many of the most disturbing symptoms of schizophrenia for the majority of patients. Nonetheless, we have a long way to go if we mean to develop a safe and effective means of preventing the appearance, and reappearance of symptoms in predisposed individuals.

For the most part, this book has presented a somewhat basic overview of schizophrenia. The uncertainty and ambiguity in defining and studying schizophrenia have been largely avoided, and little effort has been made to interpret different theories of schizophrenia as products of various researchers' scientific imagination. What concerns most of us now is whether or not we can diagnose, treat, and eventually prevent schizophrenia. While we have advanced tremendously in the past hundred years, we would not be completely honest if we were to avoid some of the major ambiguities confronting us in the search for the causes of schizophrenia.

The Question of Definition

What are some of the unknowns in the equation we have presented for schizophrenia? One serious point of discussion is the definition and diagnosis of schizophrenia. While numerous attempts have been made to standardize the means by which we arrive at a diagnosis, there is still disagreement on a definition of schizophrenia. Even if researchers decided to adopt a single diagnostic system, it would probably be many years before it could be generally used among clinicians. The research efforts to date are simply too complex and time consuming to replace traditional, well-known, and, thereby, well-entrenched diagnostic practices. What this means is that results from one study may not be generalizable to a population of schizophrenics that has been identified by a different set of criteria. For example, one study may indicate that schizophrenia, by one definition, has a strong genetic component, while another study may show that schizophrenia, by a different definition, has a negligible genetic component.

This lack of standardization presents difficulties with respect to treatment as well as with respect to the search for causes. The effects of treatment are variable, and it is reasonable to expect that different "types" of schizophrenia may account for some of this variability.

The Nature-Nurture Question

A second question involves the role genetics is thought to play in the transmission of schizophrenia. For a time it seemed as if genetics would be shown to be the major determinant of schizophrenia. More recently, however, it has become clear that while genetics may be a necessary condition for many forms of schizophrenia, it is by no means a sufficient one. We are only now turning from efforts to show that schizophrenia has a genetic component to careful examination of what the predisposition might be and what environmental events are important in precipitating schizophrenia.

In addition, no one knows what the genetic predisposition for schizophrenia actually is. We have presented what appears to be a reasonable guess. However, there is no firm evidence to support any particular predisposition. Neither do we know how such a predisposition would interact with the environment (assuming that we know which aspects of the environment are relevant) to result in schizophrenia. In short, while the diathesis-stress model of schizophrenia makes sense given what we know about schizophrenia, there is still very little with which to fill in the outlines of this theory.

One reason for these gaps in our knowledge is that much of the research on schizophrenia has been conducted with adults. By the time people have reached adulthood, there is much information about their childhoods that simply cannot be retrieved. We do not know what the long-term effects of medication are, and we cannot control fortuitous environmental circumstances. We are, in other words, limited to a rather narrow slice of the individual's life when we see that person as an adult. Therefore, making statements about childhood events, developmental patterns, or prepsychotic events that may cause schizophrenia is a risky venture at best.

Limits of Our Knowledge

While there are other points of confusion and disagreement among clinicians and researchers, the ongoing debate about definition and genetic-environmental interaction serve to illustrate the complexity involved in communicating about and studying schizophrenia. Anyone wishing to write an objective account of schizophrenia must include widely divergent points of view. To be completely accurate requires presenting a detailed, contradictory, and frequently confusing description of schizophrenia.

Instead of speculating about uncertainties existing in the schizophrenia literature, many people tend to want answers to some very specific questions. What is schizophrenia? Who is schizophrenic, and how does one know? What causes it, and how can it be treated? These are the same questions asked by patients, families, and clinicians. Unfortunately, researchers frequently cannot or will not commit themselves to providing definitive answers. More often than not, there are no single "correct" answers. As a consequence, the researcher and those interested in immediate therapy sometimes are at odds with one another.

Regardless of one's reasons for being interested in schizophrenia, there are some advantages to acknowledging the limits of our understanding. Realizing that there is still much to learn about schizophrenia may help us to avoid the self-defeating cycle of unrealistic hopes for a complete cure, followed by disappointment and depression, followed by another search. While much can be done for the schizophrenic, it is unrealistic and without demonstrated proof, for example, that huge doses of vitamins have a long-lasting beneficial effect. Even the phenothiazines, demonstrated to have positive effects on psychotic symptoms, do not have the same effect on all schizophrenics. Some schizophrenics seem to respond very favorably, others not at all or even adversely. Acknowledging this difference in drug effectivenss among various groups of schizophrenics will make us cautious about accepting blanket statements.

Another reason for being clear about the extent of our knowledge of schizophrenia is the need to make a realistic assessment of the questions researchers can fruitfully investigate and answers they can be expected to provide. Over the past several years, psychology has gained a wide audience. The number of students in psychology courses has swelled. More and more psychiatry and psychology is making its way into the general public's awareness. This increasing access to and sophistication in psychology is beneficial to the extent that people can learn about themselves and others and apply this knowledge to increase the satisfaction they get out of life. At the same time, there seems to have arisen an unrealistic expectation that psychology can solve all our problems or that we can become better individuals by simply finding the right book and method for us. One need only glance at the psychology section of any local bookstore to see what an overabundance of self-help books are available. That they continue to be published and bought reflects the need that they attempt to meet.

In the area of schizophrenia research, it is unlikely that we can "solve" the entire problem of schizophrenia to the extent that schizophrenia involves stages in development and personality formation that are simply part of the human condition. It is important to acknowledge the place of normal conflict and development in the schizophrenic's life. No amount of study is going to take away the struggle, conflict, and occasional pain that all of us must face in the process of living. To rely on psychology to eliminate problems of living seems to be a misplaced and a too ambitious expectation. What, then, can we expect from psychology and, more specifically, from the area relating to schizophrenia?

There seem to be two expectations we can place upon research. One is to identify limited behavioral disorders and to explain their causes. The research in reading disabilities, mental retardation, and deficits in various sensory systems such as blindness and deafness illustrates this type of work. These qualify as discrete disorders in that a system is not working properly, not everyone experiences a dysfunction, the disorders frequently have specific causes, and the disorders can be modified by specific treatments.

In the area of schizophrenia, one useful strategy may be to look toward a specific type of thought disorder. For example, one of the hallmarks of schizophrenia is hearing voices in the absence of any external source. This is a disorder in that it is not the usual way in which the auditory system works. Few people hear voices, and many among those who do suffer because of these voices. It may be possible one day to explain the biochemical or physiological process that underlies this experience. Similarly, it is likely that understanding this sort of deviation from normal functioning will help us either to prevent it or treat it. Thus, one goal would be to define clearly each of the psychological mechanisms that are malfunctioning in schizophrenia and to identify the physiological basis for the malfunction. Efforts to prevent or treat such specific problems would have a much greater chance of success than the present strategy of treating this complex and variable disorder as a totality.

The second goal of research is to identify problems, though not necessarily to provide the way in which to avoid them. For example, there is some evidence that the schizophrenic finds it difficult to leave the family either physically or, more importantly, psychologically. We can warn schizophrenics that any time the issue of leaving the family arises, they will experience stress. How does one avoid this or cope with the stress? These two questions cannot be answered in general terms. Every person must develop his own strategies, which take into account his unique situations. A therapist can help a person get through a difficult period, but he cannot eliminate the threat. Careful study of schizophrenics and their development can point to a set of life events, developmental crises, or social situations to which a person can be alerted. Additionally, systematic investigations of people who have successfully coped with schizophrenia may tell us what skills and behaviors the schizophrenic individual needs to learn or relearn and how best to teach them.

One of the problems in interpreting research data in schizophrenia is the confusion between the two types of research goals. While research may help us in understanding the particular problems of, for example, being deaf, such as learning to speak, we cannot eliminate the other aspects of normal development that deafness may exacerbate. Parents of deaf children, for example, may be overprotective out of a desire to make life easier for their child. When it comes time for a deaf child to form an identity of his own away from the family, the past family history of overprotectiveness will make that more difficult. We cannot say that deafness is a disorder of separating from the family. Rather, the reactions to a deaf child may make separation from the family more difficult for the deaf than for the nondeaf. When we counsel the deaf, we can use our knowledge of how other families with deaf people have acted, but we cannot avoid the conflict that arises between a person with a basic disorder and the demands placed on the person by society. It is important both for researchers and clinicians to keep common human conflicts separate from rarer disordered behavior.

Directions for Future Research

Three consistent findings have emerged from the last fifty years of research in schizophrenia. First, genetic transmission is important in some types of schizophrenia (namely, the more severe forms) but does not account for the entire development of schizophrenia. Second, schizophrenia occurs far more frequently in the lowest socioeconomic class of large, urban cities than among the middle and upper classes. Third, schizophrenics exhibit tremendous individual variability whether measured clinically or by experimental test performance. It is appropriate to reflect for a moment upon the implications of these three facts for future research.

Despite a growing body of studies supporting the role of genetic transmission and implicating environmental factors in schizophrenia, the issue of genes versus environment continues to generate heated debate.[1] The problem for most of us is not in acknowledging the importance of either genetics or environment, but rather in deciding how much each contributes to schizophrenia. Thus, while geneticists attribute the major role to heredity, the environmentalists place the most emphasis on psychological and sociological factors.

While most clinicians and researchers probably would agree that an interactionist view is the most reasonable account of schizophrenia, few have examined in detail what this heredity-environment interaction might be.[2] There are two primary forms of the gene and environment interaction theory of schizophrenia. One is a vulnerability model, which suggests that a person is generally vulnerable (either through genetic transmission or congenital accident) to serious psychiatric disorder, whose development and form are determined by environmental factors.

The second interactionist theory is more specific to schizophrenia and posits a genetic deficiency in a basic mechanism, such as thinking or the ability to experience pleasure. The person does not experience the world as others do. As a result,

1. Gottesman and Shields, 1976; Lidz, 1976.
2. Meehl, 1962; Zubin and Spring, 1977.

that person may fail to learn appropriate ways of thinking and interacting. At this stage of our understanding, it is not the detailed model in which we are interested so much as it is the need to take the interaction between genes and environment seriously.[3] One direction for schizophrenia research then is the analysis of genetic and environmental factors in the same study rather than the analysis of genetics in one study and the analysis of environment in another.[4]

How can the nature of the interaction between genetics and environment be productively explored? Longitudinal studies of people who are genetically "at risk" for schizophrenia are presently underway. In these studies efforts are made to record significant environmental features as they occur at various stages of development with the hope of eventually correlating some of these features with the emergence of schizophrenia in some of the individuals being studied. Since at present we have little evidence that one environmental event is more important than another, these researchers must begin by monitoring hundreds of variables in the hopes that they will find the significant ones. It is hoped that this strategy will produce sound hunches that will lead to hypotheses that can be systematically tested in the future.

Another consideration is the way in which we have searched for the causes of schizophrenia. Most studies have concentrated primarily on individual differences between schizophrenics and normal or psychiatric groups with which they are compared. This is illustrated, for example, in the search for the biochemical process underlying thinking disorder.

In contrast, broad-based epidemiological studies may provide equally compelling leads for the causes of schizophrenia. For example, there is a striking relationship between the occurrence of schizophrenia and low social class. There has been very little work to date that examines possible relationships linking this epidemiological finding to the individual differences in thinking demonstrated between schizophrenics and others.[5] Is there, for

3. Erlenmeyer-Kimling, 1968; Kohn, 1972; Matthysse, 1976; Murphy, 1968; Rosenthal, 1968.
4. Dohrenwend, 1976.
5. Kohn, 1972.

example, an orderly relationship between social class and measures of thought disorder? Are there experiences in low-social-class living that might lead to thinking patterns particularly susceptible to schizophrenia? These types of questions serve to point out how the eventual explanation of schizophrenia will have to take widely divergent facts into account. While it may be sufficient for now to continue the explorations in circumscribed areas such as biochemistry, physiology, and cognition, it is important to recognize the relationship between the schizophrenic as an individual and as part of society.

Finally, it may be valuable to pursue the suggestion recently made that we consider individual variability as an essential component of schizophrenia.[6] Rather than trying to ignore, statistically eliminate, or simply refer to variability in passing annoyance, schizophrenics can be classified and studied on the basis of their variability on some task. Both clinical observations and experimental studies have repeatedly reported that schizophrenics vary greatly in their behavior. Why do they vary? Under what conditions does the schizophrenic perform consistently and under what conditions does he perform variably? Do schizophrenics showing less variable behavior have better outcomes than those showing extremely variable behavior? Does variability of performance correlate with drug responsiveness? The questions are endless and are posed primarily to show the direction one could follow if one were to take seriously a finding that has been known for some time but has been ignored up to now. These questions may have important implications for therapy.

THE CLINICIAN'S VIEW

Researchers in their attempts to discover the causes and cures of schizophrenia, tend to focus on groups of people. They compare schizophrenics with nonschizophrenics, good premor-

6. Wishner, 1977.

bid schizophrenics with poor premorbid schizophrenics, phenothiazine responders with nonresponders. Clinicians, on the other hand, are concerned with the individual schizophrenic within a unique environment. As research has made tremendous gains over recent decades, so has the treatment of the individual case. To illustrate where we have been and where we are going, let us consider four cases of newly diagnosed schizophrenia, the first two of which are based on facts and the last two of which are fantasies for the future.

Janet in 1928

Janet is twenty-four years old and has been brought to the hospital by her father. Although she has been withdrawn, seclusive, and eccentric since she was eighteen, her parents have kept her at home, due to their discomfort with having a member of their family labeled as mentally ill and due to their concern for her welfare. However, Janet's mother died a year ago, and Janet's father has been unable to care for her while holding a job and providing for his other children.

The hospital to which Janet has been brought has bars on all of the windows. It is dark, impersonal, and ominous. Her father has been told that Janet is very ill and will probably have to stay for a long while.

At monthly intervals, Janet's father visits her. He comes alone, not wanting to subject his other children to the frightening atmosphere of the hospital—Janet, dressed, in a hospital gown, sitting and staring; other patients pacing, yelling, or, like Janet, just staring; the bare halls, strange sounds, and distasteful odors.

Janet's days are indistinguishable from one another. Occasionally, the ward staff speaks with her, but, getting no response, they soon hurry away. Finally, they only address her when they want her to go to bed or come for meals. At one point, shortly after her admission, she underwent insulin shock therapy during which she was given insulin until she had a seizure. This treatment, which appeared to be beneficial for some patients, was unsuccessful for Janet. The doctor told her father that there was nothing else he could do. But Janet might recover spontaneously—some patients did.

Janet does not recover. Her seclusiveness and passivity are fostered by the hospital environment. While her original symptoms remain largely unchanged, her ability to take care of herself slowly deteriorates. She no longer brushes her teeth or combs her hair. What semblance of respect she had has faded away. Finally, after two years, her father stops visiting and Janet is left alone.

Janet in 1978

Janet is nineteen years old and has been brought to the hospital by her parents. Although she has been withdrawn, seclusive, and eccentric for about a year, it was not until her refusal to look for work, or even to leave the house after high school graduation, that her parents became frightened enough to seek help. Their family physician has suggested that Janet be treated in a hospital.

The hospital to which Janet has been brought sits on a large, well-manicured tract of land. A number of people sit outside, reading or talking. It is not apparent which of these people are patients or visitors or staff members. Inside, the walls are decorated with paintings, some of them done by ex-patients. There is a snack bar and reading room which serves all of the wards. Only one hallway is locked. The hospital psychiatrist tells Janet's parents that, although she can't be certain, she feels that Janet will need to be in the hospital about six weeks. She refers them to the psychiatric social worker, who will help them plan for Janet's discharge and who suggest that they visit with her on weekends or in the evening since her days will be quite full. In response to a question from Janet's mother, the social worker explains that Janet is expected to wear her own clothes and to wash them herself in the available machines. If she needs help to do so, the ward staff will assist her.

Her parents visit a couple of times a week. Once in a while, they bring her brother and sister, pick her up, and go off grounds for a picnic. Once a week they meet with the social worker to discuss Janet's progress and to talk about what they ought to expect from her.

Janet's treatment program involves chemotherapy, meetings with her therapist, group activities, and individualized training in various personal and vocational skills. After about three weeks, she appears less withdrawn and more able to converse with her family about everyday events, although she complains about some of the medication's side effects. She is not sure whether it helps her or not. After about six weeks, her odd behaviors, like talking out loud when no one is there, are almost gone. She is still unsure about how to make friends, what sort of a job she should get, and how life will go for her. While she is still uncomfortable about taking medication, she agrees to do so when she goes home.

Shortly after Janet returns home, she is enrolled in a secretarial training program, funded through the State Office of Vocational Rehabilitation. During her months in the program she lives at home and engages in few activities outside of school. A month before graduation, she stops taking her medication. Before she can look for work her symptoms recur and she is rehospitalized. With a full therapeutic program, she is ready for discharge in only three weeks. This time, she is referred to an outpatient young people's group for continued support. Through this group she makes a number of acquaintances. After a time, she decides to share an apartment with one of her new friends, although she retains close ties with her family.

Ten years later, Janet continues to take a small dose of medication each day and remains well. She is holding a job as a clerk-typist and works as a library volunteer in the hospital in which she was treated. She is still somewhat withdrawn and never goes out with men. She has not gone to college as her parents had initially hoped she would. But she appears comfortable with her quiet, structured life.

Janet in 2028

Janet is fourteen years old and has been brought to the mental-health center by her parents. Since she has a family history of schizophrenia, her parents had been told many years ago of the possibility that they might have a child who would develop schizophrenia. They were educated about the warning signals that might alert them to its presence. Having seen some of these signals, Janet's tendency to daydream, lapses of attention, moodiness, they have decided to have her checked.

A series of medical tests confirms the diagnosis of schizophrenia and pinpoints the site and nature of the physiological disturbance. A wide array of medications have been developed, each of which controls a different type of schizophrenia and one of which is right for Janet. She is to receive an injection monthly, which will remove the symptoms with few side effects.

Since the illness has not existed long enough to rob Janet of important adolescent growing experiences, she has no need for therapy. However, for patients whose emerging illness is not detected this early a network of therapeutic social supports exist in or nearby each community, funded by revenues from the national health-insurance program. This has been made possible by massive public education, which has taught that schizophrenia is an illness that presents personal, social, and vocational problems, which, if unattacked, substantially drain the public coffers. Janet is enrolled in a class offered by the mental-health center, which teaches schizophrenics (and their families) about the illness, its treatment, and what they can do to ensure complete recovery. The family is encouraged to return if, under stress, Janet begins to experience any symptoms.

For the next few years, Janet makes her parents' life difficult, as do her teenage brother and sister. She has the usual adolescent rebellion, sometimes trying to use her illness as an excuse for all sorts of special privileges she wants. She and her brother argue over whose treatment hurts worse, her schizophrenia injection or his allergy shot. Her life has its ups and downs, to be sure, but she is not significantly impaired in her ability to adjust to them.

Janet in 2078

Janet is twenty-one years old. She has just graduated from college and is about to begin a career in journalism. When she was born, Janet was screened, as are all newborns, for the presence of an abnormal protein, which, if undetected, may produce schizophrenic symptoms later in life. Having been found to carry this protein, Janet was treated with a medication which neutralized the protein, turning it into a harmless substance excreted through the urine. She has never experienced any schizophrenic symptoms and never will.

Implications for the Future

While our last two examples are fantasies and their dates pure speculation, the progress they illustrate is well within the realm of possibility. Already major changes have occurred in our ability to treat schizophrenia and in our knowledge of its possible origins. Further gains should occur much more rapidly now that there is a basis from which to work.

Janet in 2028 has benefited from a number of significant advances. First, we expect to be able to pinpoint the physiological basis (or bases) of schizophrenic symptoms and to develop medications that specifically control these symptoms. While the present medicines have afforded many schizophrenics the opportunity to live independently, free from the most disturbing of their symptoms, our treatment now is general rather than specific. That is, the antipsychotic medications exert rather gross effects on the nervous system, causing significant discomfort, even as they ameliorate symptoms. As research provides some answers about how the medicines control symptoms, we can look forward to the production of drugs that have a more specific antipsychotic action, with fewer troubling side effects.

Further, we can expect to develop a clearer view of the environmental situations that are conducive to recovery as well as those that are stressful. We can also expect to have an understanding of which therapeutic activities are useful for which individuals. Focusing on these issues becomes particularly crucial as medicines provide schizophrenics with the wherewithal to function outside of hospitals. It is essential that the community provide individualized therapeutic work, play, and living situations for those who need them. Schizophrenics will become more and more capable of functioning in society if appropriate opportunities in the form of psychotherapy and education, residential settings, vocational training, and social support groups are made available.

The reverberations of a schizophrenic illness are dramatic and extensive, affecting parents, siblings, and children of the disturbed individual. As we become more sensitive to the fact that families, far from being "the enemy," may have endured tremendous pain and certainly have accepted great responsibility long before we knew them, we will be better able to provide the support and advice they so desperately need. Again, this is particularly important as the treatment for schizophrenia moves from a hospital-based focus to a community-based focus. While research cannot solve the problems in living that accompany schizophrenia, clinicians can provide some guidance as families attempt to cope with these problems. Thus, in our example, Janet and her family in 2028 are educated about the role of biochemistry and the role of stress in producing schizophrenic symptoms. They, and others like them, have at their disposal a system of supportive services, making the use of mental hospitals essentially obsolete.

If we are to make progress in the treatment of schizophrenia, an investment of financial and emotional support will have to be made by the community. The disturbing trend toward emptying mental hospitals without providing follow-up services will be reversed with the knoweldge that transfer of dollars from hospitals to welfare payments represents no savings. Programs providing the education, training, and support necessary to allow schizophrenics to become partially or totally self-supporting will represent a real savings in terms of dollars and lives.

Finally, at some point in the future—perhaps by 2078—we may be able to test for a predisposing biochemical deficit *before* symptom onset and to reverse that deficit. Such a strategy is already available for phenylketonuria (PKU), a genetically transmitted metabolic illness that can be detected and treated in infancy. Many genetic defects *are* reversible. And if such a defect (or defects) exists in schizophrenia, we may find it and be able to treat it some day.

Together, clinicians and researchers can tackle schizophrenia. The public can help advance our knowledge through commitment, both financially and emotionally, to the goal of one day preventing the occurrence of this stigmatizing and disabling illness that affects, directly or indirectly, many millions of people. Despite the criticism, uncertainty, and ambiguity that continue to exist in the area of schizophrenia research and therapy, there have been major advances over the last fifty years in the epidemiology, experimental study, and treatment of schizophrenia. The progress made since Bleuler first coined the term *schizophrenia* less than one hundred years ago gives us optimism for the future, tempered by the realities that we still have much to learn.

Bibliography

Angrist, B., *et al.* Amphetamine psychosis: behavioral and biochemical aspects. *Journal of Psychiatric Research,* 1974, *11,* 13–23.

Anthony W. A., *et al.* Efficacy of psychiatric rehabilitation. *Psychological Bulletin,* 1972, *78,* 447–456.

Arieti, S. An overview of schizophrenia from a predominantly psychological approach. *American Journal of Psychiatry,* 1974, *131,* 241–249.

———. Schizophrenia: the manifest symptomatology, the psychodynamic and formal mechanisms. In S. Arieti (ed.). *American Handbook of Psychiatry.* New York: Basic Books, 1959.

Astrachan, B. M., *et al.* Symptomatic outcome in schizophrenia. *Archives of General Psychiatry,* 1974, *31,* 155–160.

Astrachan, B., *et al.* A checklist for the diagnosis of schizophrenia. *British Journal of Psychiatry,* 1972, *121,* 529–539.

Axelrod, J., Perlin, S., and Szara, S. Is adrenochrome present in the blood? *American Journal of Psychiatry,* 1958, *115,* 162–163.

Ayd, F. J. A survey of drug-induced extrapyramidal reactions. *Journal of the American Medical Association,* 1961, *175,* 1054–1060.

Ban, T. A., and Lehman, H. E. Nicotinic acid in the treatment of schizophrenics: Canadian Mental Health Association Collaborative Study Progress Report II. *Canadian Psychiatric Association Journal,* 1975, *20,* 103–112.

Barker, J. C., and Baker, A. A. Deaths associated with electroplexy. *Journal of Mental Science,* 1959, *105,* 339–348.

Barnes, M. *Two Accounts of a Journey through Madness.* New York: Ballantine, 1971.

Bateson, G. *Steps to an Ecology of Mind.* New York: Ballantine, 1972.

Bateson, G., *et al.* Toward a theory of schizophrenia. In D. Jackson (ed.). *Communication, Family, and Marriage.* Palo Alto: Science and Behavior, 1968.

Beck, A. T. Reliability of psychiatric diagnoses: 1. A critique of systematic studies. *American Journal of Psychiatry,* 1962, *119,* 210–216.

Becker, A., and Schulberg, H. C. Phasing out state hospitals—a psychiatric dilemma. *New England Journal of Medicine,* 1976, *294,* 255–261.

Bellack, L. Intercultural studies in search of a disease. *Schizophrenia Bulletin,* 1975, *12,* 6–9.

Bland, R. C., Parker, J. H., and Orn, H. Prognosis in schizophrenia: a ten-year followup of first admissions. *Archives of General Psychiatry,* 1976, *33,* 949–954.

Bleuler, E. *Dementia Praecox or the Group of Schizophrenias.* Trans. J. Zinkin. New York: International Universities Press, 1950.

Bowen, M. A family concept of schizophrenia. In D. Jackson (ed.). *The Etiology of Schizophrenia.* New York: Basic Books, 1960, 346–372.

Bowers, M. *Retreat from Sanity.* Baltimore: Penguin, 1974.

Boyd, W. *An Introduction to the Study of Disease.* Philadelphia: Lea & Febiger, 1971.

Boyers, R., and Orill, R. (eds.). *R. D. Laing and Anti-psychiatry.* New York: Harper & Row, 1971.

Brežinova, V., and Kendell, R. E. Smooth pursuit eye movements of schizophrenics and normal people under stress. *British Journal of Psychiatry,* 1977, *130,* 59–63.

Broen, W. *Schizophrenia: Research and Theory.* New York: Academic Press, 1968.

Broverman, I., *et al.* Sex-role stereotypes and clinical judgments of mental health. *Journal of Consulting and Clinical Psychology,* 1970, *34,* 1–7.

Brown, G., Birley, J., and Wing, J. Influence of family life on the course of schizophrenic disorders: a replication. *British Journal of Psychiatry,* 1972, *121,* 241–258.

Brown, G., *et al. Schizophrenia and Social Care.* London: Oxford University Press, 1966.

Brown, G., and Rutter, M. The measurement of family activities and relationships: a methodological study. *Human Relations,* 1966, *19,* 241–263.

Brown, J., and Menninger, K. *Psychodynamics of Abnormal Behavior.* New York: McGraw-Hill, 1940.

Bruner, J., and Goodman, C. Value and need as organizing factors in perception. *Journal of Abnormal and Social Psychology,* 1947, *42,* 33–44.

Buchsbaum, M. Psychophysiology and schizophrenia. *Schizophrenia Bulletin,* 1977, *3,* 7–14.

————. Averaged evoked response augmenting/reducing in schizophrenia and affective disorders. In D. X. Freedman (ed.). *Biology of the Major Psychoses: A Comparative Analysis.* New York: Raven, 1975.

Cameron, N. *Personality Development and Psychopathology: A Dynamic Approach.* Boston: Houghton-Mifflin, 1963.

Carpenter, W., Strauss, J., and Bartko, J. Use of signs and symptoms for the identification of schizophrenic patients. *Schizophrenia Bulletin,* 1974, *11,* 37–49.

Chapman, L., and Chapman, J. *Disordered Thought in Schizophrenia.* Englewood Cliffs, N. J.: Prentice-Hall, 1973.

Chesler, P. *Women and Madness.* New York: Doubleday, 1972.

Cole, J. O., and Davis, J. M. Antipsychotic drugs. In L. Bellak and L. Loeb (eds.). *The Schizophrenic Syndrome.* New York: Grune and Stratton, 1969.

Cooper, B., and Morgan, H. *Epidemiological Psychiatry.* Springfield, Ill.: C. Thomas, 1973.

Creer, C., and Wing, J. Living with a schizophrenic patient. *British Journal of Hospital Medicine,* 1975, 73–83.

Creese, I., and Iversen, S. The pharmacological and anatomical substrates of the amphetamine response in the rat. *Brain Research,* 1975, *83,* 419–436.

Cromwell, R. Assessment of schizophrenia. *Annual Review of Psychology,* 1975, *26,* 593–620.

Detre, T. P., and Jarecki, H. G. *Modern Psychiatric Treatment.* Philadelphia: Lippincott, 1971.

Deutsch, A. *The Mentally Ill in America.* New York: Columbia University Press, 1937.

Diagnostic and Statistical Manual II. Washington, D.C.: American Psychiatric Association, 1968.

Dohrenwend, B. Clues to the role of socioenvironmental factors. *Schizophrenia Bulletin,* 1976, *2,* 440–444.

Dohrenwend, B., and Dohrenwend, B. *Social Status and Psychological Disorder.* New York: Wiley, 1969.

Efron, D. H. (ed.). *Psychopharmacology—a Review of Progress.* Bethesda: Public Health Service, Pub. 1836, 1968.

Ellard, J. Schizophrenia: Changing concepts of a common psychic disability. *Modern Medicine,* 1977, March 15, 61–75.

Ellinwood, E., Sudilovsky, A., and Nelson, L. Evolving behavior in the clinical and experimental amphetamine (model) psychosis. *American Journal of Psychiatry,* 1973, *130,* 1088–1093.

Engelhardt, D. M. Pharmacologic basis for use of psychotropic drugs: an overview. *New York State Journal of Medicine,* 1974, *74,* 360–366.

Engelhardt, D. M., *et al.* Phenothiazines in prevention of psychiatric hospitalization: IV. Delay or prevention of hospitalization—a reevaluation. *Archives of General Psychiatry,* 1967, *16,* 98–101.

Engelhardt, D. M., and Freedman, N. Maintenance drug therapy: the schizophrenic patient in the community. *International Psychiatry Clinics,* 1965, *2,* 933–960.

Engelhardt, D. M., and Rosen, B. Implications of drug treatment for the social rehabilitation of schizophrenic patients. *Schizophrenia Bulletin,* 1976, *2,* 454–462.

Epstein, S. Anxiety, arousal and the self-concept. Paper presented at the Conference on Anxiety and Stress, June 29–July 3, l975.

————. The self-concept revisited or a theory of a theory. *American Psychologist,* 1973, *28,* 404–416.

Epstein, S., and Coleman, M. Drive theories of schizophrenia. *Psychosomatic Medicine,* 1970, *32,* 113–140.

Erickson, G., and Hogan, T. (eds.). *Family Therapy: An Introduction to Theory and Technique.* Monterey, Calif.: Brooks/Cole, 1972.

Erikson, E. *Childhood and Society.* New York: Norton, 1950.

Erlenmeyer-Kimling, L. Studies on the offspring of two schizophrenic parents. In D. Rosenthal and S. Kety (eds.). *The Transmission of Schizophrenia.* London: Pergamon Press, 1968, 65–83.

Evans, J. L., *et al.* Premorbid adjustment, phenothiazine treatment, and remission in acute schizophrenics. *Archives of General Psychiatry,* 1972, *27,* 486–490.

Eysenck, H. Classification and the problem of diagnosis. In H. Eysenck (ed.). *Handbook of Abnormal Psychology.* London: Sir Isaac Pitman, 1960.

Farina, A., Allen, J. G., and Saul, B. B. B. The role of the stigmatized person in affecting social relationships. *Journal of Personality,* 1968, *36,* 169–182.

Farina, A., *et al.* Mental illness and the impact of believing others know about it. *Journal of Abnormal Psychology,* 1971, 77, 1–5.

Farina, A., Felner, R. D., and Boudreau, L. A. Reactions of workers to male and female mental patient job applicants. *Journal of Consulting and Clinical Psychology,* 1973, *41,* 363–372.

Feighner, J., *et al.* Diagnostic criteria for use in psychiatric research. *Archives of General Psychiatry,* 1972, *26,* 57–63.

Feinsilver, D. B., and Gunderson, J. G. Psychotherapy for schizophrenics—is it indicated? A review of the relevant literature. *Schizophrenia Bulletin*, 1971, *6*, 11–23.

Feinstein, A. *Clinical Judgment*. Baltimore: Williams & Wilkins, 1967.

Fish, B. Contributions of developmental research to a theory of schizophrenia. In J. Hellmuth (ed.). *Exceptional Infant: Studies in Abnormalities*. Vol. II. New York: Brunner/Mazel, 1971.

———. Involvement of the central nervous system in infants with schizophrenia. *Archives of Neurology*, 1960, *2*, 115–121.

———. The detection of schizophrenia in infancy. *Journal of Nervous and Mental Disease*, 1957, *125*, 1–24.

Fish, B., and Hagin, R. Visual-motor disorders in infants at risk for schizophrenia. *Archives of General Psychiatry*, 1973, *28*, 900–904.

Fish, B., *et al.* The prediction of schizophrenia in infancy: II. A ten-year follow-up report of predictions made at one month of age. In P. Hoch and J. Zubin (eds.). *Psychopathology of Schizophrenia*. New York: Grune & Stratton, 1966.

Foley, V. *An Introduction to Family Therapy*. New York: Grune & Stratton, 1974.

Frank, G. H. The role of the family in the development of psychopathology. *Psychological Bulletin*, 1965, *64*, 191–205.

Freeman, H., and Simmons, O. *The Mental Patient Comes Home*. New York: Wiley, 1963.

Freud, S. *New Introductory Lectures on Psychoanalysis*. Trans. J. Strachey. New York: Norton, 1965.

———. *A General Introduction to Psychoanalysis*. Trans. J. Riviere. New York: Washington Square Press, 1952.

Fromm-Reichmann, F. Notes on the development of treatment of schizophrenics by psychoanalytic psychotherapy. *Psychiatry*, 1948, *11*, 263–273.

Gardner, G. Role of maternal psychopathology in male and female schizophrenics. *Journal of Consulting Psychology*, 1967, *31*, 411–413.

Garmezy, N. The study of competence in children at risk for severe psychopathology. In E. J. Anthony and C. Koupernik (eds.). *The Child in His Family: Children at Psychiatric Risk*. New York: Wiley, 1974(a).

———. Children at risk: the search for the antecedents of schizophrenia. Part II: Ongoing research programs, issues, and intervention. *Schizophrenia Bulletin*, 1974(b), *9*, 55–125.

———. Process and reactive schizophrenia: some conceptions and issues. *Schizophrenia Bulletin*, 1970, *2*, 30–74.

Garmezy, N., and Streitman, S. Children at risk: the search for the antecedents of schizophrenia. Part I. Conceptual models and research methods. *Schizophrenia Bulletin,* 1974, *8,* 14–90.

Garver, D., *et al.* A schizophreniform behavioral psychosis mediated by dopamine. *American Journal of Psychiatry,* 1975, *132,* 33–38.

Gerard, R. The nosology of schizophrenia: a co-operative study. *Behavioral Science,* 1964, *9,* 311–333.

Gittelman-Klein, R., and Klein, D. F. Premorbid asocial adjustment and prognosis in schizophrenia. *Journal of Psychiatric Research,* 1969, *7,* 35–53.

———. Long-term effects of "antipsychotic" agents: a review. In Efron, D. H., *et al.* (eds.). *Psychopharmacology: A Review of Progress.* Washington: U.S. Government Printing Office, 1968.

Goffman, E. *Asylums: Essays on the Social Situation of Mental Patients and Other Inmates.* Garden City, N.Y.: Anchor, 1961.

Goldstein, M., *et al.* A method for studying social influence and coping patterns within families of disturbed adolescents. *Journal of Nervous and Mental Disease,* 1968, *147,* 233–251.

Goldstein, M., Held, J., and Cromwell, R. Premorbid adjustment and paranoid-nonparanoid status in schizophrenia. *Psychological Bulletin,* 1968, *70,* 382–386.

Goldstein, M., and Rodnick, E. The family's contribution to the etiology of schizophrenia. *Schizophrenia Bulletin,* 1975, *14,* 48–63.

Gottesman, I. Schizophrenia and genetics: Where are we? Are you sure? Paper presented at the Second Rochester International Conference on Schizophrenia, 1976 (in press).

Gottesman, I., and Shields, J. A critical review of recent adoption, twin, and family studies of schizophrenia: behavioral genetics perspectives. *Schizophrenia Bulletin,* 1976, *2,* 360–401.

———. *Schizophrenia and Genetics: A Twin Study Vantage Point.* New York: Academic Press, 1972.

Gove, W., and Tudor, J. Adult sex roles and mental illness. *American Journal of Sociology,* 1973, *78,* 812–835.

Green, H. *I Never Promised You a Rose Garden.* New York: Signet, 1964.

Griffiths, J., Oates, J., and Cavanaugh, J. Paranoid episodes induced by drugs. *Journal of the American Medical Association,* 1968, *205,* 39–46.

Grinker, R. R., and Holzman, P. S. Schizophrenic pathology in young adults. *Archives of General Psychiatry,* 1973, *28,* 168–175.

Gunderson, J. G., and Mosher, L. R. The cost of schizophrenia. *American Journal of Psychiatry,* 1975, *132,* 901–906.

Haley, J. *The Power Tactics of Jesus Christ.* New York: Grossman, 1969.

———. The family of the schizophrenic: a model system. *Journal of Nervous and Mental Disease,* 1959, *129,* 357–374.

Hare, E., Price, J. and Slater, E. Parental social class in psychiatric patients. *British Journal of Psychiatry,* 1972, *121,* 515–524.

Hayward, M. L., and Taylor, J. E. A schizophrenic patient describes the action of intensive psychotherapy. *The Psychiatric Quarterly,* 1956, *30,* 211–266.

Heath, R. G., *et al.* Effect on behavior of humans with the administration of taraxein. *American Journal of Psychiatry,* 1957, *114,* 14–24.

Higgins, J. The concept of process-reactive schizophrenia: criteria and related remarks. *Journal of Nervous and Mental Disease,* 1964, *138,* 9–25.

Hirsch, S., and Leff, J. Parental abnormalities of verbal communication in the transmission of schizophrenia. *Psychological Medicine,* 1971, *1,* 118–127.

Hoffer, A. Treatment of schizophrenia. *Journal of Orthomolecular Psychiatry,* 1974, *3,* 280–290.

Hoffer, A., and Osmond, H. *How to Live with Schizophrenia.* New York: University Books, 1969.

———. The adrenochrome model and schizophrenics. *Journal of Nervous and Mental Disease,* 1959, *128,* 18–35.

Hogarty, G. E., *et al.* Drug and sociotherapy in the aftercare of schizophrenic patients: II. Two-year relapse rate. *Archives of General Psychiatry,* 1974, *31,* 603–608.

Hogarty, G. E., Goldberg, S. C., and The Collaborative Study Group. Drug and sociotherapy in the aftercare of schizophrenic patients. *Archives of General Psychiatry,* 1973, *28,* 54–64.

Holland, R., *et al.* Adrenalin and noradrenalin in urine and plasma of schizophrenics. *Federal Proceedings,* 1958, *17,* 378.

Holzman, P., *et al.* Eye-tracking dysfunctions in schizophrenic patients and their relatives. *Archives of General Psychiatry,* 1974, *31,* 143–151.

Holzman, P., and Levy, D. Smooth pursuit eye movements and functional psychoses: a review *Schizophrenia Bulletin,* 1977, *3,* 15–27.

Itil, T. Qualitative and quantitative EEG findings in schizophrenia. *Schizophrenia Bulletin,* 1977, *3,* 61–79.

Itil, T., *et al.* Computer EEG and auditory evoked potential investigations in children at high risk for schizophrenia. *American Journal of Psychiatry,* 1974, *131,* 892–900.

Jacob, F. Evolution and tinkering. *Science,* 1977, *196,* 1161–1166.

Jacob, T. Family interaction in disturbed and normal families: a methodological and substantive review. *Psychological Bulletin,* 1975, *82,* 33–65.

Jarvis, E. On the comparative liability of males and females to insanity, and their comparative curability and mortality when insane. *American Journal of Insanity,* 1850, 7, 142–171.

Jefferson, L. *These Are My Sisters.* Tulsa: Vickers, 1948.

Kaplan, B. (ed.). *The Inner World of Mental Illness.* New York: Harper & Row, 1964.

Keith, S., *et al.* Special report: schizophrenia 1976. *Schizophrenia Bulletin,* 1976, *2,* 510–565.

Klein, D. F., and Davis, J. M. *Diagnosis and Drug Treatment of Psychiatric Disorders.* Baltimore: Williams & Wilkins, 1969.

Kobayashi, R. M. Drug therapy of tardive dyskinesia. *Medical Intelligence,* 1977, *296,* 257–259.

Koh, S., and Kayton, L. Memorization of unrelated word strings by nonpsychotic schizophrenics. *Journal of Abnormal Psychology,* 1974, *83,* 14–22.

Kohn, M. Social class and schizophrenia: a critical review and a reformulation. *Schizophrenia Bulletin,* 1973, 7, 60–79.

———. Class, family, and schizophrenia: a reformulation. *Social Forces,* 1972, *50,* 295–313.

———. Social class and schizophrenia: a critical review. In D. Rosenthal and S. Kety (eds.). *The Transmission of Schizophrenia.* London: Pergamon Press, 1968.

Kolb, L. C. *Modern Clinical Psychiatry.* Philadelphia: Saunders, 1973.

Kraepelin, E. *Lectures on Clinical Psychiatry.* New York: Wood, 1917.

Kramer, M. Population changes and schizophrenia, 1970–1985. Paper presented at the Second Rochester International Conference on Schizophrenia, Rochester, N. Y., May, 1976.

Kreitman, N. Reliability of psychiatric diagnosis. *Journal of Mental Science,* 1961, *107,* 876–886.

Laing, R. *The Politics of Experience.* New York: Ballantine, 1967.

———. *The Divided Self: An Existential Study in Sanity and Madness.* London: Tavistock Publications Ltd, 1960.

Laing, R., and Esterson, A. *Sanity, Madness and the Family.* London: Penguin, 1964.

Lamb, H. R., and Goertzel, V. Discharged mental patients— are they really in the community? *Archives of General Psychiatry,* 1971, *24,* 29–34.

Landy, D., and Griffith, W. D. Employer receptivity toward hiring psychiatric patients. *Mental Hygiene,* 1958, *42,* 383–390.

Lazarus, M. *Momma.* Field Enterprises, Inc., June 5, 1977.

Leff, J. Schizophrenia and sensitivity to the family environment. *Schizophrenia Bulletin,* 1976, *2,* 566–574.

Lewine, R., Strauss, J., and Gift, T. Sex differences in schizophrenia. Submitted for presentation at the American Psychiatric Association Convention. February, 1978.

Lidz, T. Commentary on "A critical review of recent adoption, twin, and family studies of schizophrenia: behavioral genetics perspectives." *Schizophrenia Bulletin,* 1976, *2,* 402–412.

————. Schizophrenia and the family. *Psychiatry,* 1958, *21,* 21–27.

Lidz, T., *et al.* The intrafamilial environment of schizophrenic patients: II. Marital schism and marital skew. *American Journal of Psychiatry,* 1957, *114,* 241–248.

Lidz, T., Fleck, S., and Cornelison, A. (eds.). *Schizophrenia and the Family.* New York: International Universities Press, 1965.

Linn, L. Physician characteristics and attitudes toward legitimate use of psychotherapeutic drugs. *Journal of Health and Social Behavior,* 1971, *12,* 132–140.

Lorr, M., Klett, C., and McNair, D. *Syndromes of Psychosis.* Oxford: Pergamon Press, 1963.

Luborsky, L., *et al.* Factors influencing the outcome of psychotherapy: A review of quantitative research. *Psychological Bulletin,* 1971, *75,* 145–185.

McAndrew, I. Children with a handicap and their families. *Child Care Health Development,* 1976, *2,* 213–218.

McCabe, M. Demographic differences in functional psychoses. *British Journal of Psychiatry,* 1975, *127,* 320–323.

MacDonald, N. Living with schizophrenia. *Canadian Medical Association Journal,* 1960, *82,* 218–221, 678–681.

McGhie, A. *Pathology of Attention.* Baltimore: Penguin, 1969.

McGhie, A., and Chapman, J. Disorders of attention and perception in early schizophrenia. *British Journal of Medical Psychology,* 1961, *34,* 103–116.

McKenzie, K. G., and Kaczanowski, G. Prefrontal leukotomy: a five-year controlled study. *Canadian Medical Association Journal,* 1964, *91,* 1193–1196.

MacLane, M. *The Story of Mary MacLane.* New York: Stone, 1902.

Maher, B. (ed.). *Clinical Psychology and Personality—the Selected Papers of George Kelly.* New York: Wiley, 1969.

Maher, B. *Principles of Psychopathology.* New York: McGraw-Hill, 1966.

Matthysse, S. Theoretical commentary on Gottesman and Shields' review. *Schizophrenia Bulletin,* 1976, *2,* 445–446.

May, P. R. A., *et al.* Schizophrenia—a follow-up study of results of treatment. II: Hospital stay over two to five years. *Archives of General Psychiatry,* 1976(b), *33,* 481–486.

May, P. R. A., Tuma, A. H., and Dixon, W. J. Schizophrenia—a follow-up study of results of treatment. I: Design and other problems. *Archives of General Psychiatry,* 1976(a), *33,* 474–478.

Mednick, S. Breakdown in individuals at high risk for schizophrenia: possible predispositional perinatal factors. *Mental Hygiene,* 1970, *54,* 50–63.

Mednick, S., *et al.* Erratum and further analysis: perinatal conditions and infant development in children with schizophrenic parents. *Social Biology,* 1971, *18* (Sept. supplement), S103–S113.

Mednick, S., and McNeil, T. Current methodology in research on the etiology of schizophrenia: serious difficulties which suggest the use of the high-risk group method. *Psychological Bulletin,* 1968, *70,* 681–693.

Meehl, P. Schizotaxia, schizotypy, schizophrenia. *American Psychologist,* 1962, *17,* 827–838.

Meltzer, H., and Stahl, S. The dopamine hypothesis of schizophrenia: a review. *Schizophrenia Bulletin,* 1976, *2,* 19–76.

Meyer, A. The dynamic interpretation of dementia praecox. *American Journal of Psychology,* 1910, *21,* 385–403.

Meyer, E., and Covi, L. The experience of depersonalization: a written report by a patient. *Psychiatry,* 1960, *23,* 215–217.

Mirsky, A. F., and Kornetsky, C. The effect of centrally-acting drugs on attention. In D. H. Efron (ed.). *Psychopharmacology: A Review of Progress.* Bethesda: Public Health Service, 1968.

Morris, D., Soroker, E., and Burruss, G. Follow-up studies of shy, withdrawn children: evaluation of later adjustment. *American Journal of Orthopsychiatry,* 1954, *24,* 743–755.

Mosher, L. A research design to evaluate psychosocial treatment of schizophrenia. *Hospital and Community Psychiatry,* 1972, *23,* 229–234.

Mosher, L., *et al. Special Report on Schizophrenia.* Pub. No. (HSM) 72–9007. Washington, D.C.: U.S. Government Printing Office, 1971.

Mosher, L., Menn, A., and Matthews, S. Soteria: evaluation of a home-based treatment for schizophrenia. *American Journal of Orthopsychiatry,* 1975, *45,* 455–467.

Mowrer, O. H. "Sin," the lesser of two evils. *American Psychologist,* 1960, *15,* 301–304.

Murphy, H. Cultural factors in the genesis of schizophrenia. In D. Rosenthal and S. Kety (eds.). *The Transmission of Schizophrenia.* London: Pergamon Press, 1968.

Nameche, G., Waring, M., and Ricks, D. Early indicators of outcome in schizophrenia. *Journal of Nervous and Mental Disease,* 1964, *139,* 232–240.

National Institute of Mental Health. Psychopharmacology Service Center Collaborative Study Group: phenothiazine treatment in acute schizophrenia. *Archives of General Psychiatry,* 1964, *10,* 246–261.

Nunally, J. C., Jr. *Popular Conceptions of Mental Health.* New York: Holt, Rinehart & Winston, 1961.

Ødegaard, O. Emigration and mental health. *Mental Hygiene,* 1936, *20,* 546–553.

Olson, G. Q., and Peterson, D. B. Sudden removal of tranquilizing drugs from chronic psychiatric patients. *Journal of Nervous and Mental Disease,* 1960, *131,* 252–255.

Orne, M. The nature of hypnosis: artifact and essence. In R. Shor and M. Orne (eds.). *The Nature of Hypnosis.* New York: Holt, Rinehart & Winston, 1965, 89–123.

Pasamanick, B., Scarpitti, F. R., and Dinitz, S. *Schizophrenics in the Community.* New York: Appleton-Century-Crofts, 1967.

Phillips, L. Case history data and prognosis in schizophrenia. *Journal of Nervous and Mental Disease,* 1953, *117,* 515–525.

Piaget, J. *The Origins of Intelligence.* Trans. M. Cook. New York: International Universities Press, 1952.

Pokorny, A. D. Suicide rates in various psychiatric disorders. *Journal of Nervous and Mental Disease,* 1964, *139,* 499–506.

Pollack, M., Levenstein, S., and Klein, D. A three-year follow-up of adolescent and adult schizophrenics. *American Journal of Orthopsychiatry,* 1968, *38,* 94–109.

Pollin, W., and Stabenau, J. Biological, psychological and historical differences in a series of monozygotic twins discordant for schizophrenia. In D. Rosenthal and S. Kety (eds.). *The Transmission of Schizophrenia.* London: Pergamon Press, 1968.

Prien, R. F., Cole, J. O., and Belkin, N. F. Relapse in chronic schizophrenics following abrupt withdrawal of tranquilizing medication. *British Journal of Psychiatry,* 1969, *115,* 679–686.

Professional staff of the United States–United Kingdom Cross-National Project. The diagnosis and psychopathology of schizophrenia in New York and London. *Schizophrenia Bulletin,* 1974, *11,* 80–102.

Randrup, A., and Munkvard, I. Biochemical, anatomaical and psychological investigations of stereotyped behavior induced by amphetamines. In E. Costa and S. Garattini (eds.). *Amphetamines and Related Compounds.* New York: Raven, 1970, 695–713.

Rappaport, M. Competing voice messages: effect of message load and drugs on the ability of acute schizophrenics to attend. *Archives of General Psychiatry,* 1967, *17,* 97–103.

Rappaport, M., *et al.* Phenothiazine effects on auditory signal detection in paranoid and nonparanoid schizophrenics. *Science,* 1971, *174,* 723–725.

Raskin, A., and Golob, R. Occurrence of sex and social class differences in premorbid competence, symptom and outcome measures in acute schizophrenia. *Psychological Reports,* 1966, *18,* 11–22.

Ricks, D. Life history research in psychopathology: retrospect and prospect. In M. Roff and D. Ricks (eds.). *Life History Research in Psychopathology.* Minneapolis: University of Minnesota Press, 1970.

Ricks, D., and Berry, J. Family and symptom patterns that precede schizophrenia. In M. Roff and D. Ricks (eds.). *Life History Research in Psychopathology.* Minneapolis: University of Minnesota Press, 1970.

Riskin, J., and Faunce, E. An evaluative review of family interaction research. *Family Process,* 1972, *11,* 365–456.

Roberts, S. V. And another: what about the halfway home idea? *New York Times,* March 19, 1978, p. 10E.

Robins, L. *Deviant Children Grown Up.* Baltimore: Williams & Wilkins, 1966.

Rosen, B., Klein, D. F., and Gittelman-Klein, R. The prediction of rehospitlization: the relationship between age of first psychiatric treatment contact, marital status and premorbid asocial adjustment. *Journal of Nervous and Mental Disease,* 1971, *152,* 17–22.

Rosenhan, D. On being sane in insane places. *Science,* 1973, *179,* 250–258.

Rosenthal, D. Discussion: the concept of subschizophrenic disorders. In R. R. Fieve, D. Rosenthal, and H. Brill (eds.). *Genetic Research in Psychiatry.* Baltimore: Johns Hopkins University Press, 1975.

———. *Genetics of Psychopathology.* New York: McGraw-Hill, 1971.

———. The heredity-environment issue in schizophrenia. In D. Rosenthal and S. Kety (eds.). *The Transmission of Schizophrenia.* London: Pergamon Press, 1968.

———. Familial concordance by sex with respect to schizophrenia. *Psychological Bulletin,* 1962, *59,* 401–421.

Rosenthal, D. (ed.). *The Genain Quadruplets.* New York: Basic Books, 1963.

Rosenthal, D., and Kety, S. (eds.). *The Transmission of Schizophrenia.* London: Pergamon Press, 1968.

Roueché, B. *Eleven Blue Men.* New York: Berkeley Medallion Books, 1947.

Russell, P., Bannatyne, P., and Smith, J. Associative strength as a mode of organization in recall and recognition: a comparison of schizophrenics and normals. *Journal of Abnormal Psychology,* 1975, *84,* 122–128.

Rutter, M. Children of sick parents: an environmental and psychiatric study. *Maudsley Monograph,* No. 16, 1966.

Rutter, M., and Brown, G. The reliability and validity of measures of family life and relationships in families containing a psychiatric patient. *Social Psychiatry,* 1966, *1,* 38–53.

Saenger, G. Patterns of change among "treated" and "untreated" patients seen in psychiatric community mental health clinics. *Journal of Nervous and Mental Disease,* 1970, *150,* 37–50.

Salzinger, K. *Schizophrenia: Behavioral Aspects.* New York: Wiley, 1973.

Sameroff, A., and Zax, M. Neonatal factors in serious mental disorder. Progress report. NIMH Grant 16544 University of Rochester School of Medicine, Rochester, N.Y., June, 1972.

Sarbin, T. Schizophrenia is a myth, born of metaphor, meaningless. *Psychology Today,* 1972, 18–27.

Schmidt, H., and Fonda, C. The realiability of psychiatric diagnosis: a new look. *Journal of Abnormal and Social Psychology,* 1956, *52,* 262–267.

Schneider, K. *Clinical Psychopathology.* Trans. M. Hamilton. New York: Grune & Stratton, 1959.

Schuham, A. The double-bind hypothesis a decade later. *Psychological Bulletin,* 1967, *68,* 409–416.

Schwab, J., and Schwab, R. The epidemiology of mental illness. Paper presented at the American College of Psychiatrists' Sixth Annual Seminar for Continuing Education of Psychiatrists, New Orleans, January 24–28, 1973.

Sechehaye, M. A. *Journal d'une schizophrène.* Paris: Presses Universitaires de France, 1950.

Selling, L. *Men against Madness.* New York: New Home Library, 1940.

Sendev, H. S., and Olson, J. L. Nicotinic acid therapy in chronic schizophrenia. *Comprehensive Psychiatry,* 1974, *15,* 511–517.

Serban, G., and Thomas, A. Attitudes and behaviors of acute and chronic schizophrenic patients regarding ambulatory care. *American Journal of Psychiatry,* 1974, *131,* 991–995.

Shakow, D. Some observations on the psychology (and some fewer, on the biology) of schizophrenia. *Journal of Nervous and Mental Disease,* 1971, *153,* 300–317.

————. Psychological deficit in schizophrenia. *Behavioral Science,* 1963, *8,* 275–305.

Sheehy, G. *Predictable Crises of Adult Life.* New York: Dutton, 1974.

Silverman, J., Buchsbaum, M., and Henkin, R. Stimulus sensitivity and stimulus intensity control. *Perceptual and Motor Skills,* 1969, *28,* 71–78.

Slater, E. A review of earlier evidence on genetic factors in schizophrenia. In D. Rosenthal and S. Kety (eds.). *The Transmission of Schizophrenia.* London: Pergamon Press, 1968.

Slater, E., and Cowie, V. *The Genetics of Mental Disorders.* London: Oxford University Press, 1971.

Slone, D., *et al.* Antenatal exposure to the phenothiazines in relation to congenital malformations, perinatal mortality rate, birth weight, and intelligence quotient score. *American Journal of Obstetrical Gynecology,* 1977, *128,* 486–488.

Spadoni, A. J., and Smith, J. A. Milieu therapy in schizophrenia: negative result. *Archives of General Psychiatry,* 1969, *20,* 547–551.

Spitzer, R., and Endicott, J. DIAGNO: a computer program for psychiatric diagnosis utilizing the differential diagnostic procedure. *Archives of General Psychiatry,* 1968, *18,* 746–756.

Spohn, H. E., *et al.* Phenothiazine effects on psychological and psychophysiological dysfunction in chronic schizophrenics. *Archives of General Psychiatry,* 1977, *34,* 633–644.

Squire, L. R., and Chace, P. M. Memory functions six to nine months after electroconvulsive therapy. *Archives of General Psychiatry,* 1975, *32,* 1557–1564.

Stein, L. Neurochemistry of reward and punishment: some implications for the etiology of schizophrenia. *Journal of Psychiatric Research,* 1971, *8,* 345–361.

Stein, L. I., and Test, M. A. Training in community living: one year evaluation. Paper presented at the Annual Meeting of the American Psychiatric Association, Anaheim, California, May, 1975.

Stephens, J. Long-term course and prognosis in schizophrenia. *Seminars in Psychiatry,* 1970, *2,* 464–485.

Stephens, J., and Astrup, C. Prognosis in "process" and "nonprocess" schizophrenia. *American Journal of Psychiatry,* 1963, *119,* 945–953.

Stone, A. A. *Mental Health and Law: A System in Transition.* New York: Aronson, 1976.

Strauss, J. A comprehensive approach to psychiatric diagnosis. *American Journal of Psychiatry,* 1975, *132,* 1193–1197.

Strauss, J., and Carpenter, W. T. Characteristic symptoms and outcome in schizophrenia. *Archives of General Psychiatry,* 1974, *30,* 429–434.

———. The prediction of outcome in schizophrenia. II. Relationships between predictor and outcome variables: a report from the WHO international pilot study of schizophrenia. *Archives of General Psychiatry,* 1974, *31,* 37–41.

Strauss, J., Carpenter, W., and Bartko, J. Schizophrenic symptoms and signs. *Schizophrenia Bulletin,* 1974, *11,* 61–79.

Sullivan, H. *The Interpersonal Theory of Psychiatry.* New York: Norton, 1953.

Szasz, T. *The Myth of Mental Illness.* New York: Dell, 1961.

Taubel, D. E. Mellaril: ejaculation disorders. *American Journal of Psychiatry,* 1962, *119,* 87–91.

Temoche, A., Pugh, T., and MacMahon, B. Suicide rates among current and former mental institution patients. *Journal of Nervous and Mental Disease,* 1964, *138,* 124–130.

Turner, R. Social mobility and schizophrenia. *Journal of Health and Social Behavior,* 1968, *9,* 194–203.

Turner, R., and Wagenfeld, M. Occupational mobility and schizophrenia: an assessment of the social causation and social selection hypotheses. *American Sociological Review,* 1967, *32,* 104–113.

Vaillant, G. An historical review of the remitting schizophrenias. *Journal of Nervous and Mental Disease,* 1964, *138,* 48–56.

———. The natural history of the remitting schizophrenias. *American Journal of Psychiatry,* 1963, *120,* 367–376.

Van Putten, T. Why do schizophrenic patients refuse to take their drugs? *Archives of General Psychiatry,* 1974, *31,* 67–72.

Van Putten, T., Crumpton, E., and Yale, C. Drug refusal in schizophrenia and the wish to be crazy. *Archives of General Psychiatry,* 1976, *33,* 1443–1446.

Vaughn, C., and Leff, J. The influence of family and social factors on the course of psychiatric illness. *British Journal of Psychiatry,* 1976, *129,* 125–137.

Venables, P. The electrodermal psychophysiology of schizophrenics and children at risk for schizophrenia: controversies and developments. *Schizophrenia Bulletin,* 1977, *3,* 28–48.

Vonnegut, M. *The Eden Express.* New York: Praeger, 1975.

Wahl, O. F. The Mad and the Misinformed: A Guide to Common Misconceptions about Mental Hospitals and Mental Patients. Unpublished manuscript, 1977.

Watt, N. Longitudinal changes in the social behavior of children hospitalized for schizophrenia as adults. *Journal of Nervous and Mental Disease,* 1972, *155,* 42–54.

Watt, N., *et al.* School adjustment and behavior of children hospitalized for schizophrenia as adults. *American Journal of Orthopsychiatry,* 1970, *40,* 637–657.

Waxler, N. The normality of deviance: an alternate explanation of schizophrenia in the family. *Schizophrenia Bulletin,* 1975, *14,* 38–47.

Weinman, B., and Kleiner, R. Measuring the effectiveness of community treatment of chronic patients. Paper presented at the Annual Meeting of the American Psychiatric Association, New Orleans, Louisiana, September, 1974.

Wender, P., *et al.* Social class and psychopathology in adoptees: a natural experimental method for separating the roles of genetic and experiential factors. *Archives of General Psychiatry,* 1974, *28,* 318–325.

Werner, H. *Comparative Psychology of Mental Development.* New York: International Universities Press, 1948.

White, R., and Watt, N. *The Abnormal Personality,* 4th ed. New York: Ronald, 1973.

White, W. *Outlines of Psychiatry.* Washington, D.C.: Nervous and Mental Disease Publishing Company, 1926.

Williams, J. *Psychology of Women: Behavior in a Biosocial Context.* New York: Norton, 1977.

Wing, J. The management of schizophrenia in the community. Paper presented at the Annual Meeting of the American College of Psychiatrists, Atlanta, Georgia, February, 1977.

———. Preliminary communication: a technique for studying psychiatric morbidity in in-patient and out-patient series and in general population samples. *Psychological Medicine,* 1976, *6,* 665–671.

Wishner, J. Workshop on Attention in Schizophrenia. Paper presented at the Eastern Psychological Association Meeting, May, 1977.

————. Convergent trends in psychopathology. Paper presented at the symposium on "Research Extensions of Clinical Psychology—Emphasis on Prevention," International Congress of Applied Psychology, July 25–30, 1971.

————. Efficiency in schizophrenia. Paper presented at the symposium on "Clinical Psychology and Experimental Psychopathology," International Congress of Applied Psychology, August 3, 1964.

World Health Organization. *Report of the International Pilot Study of Schizophrenia.* Geneva: World Health Organization, 1973.

Wyatt, R., and Murphy, D. Low platelet monoamine oxidase activity and schizophrenia. *Schizophrenia Bulletin,* 1976, *2,* 77–89.

Wynne, L., *et al.* Schizophrenics and their families: recent research on parental communication. In J. Tanner (ed.). *Psychiatric Research: The Widening Perspective.* New York: International Universities Press, 1975.

Wynne, L., *et al.* Pseudomutuality in the family relations of schizophrenics. *Psychiatry,* 1958, *21,* 205–222.

Zahn, T. Autonomic nervous system characteristics possibly related to a genetic predisposition to schizophrenia. *Schizophrenia Bulletin,* 1977, *3,* 49–60.

Zilboorg, G. *A History of Medical Psychology.* New York: Norton, 1941.

Zubin, J., and Spring, B. Vulnerability—a new view of schizophrenia. *Journal of Abnormal Psychology,* 1977, *86,* 103–126.

Index

247